For Honor, Country, and God

Los Niños Héroes

A New Look at Mexico's Cadets
"Vayan Con Dios"
Chapultepec, September 13, 1847

Also by this author

Nat Turner's Holy War To Destroy Slavery
America's Female Buffalo Soldier
Miller Cornfield at Antietam
Pickett's Charge
Death at the Little Bighorn
Barksdale's Charge
Storming Little Round Top
Exodus From The Alamo
Emily D. West and the "Yellow Rose of Texas" Myth
The South's Finest
George Washington's Surprise Attack
How The Irish Won The American Revolution
Why Custer Was Never Warned
The Alamo's Forgotten Defenders
Irish Confederates
God Help The Irish!
Burnside's Bridge
The Final Fury
Westerners In Gray
Alexander Hamilton's Revolution
The Confederacy's Fighting Chaplain
Cubans In The Confederacy
Forgotten Stonewall of the West
From Auction Block To Glory
The Important Role of the Irish in the American Revolution
The 1862 Plot to Kidnap Jefferson Davis.
Anne Bonny: The Infamous Female Pirate
America's Forgotten First War for Slavery and Genesis of The Alamo Vol I and II

For Honor, Country, and God

Los Niños Héroes

A New Look at Mexico's Cadets
"Vayan Con Dios"
Chapultepec, September 13, 1847

Phillip Thomas Tucker, Ph.D.

Copyright © 2017 Phillip Thomas Tucker

2nd Edition 2018

All rights reserved, including the right to reproduce this book, or portions thereof in any form. No part of this text may be reproduced, transmitted, downloaded, decompiled, reverse engineered, or stored, in any form or introduced into any information storage and retrieval system, in any form or by any means, whether electronic or mechanical without the express written permission of the author.

The views expressed in this work are solely those of the author and do not necessarily reflect the views of the publisher, and the publisher hereby disclaims any responsibility for them.

Front cover images from author's collection
Bottom: Battle of Chapultepec
Top: From a Bank of Mexico 5000 peso note

ISBN: 978-1-387-34971-5

PublishNation LLC
www.publishnation.net

To the People of Mexico

Table of Contents

Foreword by Mario Marcel Salas	viii
Introduction	1
Prologue	21
Chapter I: Lost Golden Land of Texas Leads to War	30
Chapter II: The Looming Heights of Chapultepec	48
Chapter III: The Great Assault Released	125
Chapter IV: A Heroic Final Act of Defiance	189
Epilogue	216
About the Author	220
Bibliography	222

Foreword by Mario Marcel Salas

We live in an era where historical narratives and research is uncovering the details of what was never thoroughly and wholly evaluated. Foundational works were often accepted which ignored the underlying reasons that would have explained a historical event in more precise detail. If the underlying evidence supported an alternative historical view, a view that went against the grain of the accepted norms of society, it was ignored. Any evidence that would bring into question the role of racialized thought or motives, gendered biases, or class inequalities as reasons behind some historical event was simply ignored. For a historical description or event to remain in mainstream acceptance, it had to be devoid of evidence that would point to an unjust reason for its occurrence. We were expected to ignore the synchronicity between dominant racial formulations and events that shaped history. In this well-researched book, Dr. Phillip Thomas Tucker provides us with synchronous connections between what social forces were materializing, arising, or existing at precisely the same time that the United States decided to engage upon in what could only be described as an unjust war of imperialism against the Republic of Mexico.

Many events remain without scrutiny and are not the subject of more in-depth analysis and are thus anchored in place by simple popular ignorance put there by those wishing to sweep under the historical rug an established but inaccurate view. More in-depth views often provided an outright reversal of the accepted patterns of a non-historicity. Millions of unsuspecting, teachers, students and everyday people have grown up in a society where the historical record was written by those with a hidden agenda. These pseudo-historians sought to write about events colored by biases that reflected the dominate view. Myths abound, and have become the foundations of societies across the earth, but here we are concerned with the United States invasion of Mexico. If ever there was an unjustified war one could make that claim about the Mexican-American War of 1846. It was opposed by many well-informed

Americans who saw it as a land grab to set the Mexican border at the Rio Bravo (Rio Grande) and to completely remove Mexico from its established territories. "Manifest Destiny" was surely at work in this war; a religious, raced-based, and political doctrine that had its roots in the extension of slavery and the genocide and removal of Indigenous People.

The "boys," or "The Niños Héroes" as they are known, took up the call of history by fighting against the North American invasion of their country. Dr. Tucker has once again shown that what is ignored by historians has a foundational effect in establishing a woven web of historical fabrication. All societies invent myths, but in this aggressive country the myths were tainted with bellicose nationalism and racial fabrications that bolstered the narratives of white supremacy. The conquering of North America and Mexico has its origins early on in the ideas of what was once known as "Continentalism." One is reminded that the early governmental form made use of the term "Continental Congress" during the American Revolution from 1775 to 1783. Of course, one could argue that this term was accidental, or only a geographical reference, but the 13 colonies clearly had other ideas, especially since the British promoted anti-slavery policies. The desire to expand across the continent would later serve the interests of those whose racial and class motives were fused with territorial conquest. This belief set the stage for France, Spain, Canada, Russia, and others to be removed by conquest or through Machiavellian political maneuvers sometimes aimed at igniting wars or exploiting natural resources, or both.

God was of course added to the formula as the idea of "American Exceptionalism" took on economic and imperialistic designs. Although the idea of Manifest Destiny had no compacted written set of aspirations, it nevertheless was the symbolic fountainhead of dreams of conquest. The conquest of Mexico had little to do with morals and democratic virtues, but the power of its imagery served several goals. It would in later years eventually morph into the "Lost Cause" of the "Redeemer Movement," of the slave owning states after the Civil War. Even though the rebel states of the Confederacy lost the 1861-1865 war they sought to redeem the South by inventing themselves as "noble gentlemen" that fought a war unconnected to slavery and white supremacy.

In a similar vein the United States invasion of Mexico, and the Battle of Chapultepec on September 13, 1847, was an unjust war that carried forward the ideas of a "morality" that was ill-conceived and racialized. The Mexican-American War (called the Invasion in Mexico) was the ideological and religious fuel that became a part of what was then a very different "American Dream." The "virtues" and missions associated with this war impregnated a false morality and an extremely limited democracy among a population that was made to feel superior to others. These ideological shadows of specified moralities, infused into the minds of thousands, were in the form of a hollow political pointillism, blending into the inner eye an ideal, yet socially, morally, and politically inhibited by the actualities of slavery and racialized thought. God was made into the glue that sanctioned this war.

From the early days of American colonialization and the establishment of the English settlements in North America, the drive to extend slavery and to remove or control all non-white people from the continent was dominant. This colonial determination and expansion placed racial ideology and God in the same dimension; which was but the extension of scientific racism invented in Europe by Carl Linnaeus, Johann Blumenbach, Christoph Meiners, and others a hundred years or more before the 1846 invasion of Mexico. The mission of these racialized expansionists was to provide "holy" justifications that claimed a Godly approval, in redeeming the agricultural foundations of American life. Hence, the conquering of Mexico was wedded to a functional ideal that was destined to bring misery to the American and Mexican frontier and to generations of Mexicans, blacks, and Indigenous People.

In fulfilling the dreams of expansionism in early 1847, President James K. Polk sent a mighty army and armada to capture Veracruz in order to provide a beachhead to push inland and all the way to Mexico City. Upon approaching Mexico City, United States forces overwhelmed the small garrison, including the young cadets of the Military College, at Chapultepec on the morning of September 13, 1847. Unknown too many, the United States Marine Corps Anthem that includes the words, "From the Halls of Montezuma" refers to the hard-fought battle at Chapultepec Castle. Why is this important? When history is ignored or erased and purposefully left untold, then human dignity can be cast away like an unimportant tidbit. A song made on the basis of brutality, racism, and injustice should not be stripped of its origins to provide a cover for an injustice. Some may argue that Mexico's history is slanted in favor of their own interpretations. There is always some truth to such charges levied against any country, but when it is done to create false narratives and fabricated history by superior forces it is quite another matter. The victims of manifest destiny, including the cadets of Chapultepec, have shed real blood because of such ideological juggernauts. There are always the myths of the conquerors and the conquered. However, there is a world or difference between the mythology of the oppressed and that of the oppressor.

The cadet boys of Mexico's garrison that defended Chapultepec's summit would go down in history as heroes, as would the Irishmen and others who left the ranks of the expansionist army to form the famous San Patricio Battalion and would be executed on September 13, 1847 under orders by men (Southerners) who would later betray the United States in the Civil War. The pride of Mexico, its flag, fell into the lap of one of those young cadets (Cadet Juan Escutia) who saved the Mexican flag from those who made songs of conquests at their expense.

Devoted to telling the true story of the young cadets of Chapultepec, this book is but another well documented resource for those who now question the bogus historical accounts, including those of reactionaries who have recently questioned the cadets' heroism, that have long been used as foundation myth. This research is needed and part of the desire of 21st Century historians to uncover that which has been purposefully subverted and erased.

Mario Marcel Salas
Assistant Professor of Political Science (Ret)
Lecturer, University of Texas at San Antonio

Introduction

In the annals of western history, the last stand of the 300 Spartan warriors at Thermopylae in 480 BC has been immortalized as the epitome of courage and self-sacrifice to inspire generations of western fighting men over the centuries. The deaths of the 300 Spartans on a small 'hillock" located near the pounding surf of the sea by the seemingly endless tide of Xerxes' Persian fighting men was a legendary noble sacrifice. This handful of Spartans bought precious time for saving the threatened ancient Greek homeland from the mightiest army that had ever invaded European soil.

In a clash between Europe and Asia, the Spartans of Thermopylae faced warriors of a different race, civilization, and religion. With the death of the last Spartan at Thermopylae, the martial tradition of noble self-sacrifice—dying heroically for the salvation of a unique western civilization and a distinctive freedom-loving people—was born, helping to unite Greece to eventually hurl the invader back into vastness of Asia.

Like the dramatic showdown at Thermopylae, so a few good men and boys of the Republic of Mexico defended another hill of destiny (higher than the Spartans' "hillock" near the sea) against the seemingly invincible invaders of a different race and religion, when their Mexican homeland and capital of Mexico City were facing their greatest threat in February 1847. Just as the famous pass of Thermopylae was defended so that "the whole of Hellas may be sheltered from the war," in the words of the ancient historian Herodotus, so the desperate defense of Chapultepec by the Boy Cadets and soldados (regulars and National Guardsmen) was orchestrated to shelter the people of Mexico City from harm and save the reeling republic that faced its greatest threat.

The Mexican-American War of 1846-1848 was America's first foreign war and it was an especially ugly one. But more ominously, this conflict was also America's most artificially manufactured war. This cruel conflict was created by the Manifest Destiny-inspired Democratic Administration of President James K. Polk, who led the

1

way for national expansion to the Pacific's shores at Mexico's expense. This grossly unjust war was declared against a peaceful neighboring republic for fabricated reasons to acquire some of Mexico's choice territories, especially California, while violating America's core republican and moral principles. Unlike in Mexico to this day and certainly no coincidence, America's most unjust war has also become one the most forgotten conflicts in United States history, despite having served as a training ground for the most famous leaders of both sides during the Civil War.

Indeed, this tragic war revealed some of the most unsavory aspects of the American experience, including imperialism, greed for a neighboring republic's lands, and the spread of slavery. Because of such reasons, America's most misunderstood and controversial war has been largely silenced to leave a giant void (unlike in today's Republic of Mexico) in the nation's collective historical memory and consciousness. There was little, if anything at all, about the Mexican-American War that has warranted it the designation of a "good war" like when America fought against the relentless march of fascism during the Second World War. Therefore, the American people have long possessed a historical amnesia in regard to the Mexican-American War, and for ample good reason.

Young Ulysses S. Grant was one participant of the conflict that bought so much suffering and misery to Mexico, winning recognition not long after graduating from the United States Military Academy (Class of 1843) at New Point, New York. In a crusade in which the American battle-cry was "To the Halls of Montezuma" (the most famous Aztec ruler whose ill-fate was to have governed his empire when the Spanish Conquistadors arrived in 1519 with fire, lust, and sword) and many American soldiers carried their prized volumes of *Cortéz's Conquest of Mexico*, Lieutenant Grant first earned distinction in this conflict that he correctly called a "wicked" war. The ugliness of this conflict against a vulnerable and weak Mexico was demonstrated by a no quarter (unofficial) policy by American soldiers, when they overran the strategic high ground of Chapultepec, a native Nahuatl, or Nahua, Aztec (the original Mexicas) word, on the morning of September 13, 1847.

Like other long-overlooked aspects of the battle, this massacre was one of the forgotten chapters of the struggle for possession of the highest hill in the area during the engagement that effectively ended the fighting for possession of Mexico City, although the final treaty was not signed until months later.

Located just over a mile southwest of Mexico City (the "city of Montezuma") as the Mexican Crow flies and dominated by the so-called Castle that stood in magnificent fashion atop its lofty flat summit, Chapultepec fell to a dramatic assault on a bloody Monday morning just before mid-September. Chapultepec was also the home of Mexico's Military College, which trained its best and brightest in the art of war. However, the full story, including the massacre of many soldados, who had attempted in vain to surrender, of Chapultepec has not been previously told until the publication of this book.

Therefore, more than 170 years after the war's conclusion, it is now time to take a fresh "new look" at the story of "Los Niños Héroes," or "the Child Heroes," who were members of the Cadet Corps of the Military College. Like these young men themselves, so the final showdown at Chapultepec has been long dominated by misconceptions and distortions that have obscured the historical record.

First, the students of Mexico's Military College were not boys as so often alleged. In truth, they were typical young men who were serving their country as cadets at their nation's premier Military College. In 1847, they were being groomed as officers in the Mexican Army and future leaders of their beloved republic, before the war itself suddenly descended upon the Military College.

Like no other event of this disastrous war, the people of Mexico have long honored the brave performance and noble sacrifice of these dedicated cadets, who have won famed as the Boy Heroes, of Chapultepec. These young men, who were among Mexico's best and brightest, represented a new generation of promising youth, who prepared for the stern future challenges.

Unfortunately, much of the story of the Boy Cadets (around 200 soldiers at the time of the overpowering American attack) has been romanticized, evolving into what some historians have incorrectly considered a popular myth. Consequently, now is the time to separate the ample amount of romantic fiction from fact as much as possible to present a much more accurate and honest view of these heroic young men, who defended Chapultepec with great spirit and courage against impossible odds.

These cadets were mostly teenagers of Mexico's premier military academy at the Castle, which contained the viceroy's old residence. The Military College was located in the Castle's southeast section, standing atop the last hill before Mexico City in guardian fashion like a silent sentinel. Mexico's Military College was a direct counterpart to the United States Military Academy at West Point, New York: another irony of this bitter war between two neighboring republics that had won their independence from European Powers.

Transferred from Perote, Mexico, in 1841, Chapultepec was officially designated as the site of the Military College at that time. As mentioned, this resplendent Castle had been built as the residence for Spanish royalty, serving as the Viceroy's summer palace. In addition, the beautiful hill of Chapultepec had also once been the summer residence of Aztec royalty. A picturesque and cool place had been provided by an attractive Mexican Cypress forest of towering virgin timber, which was located at the foot of "Grasshopper Hill."

The vice-regal palace housed the Military College atop the summit that overlooked Mexico City just to the northeast. The Castle, built by the Spanish (Spanish engineers who used cheap Indian labor) of gray stone, stood atop the hill of the ancient Aztec in commanding fashion. The Chapultepec complex situated on the flat summit was distinguished by an elegant tower, called the Caballero Alto, located on the summit's east side.

Wearing distinctive French-style blue forage caps piped in red near the top, these dedicated cadets of the "Colegio Militar" (Military College) wore a light gray frock coat (service dress) with brass buttons marked, "Colegio Militar." But they wore a gray service uniform, which included gray trousers with a wide red stripe down each leg, during the battle of Chapultepec. A high, stiff gray collar of their service uniform was trimmed in red to highlight a stylish and close-fitting uniform. On fateful September 13, 1847, the young men of the around 200-man Cadet Corps also wore black leather cross belts. A plain brass rectangular belt buckle lay over the center of their chests, where the belts crossed and were held in place by the buckle. Neat and tidy, these snappy cadet service uniforms of gray made these teenagers look older than their actual years.

During the September 13 battle, this distinctive appearance of the gray uniform (other Mexican defenders wore blue uniform coats) made the cadets' appearance more distinctive from other soldados and fair game to incensed Americans at the height of the assault. The final tally of the losses on September 13 told an ugly story: around 675 defenders of Chapultepec were killed and only 100 wounded and another 100 captured: gross proportional distortions compared to usual losses in a conventional battle. Clearly, the high number of fatalities revealed an ugly no-quarter (not official) policy on the morning September 13, which made the battle more nightmarish and far bloodier than a traditional battle.

While the Mexican people have long revered the Boy Cadets of Chapultepec as national heroes and cultural icons—Los Niños Héroes, or the Boy Heroes— the American people know relatively little, if anything, about them and their heroic sacrifice for God and country. Indeed, the dramatic story of Chapultepec has become a forgotten chapter to modern Americans. Even the final resting places of the bodies of the American soldiers who stormed the 200-foot high hill of Chapultepec have been long forgotten today by their own people or country.

Chapultepec was the last high ground that stood before the colonial urban center of Mexico City, distinguished by its magnificent Cathedral and its baroque buildings less than two miles away. This strategic hill guarded the western approaches to the beautiful city that looked much like a metropolis in Spain. Here, the heroics demonstrated by the cadets on a unforgettable September morning represented a noble, but tragic, sacrifice of a proud nation in the throes of defeat.

The cost of overrunning Chapultepec that morning was high. More than 850 American attackers were killed and more than 2,500 men fell wounded. Today, located in the heart of bustling Mexico City, a small American cemetery contains the bodies of 750 United States soldiers, including those men who fell in the seemingly doomed assault launched against what appeared impregnable to the majority of men on both sides, Chapultepec.

Nestled amid a peaceful residential neighborhood today known as San Rafael amid the sprawling city of more than 22 million people of Greater Mexico City and the largest urban area on the North American continent, this tiny cemetery of only one acre (owned by the United States) is virtually hidden from view today. Very few of Mexico City's residents are even aware of the location of the officially designated United States National Cemetery.

Ironically, this lack of knowledge about the cemetery's location is mirrored by the overall historical amnesia and negligence of the American people about the war and Chapultepec. They long ago forgot about these fallen soldiers, despite fully aware that the United States Marine Corps' anthem (a slightly more than 100-man detachment was engaged in its largest battle during the Marine Corps' 72-year history) that emphasized September 13 heroics "From the halls of Montezuma" This famous battle cry pertained to the bitter fighting at Chapultepec that had been turned into a slaughter: the once-serene elevated hilltop that had once served as the summer home of Aztec (Mexica) royalty and then the colonial viceroy, looming high above the surrounding humid lowlands of swamps and lakes, including S-shaped Lake Texcoco.

In 1851, the United States Congress had voted to establish a cemetery for the multitudes of American dead who fell around Mexico City. Then, the "bones were collected," and the last remains of America's soldiers were then buried without ceremony in a common grave of unknown soldiers along a main road leading to Mexico City, the Calzada Verónica (Verónica Causeway). The wooden crosses upon which the names (carved by their comrades' knives and bayonets) of America's war dead had been eroded or torn down in the years after the war, which made positive identification impossible.

Ironically, the United States people or government never ensured the proper burial of its war dead on other Mexican battlefields, except for this one exception—the U.S. National Cemetery in Mexico City. This glaring neglect is in striking contrast to the continued respect paid by the Mexican people, who still routinely bring ceremonial flowers, foods, and drinks to the graves of their ancestors and their fallen fighting men like in the days of their Aztec ancestors. As mentioned, few people—Americans or Mexicans—

know today about the location of the small cemetery that has been seemingly deliberately hidden amid the urban sprawl of Mexico City.

Today, the Mexican people are generally not concerned about this central location of so many enemy dead, but some residents of the area believe that the United States dead should be removed to their own country: not unlike when dozens of captured Mexican flags were officially returned to Mexico from the United States. Opinions of Mexican citizens about the location of this small United States cemetery have continued to be divided to this day.

Unlike on battlefields located on other distant lands, such as European battlegrounds like Normandy, France, American military cemeteries do not exist on battlefields such as Buena Vista and Monterey in northern Mexico, or even at battlefields located in the United States like Palo Alto (situated just north of Brownsville, Texas).Therefore, the vast majority of America's dead (far more died of disease than in battle) today lay in unmarked graves across Mexico.

In many cases during General Winfield Scott's fast-paced 1847 campaign that resulted in the capture of Mexico City, there had been no time for their comrades to even construct caskets for the American dead. Most dead, therefore, were laid to rest in dirty and worn army blankets when buried in Mexican soil. In the words of one saddened Mississippi officer who lamented how the common soldiers were buried "in their blankets without coffins [and] Hundreds of America's noble and generous sons sleep in this soil without having received the rites or the decencies of Scripture"—or proper Christian burials. To this day, the final resting places of thousands of young American men and boys who died from 1846-1848 are known only to God.

In striking contrast and as noted, the Mexican people have never forgotten their brave sons who died in the defense of Mexico City and their republic: ironically, a heroic, but failed, defensive stand at Chapultepec has been long remembered by the people of Mexico, while the American public simply forgot about their deceased soldiers in a victorious war.

The dramatic true story of the cadets, especially the six young men who were killed, is truly deserving of lavish praise on multiple levels. First, they defiantly refused to leave the doomed hilltop, after having been directed by their commandant that it would be best for them to forsake the defense of their beloved Military College. All in all, the cadets' distinguished role at Chapultepec can be compared to the most famous last stand by the brave Greek defenders of western civilization (the city-states of ancient Greece) at Thermopylae in 480 B.C. At the strategic pass of Thermopylae, the 300 Spartan warriors (hoplites), who hailed from the lands of the fertile Eurotas River Valley, fought against the impossible odds of a mighty invader.

Here, at the so-called "Hot Gates," the Spartans of Thermopylae died in a last stand to save their western, or European, civilization from destruction, autocratic rule, and slavery, if the Greek city-states were conquered by King Xerxes and his immense Persian Army. Like the Boy Cadets, these long-haired Spartan warriors were bound together by a sacred oath that placed duty, honor, and God before life itself. At Chapultepec and to the very end, the six Boy Cadets remained true to themselves, their often-defeated army, and Mexico by dying for their beleaguered country when hope no longer remained.

Ironically, generations of Texas and the United States historians have usurped the designation of Thermopylae for their own last stand of a relative handful of Anglo-Celtic rebels, less than 200 men, at the Alamo, at San Antonio de Béxar, Texas. On the early morning (just before dawn) on March 6, 1836, Mexican troops under General Antonio Lopéz de Santa Anna (who was the overall commander in charge of defending Mexico City in 1847) killed around 185 Alamo defenders to the last man. Santa Anna was attempting to regain control of Texas by defeating the rebellious Texans, who had revolted in early October 1835.

Generations of writers (historians and novelists), movies, and television have played a large role in creating the mythical Alamo based on the popular Thermopylae analogy that was emphasized at the time and even to this day. In fact, no chapter in American history has been more romantically embellished to deviate from the historical facts about the Alamo's story: the self-congratulatory fabrication and glorification of the Texas creation myth that conveniently left the supreme importance of slavery out of the historical equation in order to keep the romantic myths alive and, most importantly, to falsely claim the moral high ground, although the Republic of Mexico (President Vincente Guerrero) had abolished slavery on September 15, 1829 to its great credit.

No small part of the Alamo myth has been based on the pervasive anti-Mexican stereotypes, an overt racism, Anglo-Saxon myths, and anti-Catholicism that had endured in the United States for generations. But new research has revealed that instead of the fabled last stand, a large percentage of the Alamo garrison actually fled the attack by escaping the Alamo compound (a death-trap) only to be cut down by Mexican cavalry that Santa Anna had ordered in place for this express purpose, on the open wintertime prairies outside the Alamo. In contrast, the Boy Cadets, around 200 men of the Cadet Corps, had decided on their own to stay at their defensive positions when their superior officer suggested for them to depart the doomed hill of Chapultepec.

In these sense, the story of the Boy Cadets actually revealed more genuine heroism on the fateful on September 13, 1847 than what had been exhibited by the Anglo-Celts on the morning of March 6, 1836 (another bloody morning), because the Alamo defenders had been surprised and trapped (they had no choice about departing the surrounded old Franciscan mission unlike the six Boy Cadets who could have safely departed to save their lives) by Santa Anna's Army. Again and as noted, this was not the case of the young cadets, who declined to save themselves unlike the citizen-soldiers of the Alamo garrison, before the massive assault on Chapultepec when they had the opportunity to do so.

What cannot be denied was the fact that the cadets' heroics were performed against impossible odds and in a no-win situation, because the inadequately-manned Chapultepec was doomed from the beginning. Even more, the cadets' high sacrifice came in an unjust war that the badly-divided (between federalists and centralists) nation never had a realistic chance of winning against a far more powerful United States military machine. As mentioned, when the Boy Cadets received the recommendation from the Military College's commandant, General José Mariano Monterde, that they should return home to avoid the carnage that was only a matter of time, they declined to depart the academy that they loved.

Also, some evidence exists that when some cadets were ordered by the commanding officer (Major General Nicholás Bravo Rueda) at Chapultepec to join the defenders' retreat from their assigned defensive positions that were about to be overwhelmed on the morning of September 13. But they refused to fall back with their retiring comrades and defiantly remained at their assigned defensive positions. Fighting to the bitter end, six cadets died in a righteous and heroic defense of Chapultepec, their school, and capital.

Therefore, the young cadets were not unlike the ancient Spartan warriors, whose greatest sin had been to discard their heavy battle shields and assigned places in a tight formation, because it endangered fellow warriors whose lives depended upon a solid, unified shield defense in their tactical formation, the phalanx. In this sense, the Military College, Mexico City, and families represented the Spartan shield and explained why the cadets had decided to remain in harm's way by choosing not to return home, as suggested by their commandant, and then ignored the orders to retreat from General Bravo in the heat of battle. But like the ancient Spartans who died for the people, including wives, parents, and children, of their city-state and Greece, so the cadets died for the people of Mexico and the nearby capital city.

In addition, in a long-overlooked sacrifice that above all emphasized still another moral aspect of this vicious struggle, the half dozen cadets perished for a Mexico that had abolished slavery (unlike the United States until the Civil War) in mid-September 1829. What has been most forgotten was that the Texans and their allies—American volunteers from across the United States—fought largely to save slavery. At this time, a vibrant institution of slavery served as the foundation of the robust Texian economy based on cotton cultivation).Therefore, in 1836, Santa Anna and his soldados had liberated Texas slaves according to not only the nation's moral and egalitarian principles, but also the national law from President Guerrero's September 15, 1829 decree that had freed all of Mexico's slaves.

Ironically, the miserable defeat and slaughter at the Alamo—the so-called modern Thermopylae of Texas history—rallied the Texians and their United States volunteer allies in sufficient numbers to win the decisive battle of San Jacinto on April 21, 1836, guaranteeing the loss of the bountiful of Texas to the republic. A captured General Santa Anna, whose life was under threat, was forced to accept Texas independence to gain his release. But the outraged statesmen of the Mexican Congress refused to abide by the outrageous stealing of Texas by a well-organized filibuster effort that was fueled and funded primarily by wealthy, pro-slavery citizens across the United States, especially New Orleans, Louisiana.

Therefore, when Texas was annexed by the United States Congress a decade later and accepted the bogus Texans' claim that its boundary extended all the way south to the Río Grande River, then this travesty led directly to the outbreak of war in the spring of 1846. Mexican troops dutifully defended their nation's sacred soil just north of the Río Grande River (also called the Río Bravo) and attacked an interloping reconnaissance column of United States cavalrymen not far from the city of Matamoros, Mexico. Here, on the north bank of the Río Grande River northwest of Matamoros, the opening shots of the Mexican-American War were fired. Having been handed the long-awaited and convenient excuse, President James K. Polk appealed to Congress to declare war because allegedly American blood had been shed on American soil, which of course was actually Mexican soil!

This bogus excuse for unleashing the invasion of Mexico eventually led all the way to the assault on Chapultepec by September 1847. Consequently, the Boy Cadets also fought against the race-based concept of Manifest Destiny (ironically, like the race-based crusading spirit of the Spanish Conquistadors more than three centuries before), which proclaimed that the Anglo-Saxon race had been sanctioned by God to possess the entire North American continent.

In the end, what has been most forgotten was that the Boy Cadets had fought in part to stop the march of slavery ever-southward because it was such an integral part of American expansionism, after Texas had become a slave state. If Mexico was conquered and annexed by the United States, then slavery would be once again introduced into a land that had known freedom for people of all colors since mid-September 1829.

Symbolically, the 1st Mississippi Volunteer Regiment, that won distinction at the battle of Buena Vista in helping to repulse Santa Anna's attack on February 23, 1847, consisted of the wealthy sons of leading planters and slave-owners. The volunteer regiment of

Mississippians was commanded by the aristocratic planter and large slave-owner who became the first president of the Confederacy, Colonel Jefferson Davis. Of course, the Confederacy went to war in April 1861 to defend what had long cursed the American experiment in democracy, slavery.

Clearly, in matters of race, the two countries—the United States and Mexico—could not have been more different: basically, they were very much polar opposites, despite neighboring republics which had been founded on the idealism of Age of Enlightenment ideologies. One people's republic was largely Anglo-Saxon, and the other largely mestizo, who were the descendants of Spaniards and pre-Columbians, or Aztec, who were also known as the Mexica. In general, the mixed-race mestizos (the majority of Mexicans by 1846) were more Indian than Spanish, and they had inherited both the good and bad of the conquering Spanish.

Both neighboring republics that were so different had been created from the fiery forge of revolution, after successful people's uprisings against their respective European mother countries. Much to its ever-lasting credit in the history of the progressive course of humanity, one country had abolished slavery before the Mexican-American War and celebrated a distinctive mixed-race heritage, while the people of the other nation had long considered the mixing of races as the greatest taboo, since the republic's founding in Philadelphia, Pennsylvania, on July 4, 1776. Early bestowed to the United States by mass migrations across the Atlantic, this cultural legacy had been largely inherited from an isolated, xenophobic island nation of Anglo-Saxons. But while the thirteen English colonies had gained strength and unity from a homogenous English culture and heritage that was on a dramatic ascent during the 1840s, the Mexican people had inherited some of the weaknesses of a decadent Spain on the decline. In overall terms, this inheritance made Mexico less capable of resisting the armies of invaders from the north.

In purely moral terms and because of Texas slavery that was a flourishing institution, consequently, the Thermopylae analogy actually applied more to the last stand of the cadets at their Military College at Chapultepec (an anti-slavery defense) than to the battle of the Alamo (a pro-slavery defense at an old Franciscan mission and stone church) barely a decade before.

Therefore, the Boy Cadets were more truly freedom fighters who were in fact truly deserving of more genuine respect than the Alamo defenders. In this sense, the cadets were actually in the mainstream of the international anti-slavery movement and moral progressivism of the most civilized nations of the western world, like Great Britain that had already abolished slavery like Mexico.

Significantly, in regard to what they fought for and the moral implications of their heroic sacrifice on September 13, the Boy Cadets were less mythical in overall historical terms than the Alamo defenders, who battled primarily to save an antiquated institution that had existed from times immemorial (the first war captives became slaves) quite unlike the young students of Mexico's military college.

In addition, the sacrifice of the Boy Cadets symbolically represented Mexico's loss of national innocence. In the end, this tragic reality was personified when the last surviving cadet, seventeen-year-old Juan Baptist Pascasio Escutia, who had been born in Tepic, Mexico, leaped to his death when he fell to the rocky eastern slope. When it was obvious that all was lost and Chapultepec was about to fall to the hordes of cheering Americans, the young cadet jumped from the highest point of the Castle's eastern side, while wrapped in the flapping Mexican banner to save it from Yankee hands.

As presented in this book, American soldier accounts have verified the truth of desperate Mexican soldiers attempting to escape the slaughter by jumping from windows and rooftops. Like the life of Cadet Juan Escutia who had been admitted to the Military College only five days before on September 8, so too Mexico was tragically sacrificed on the altar of a more aggressive nation's ambitions and imperialism based largely primarily on race and the quest for another republic's lands.

However, this is an inappropriate analogy about Mexico losing its innocence in this brutal conflict. After all, it was actually the United States that had lost its innocence in waging an aggressive war (in violation of George Washington's words of caution to avoid foreign entanglements, especially immoral ones) against a neighboring republic. The United States had launched its most unjust war in its history in the name of national greatness against a weak opponent in a deliberately manufactured war orchestrated from the White House that resulted in the stripping away of around half of Mexico's territory—today's American Southwest, including California—in the Treaty of Guadalupe Hidalgo. An easy target and inevitable victim, Mexico was exceptionally weak, especially in regard to nationalism, after having inherited Spain's feudal-like institutions to ensure social, political, and economic underdevelopment unlike the more unified and homogeneous United States. But Mexico was more advanced and progressive than the United States in regard to race, especially in regard to having abolished slavery.

Therefore, what has been most forgotten about the deaths of the Boy Heroes at Chapultepec was that they died in part because they were standing up against the march of slavery that might have been reestablished across Mexico by the victors, if the nation was conquered. Indeed, if the United States Congress had decided to annex (this movement was part of the nation's Manifest Destiny-inspired visions) all of Mexico, then slavery would be re-imposed in Mexico.

While America, especially the South because of its cotton-based economy and agrarian society, had long profited from slavery, Mexico benefitted economically from the debt peonage system that ensured lifetime labor of many native inhabitants. Tragically, to make the wealthy class even richer, the economic systems of both nations were based on the exploitation of the labor of darker-skinned people of two subjugated races, one native of the New World and the other native of far-away Africa.

These grim historical realities, especially in regard to slavery if re-imposed in Mexico, have now placed the dramatic story of the Boy Cadets in a proper and more striking historical context than previously thought. As mentioned, the Thermopylae analogy was actually more on target in regard to Chapultepec's cadets than initially realized, because if Mexico had been annexed (a distinct possibility that was ultimately defeated), then slavery would have become the law of the land throughout Mexico, just as Texas had become part of a vast slave empire, after Santa Anna's decisive defeat at San Jacinto. Symbolically, had the Greek city-states had been conquered, then King Xerxes and his Persians would have made slaves of the vanquished Greeks, including the Spartans, spreading slavery like if the United States had annexed all Mexico, as many Americans had envisioned.

Ironically, the first governor of the Massachusetts Colony, John Winthrop, proclaimed that the religious refugees (the Puritans) from England were ordained by God to create a great shining "city on a hill": a biblical metaphor for an oppressive people's regeneration in the New World far from the Old War's evils and decadence. What evolved from this initial idealistic concept was the growth of a race-based expansionism, fueling westward expansion, the stealing of Texas (first by Anglo-Celtic rebels and their United States allies, and then annexation of Texas by the United States to spark the conflict. But America betrayed herself, and this fundamental betrayal was best symbolized by what happened at Chapultepec, including the tragic deaths of a half dozen young cadets who perished in defense of their beloved republic.

For many such reasons and especially to present a fresh and new view for the first part of the twenty-first century, therefore, the fascinating story of the Boy Cadets of Chapultepec needs to be presented to the American people for the first time and in a proper historical perspective. After all, this is a timeless story of heroism and sacrifice for God, honor, and country.

Therefore, this is the first book in English to tell the full story about the young cadets and their role at Chapultepec. As much as possible, the usual romance and mythology has been eliminated from this work, because some myths surrounding the Boy Cadets were created to derive a sense of glory from a humiliating past, including decisive defeat in this battle and the war.

The unvarnished truth (for instance, ample xenophobia, racism, and intolerance in fact existed on both sides as in any conflict between nations so vastly different) will be presented in this book, including how the Boy Cadets died in no small part from the results of the combined effects of bitter political in-fighting, incompetence, and deep internal divisions and failures of military leadership. In this sense, the Boy Cadets died for the sins and failures of the nation for which they so gallantry defended with their young lives. Nevertheless, they died for a noble and worthy cause: fighting with heart and soul in a desperate bid to save Mexico City and their people from the nightmare of foreign conquest and to avoid the worst of all fates for Mexico, which was losing half of its territory.

While the Boy Cadets are revered today as national heroes across Mexico and as noted, their timeless story is still not known today in the United States, despite its ever-growing Latino population. As mentioned, this is the first book about the Boy Cadets that has been presented by any American author, but one who had long visited and researched Mexican-American War battlefields on both sides of the Rio Grande River.

At this late date, Americans and the English speaking world in general should know about the many hidden truths, including some of the most uncomfortable ones to both Americans and Mexicans (each side was guilty of committing atrocities in this brutal conflict) about the war that was fought so long ago.

Ironically, this book was inspired in a rather unusual, if not entirely strange, way. The initial idea to write this book largely stemmed from the words of a well-meaning National Park Service ranger at a Mexican-American War Battlefield National Historical Park located in south Texas and just north of the Rio Grande River. This well-educated expert on the Mexican-American War emphasized to this author in no uncertain terms in December 2011 that the remarkable story of the Boy Cadets simply did not deserve a full-book treatment because it was nothing more than a romantic myth.

For whatever reason but perhaps because these young men in grey uniforms have become so iconic to the Mexican nation and people to this day, a number of rather dark counter myths have recently developed to deny the fundamental truths about the role and sacrifice of the Boy Cadets on that fateful September morning.

This rather surprising reaction to what has been documented in the historical record has been calculated to deny the Boy Cadets' courage and sacrifice, revealing an attempt to silence and erase history. Consequently, this book has been written to dispel the rise of these prevalent counter-myths of reactionaries, contrarian-minded individuals, and non-professional historians, while permanently placing the heroic sacrifice of the young cadets in a proper historical perspective. After all, the ample amount of existing documentation and evidence about the sacrifice of the Boy Cadets on September 13, 1847 is certainly more than sufficient to silence these critics and reactionaries, who have been motivated in fostering counter myths primarily because of personal and political agendas that have little, if anything, to do with the historical facts.

Therefore, this book has been written to prove that what happened in the cadets' spirited defense of the Military College was not a myth and to preserve an important chapter of Mexico's storied history in the nation's most tragic war.

Significantly, President Harry Truman, a World War I veteran of the western front in France and an artillery officer from Missouri who trained at Camp Doniphan which was named after the Mexican-American War hero Colonel Alexander Doniphan and his Missouri men who captured El Paso and Chihuahua, certainly did <u>not</u> believe that the story of the Boy Cadets was a myth.

On March 4, 1947 and before a Mexican honor guard, President Truman solemnly laid a memorial wreath at the monument to the Boy Cadets located at the foot of Chapultepec hill: the bestowal of a heartfelt recognition and sincere respect by the Missourian that won the hearts of the Mexican people. When asked why he had honored of these fallen heroes of the Republic of Mexico, President Truman emphasized in no uncertain terms how: "Brave men don't belong to any one country. I respect bravery wherever I see it." And the Boy Cadets demonstrated a great deal of bravery against the odds on the bloody morning of September 13, 1847, impressing not only successive Mexican presidents, but also United States presidents.

Truman was the first United States president to acknowledge and pay an appropriate tribute to the six fallen cadets at a hallowed national shrine. What was significant was the fact that this native Missourian (who was raised near where Colonel Doniphan had lived in the Missouri River country) displayed an inordinate degree of respect and empathy to the warm, dignified people of a weaker nation that lost so much of its treasure in manhood and territory during that terrible conflict.

While the people of America quickly forgot about its most unjust war, the Mexican people never forgot this most tragic of conflicts or the heroic Boy Cadets of Chapultepec. Here, the ancient Aztec War Eagle clashed with the American bald eagle in a dramatic showdown, when Mexico's life was at stake as never before.

Most importantly, the heroic deaths of the Boy Cadets in attempting to defend their Military College symbolized the loss of the some of its best and brightest. For such reasons, this book has been dedicated to telling the true story of the Boy Cadets and what exactly happened on that awful morning at Chapultepec. For example, while the role of the Boy Cadets had been embellished by many historians, the far higher sacrifice (both in numbers and percentage of loss) made by the National Guardsmen of the San Blas Battalion at Chapultepec has been forgotten: just another one of the paradoxes of the hard-fought battle that paved the way to Mexico City's fall.

In presenting the unvarnished "new look" perspective, the good, bad, and the ugly have been revealed in this book to bring forth as much truth about the climactic battle and cadets as much as possible. For instance, one of the long-recognized six cadets who were killed on September 13, 1847 was not even a cadet, Lieutenant Juan de la Barrera. However, de la Barrera had spent most of his military career as a cadet, before being assigned to a combat engineer battalion shortly before the battle, after having just completed his difficult engineering studies at the Military College.

However, Lieutenant de la Barrera's heart and soul still lay with his beloved Military College on the early morning when the Americans pounded Chapultepec with an artillery bombardment and then attacked in overwhelming numbers. Unfortunately, relatively little information can be found about Juan Baptist Pascasio Escutia, because primary documentation about the young man has been lost from the Military College's records in part because he was the newest cadet admitted to the prestigious institution. He had been admitted as a student only five days before the final assault when the Americans went for broke to carry the high ground.

Young Juan Escutia evidently either volunteered to fight beside the cadets or had been assigned to the task of defending the Military College by General José Mariano Monterde. In a speech that he presented only a few years later, Monterde mentioned that he had informally admitted Escutia to the Military College on September 8, after the San Blas Battalion had been assigned to defend Chapultepec.

Consequently, it seems that Escutia had been a member of the San Blas Battalion, which had been raised in his home area, to the Military College. Almost certainly, Escutia had been admitted because of the emergency situation and to bolster the cadets' thin ranks when the Americans were about to attack, or to replace those cadets who had been

18

wounded in the artillery bombardment on either September 12 or on the early morning of September 13.

This is an important distinction because Escutia has been long celebrated as having sacrificed his life by jumping to this death to save the Mexican flag, which he had wrapped around his body, from capture. It is not known but perhaps because of the chaos, thick smoke, and confusion that provided no eyewitnesses about the closing scenes of the bloody fight, Cadet Agustín Melgar might have actually been the one who performed this celebrated gallant act to keep the sacred national banner out of the Yankees' hands, because his body lay next to Escutia on the eastern slope of Chapultepec, after the fighting ended.

Most significant and as mentioned, ample primary evidence from American soldier accounts have revealed that a number of desperate Mexican fighting men attempted to escape out of the windows of the easternmost building of Chapultepec, and then fell to the ground of the rocky eastern slope. But the best existing evidence has revealed that Cadet Escutia almost certainly jumped to his death, after he had received a fatal wound from an attacker.

But most of all, this book was been dedicated not only to the people of Mexico, but also to the heroic actions and sacrifice of the young men ("Los Niños Héroes) of what can be considered Mexico's West Point. Consequently, this work has praised the valor and sacrifice of young cadets like Juan Baptist Pascasio Escutia, who fought and died beside his fellow cadets, when Mexico's life was at stake.

Mexico's best and brightest had no idea about the key roles that they were destined to play in the bloody defense of Chapultepec, when they were first admitted to their nation's premier Military College with a bright-eyed innocence and hope for the shining future that partly revealed their lack of knowledge about the horrors of war. Therefore, this book has presented not only the unforgettable story of great heroism of Mexico's youngest fighters, but also the dark, insidious side of American expansionism and imperialism at the expense of the Republic of Mexico.

In one of the war's most tragic chapters, the cadets were little more than sacrificial lambs in the doomed defense of Mexico City. But most importantly, the enduring inspirational legacy of Mexico's cadets was destined to rise from the ashes of a disastrous defeat like the proverbial phoenix. Like the ancient Spartan warriors at Thermopylae who died to keep the hordes of Persians from invading their native homeland, so the young cadets, known today as "the Child Heroes," were among the last guardians of the gate and the roads that led to Mexico City.

Phillip Thomas Tucker, Ph.D.
Washington, D.C.
July 22, 2017

Prologue

Month after month on the elevated stage of the flat summit of Chapultepec, the young men of the Cadet Corps of Mexico's premier Military College drilled and trained on the wide parade ground. The parade ground was situated atop the high stone terrace located on the south side of the prestigious academy at the Castle's southeast section and near where its ornate main entrance stood. Symbolically, when peering from the edge of the parade ground (the plaza of Chapultepec), the cadets viewed the sprawling expanse of Mexico City that extended over a wide area in the valley below to the northeast.

Not long after the Mexican Republic that had won its independence from Spain in 1821 during a brutal war for liberation that was based on the egalitarian principles of the American and French Revolutions, the Colegio Militar (Military College) was founded in 1823. The Military College was housed in the southeast section of the so-called Castle (Spain's colonial viceroy's residence) at Chapultepec by 1841.

Most importantly, the Military College represented a new day and brighter future for the republic. Here, some of the best and brightest young men of Mexico were educated to become future leaders in service for the common good of the nation.

This standard practice of preparing talented young men for future professional military careers and leadership roles at a military academy had been first created in France by Napoleon Bonaparte. He had established the Saint-Cyr Military College on May 1, 1802. Consisting of some of France's best and brightest like at Mexico's Military College by early September 1847, Saint-Cyr had long graduated promising cadets that helped to make Napoleon's Armies better trained and more formidable. The French cadets lived by the motto of "They Study to Win" in the game of war. In this sense, the Boy Cadets were part of an enduring legacy left by Napoleon, who had died in exile in the same year (1821) that Mexico won its independence.

These young men of Mexico's premier Military College were imbued with the republican and egalitarian faith of the young nation. After all, the Military College had been first established for the creation of virtuous and moral republican leaders, military and civilian. This was an increasingly pressing concern for the troubled republic. The aristocratic and luxury-loving General Antonio López de Santa Anna, a ruthless strongman in successive decades, was destined to lead Mexico to decisive defeat and national humiliation in 1847.

In fact, no leader in Mexico's history caused the republic so much pain, grief, and territorial loss than Santa Anna. Overly ambitious and self-serving, he was a pompous criollo, who proudly claimed pure Spanish blood like a badge of honor. As revealed by Santa Anna's repeated rise to power, Mexico needed promising young men like the Boy Cadets to rise to prominence in the future, so that there would be no more corrupt Santa Anna's to lead the nation to disaster.

In striking contrast to Santa Anna, General José Mariano Monterde, born in 1812 and now serving in his first term as the Military College's commandant, was a decent man of honor. The general loved Mexico more than himself, and he was supremely devoted to the national good. Therefore, Monterde was highly respected by the young men who trained day after day at the Military College. General Monterde was a model officer and commander, who the cadets looked up to as an inspiring example to emulate.

Hailing from various towns across Mexico, including Mexico City, the cadets of the Military College were the sons of military men, including generals. First officially approved in 1823 and much like the United States Military Academy at West Point, New York, that was so vital to creating a strong military to protect the United States, the Military College had been relocated at Chapultepec from Perote, Mexico, in 1841. The level plateau atop the commanding flat crest of "Grasshopper Hill" (as named by the Aztec who had worshiped at this special place) served as an ideal parade ground for the cadets to drill and learn their trade.

Prophetically, in 1843, the first cannon of the Mexican artillery had been hauled up the dusty road that led up the steep hillside of Chapultepec for placement on the commanding summit to protect the Castle and the Military College. These guns would roar their angry defiance in less than four years later, when a determined enemy advanced with audacity all the way to the gates of Mexico City: a shocking development long considered impossible by Mexican military and civilian leadership.

By the time that the Americans attacked on the morning of September 13, 1847, around 200 cadets defended the Military College and Chapultepec with their lives. As a sad fate would have it, six of the most promising cadets of the two cadet companies, which were headed by a seasoned infantry captain, were destined for untimely deaths on that awful morning. The heroic deaths of these cadets, whose ages spanned from 13 to 19, in defending the Military College and Chapultepec were representative and symbolic, because these promising future leaders hailed from across Mexico, Tepic, Chihuahua, Puebla, Mexico City, Azcapotzalco, and Guadalajara.

But most of all on this fateful morning of September 13 just southwest of Mexico City, the cadets were now united as one by love of country and a deep sense of patriotism. No longer wearing their dress uniforms that consisted of blue uniform coats, distinguished by a single row of brass buttons, and white trousers that had been assigned for cadet attire since December 1843, they were now dressed in battle clothes--a gray service uniform. As well-known by the common soldados of Santa Anna's regiments, these young men were the promising sons of a people's revolution and the War for Independence and represented destiny itself.

Symbolically and as demonstrated at Chapultepec, it was their solemn duty of these young men to not allow the sacred legacy of generations of courageous Mexican revolutionaries and freedom fighters succumb to an untimely death. Quite simply, the Military College's students represented the future of Mexico, especially when the republic's life was at stake on September 13.

For the cadets, the Military College had become their surrogate homes, after having left their families to faithfully serve the country that they loved with all their hearts. They had dedicated themselves to a strict military life and a Mexico that they hoped to shape in the future. The six companies of the Cadet Corps consisted of squads of cadets who served under a cadet corporal. Each squad of cadets was commanded by a cadet sergeant. The cadets were grouped together by stature that had been a standard procedure employed by

Napoleon, when he led the finest fighting machine ever seen on the European continent. The First Company consisted of the tallest cadets, while the Second Company contained young men of the shortest stature, which included the youngest cadets.

The prestigious military college located high atop the hill that towered above the wide plain also possessed a small corps of musicians: four drummer boys and two buglers, who all wore green uniform coats. But as mentioned for the dramatic showdown at Chapultepec, the cadets wore their neat service dress uniform: a light gray frock coat that was distinguished by red trim, or piping, around the collar, and a red stripe that extended down each leg of the gray trousers to bestow a natty look. Along with their youth, this distinctive appearance set the cadets apart from the blue-coated regulars and National Guard troops. While the Americans wore white cross-belts over their blue uniform coats, the cadets wore black cross-belts with a rectangular brass plate. This plan brass plate was situated on their chests, where the two belts crossed and were held together.

By this time, the Military College meant as much to these young men as their beloved republic. As they fully realized, the cadets were being educated in preparation not only for military careers, but also for lofty places in the military establishment by becoming proper officers and a gentlemen. To the cadets, the Military College was worth defending and even dying for if necessary. In fact, this was a sacred trust which guaranteed that the cadets defended Chapultepec and the Military College with their lives during a supreme crisis.

Bonds of comradeship with other cadets created familial-like associations among the young men, who received excellent educations while studying atop the picturesque hill. As teenagers away from their fathers, sisters, and brothers for the first time in their lives, the bonds forged among the cadets—literally a band of brothers—were especially close and tight. The past months of receiving their educations and learning how to become faithful soldiers of the republic had forged a strong sense of camaraderie, close bonds of trust, and feelings that ran deep. Quite simply, the cadets felt personally responsible for the welfare and safety of their military academy situated atop the picturesque summit like a beacon, because it was part of their very being by September 1847.

First and foremost, the military college taught the value of the golden rules of duty, fidelity, and honor. These time-honored military virtues had been learned by the cadets by intense study in their classrooms and student quarters. Of course, such stern demands were far more than what was required of the conscripted lower class soldados, who were mostly of Indian ancestry, of the Mexican Army. The demands made upon the average soldado of the national army were far more lenient in discipline and standards compared to the Military College's exceptionally high requirements.

While sitting in the classroom or standing at attention in a neat line amid formation, the cadets of the two companies were indoctrinated into the finer points of military science, especially tactics. This was a time of intense study and learning for these young men. While drilling by the guidelines of the 1841 Light Infantry tactics manual and the French system of bayonet drill on the parade ground atop the high terrace before the front of the Military College, the cadets learned about the art of war.

Most importantly, the cadets possessed a great sense of pride not only in their nation, but also in the Military College. Here, atop the summit of Chapultepec, they were coming of age in many ways. But now with the invaders—the Protestant heathen "barbarians" as the northerners were called by the Mexican people--from the United States having advanced nearly to the gates of Mexico City, the cadets' lives were about to change forever.

But they had not forgotten what they had been taught month after month at Chapultepec. The Military College was the honored place where the cadets had learned the supreme importance of the military values of honor and patriotism. Along with the fact that his nation was now engaged in a life-or-death struggle with the invader, time-honored traditional values were a primary reason why Agustín Melgar had entered the Military College with solemn commitment on November 4, 1846.

This deep sense of honor to the republic and the Military College caused teenage Agustín Melgar to have recently, and quite unexpectedly, reappear at the academy's front door, after having just returned from an unauthorized absence and a brief reentry into civilian life since May 4, 1847. The young man had departed

Chapultepec because of either financial reasons to assist family members or romantic reasons or perhaps both.

At great risk because of the inevitable disciplinary actions that followed any unauthorized leave of absence and especially an extended one, Melgar had suddenly returned to the Military College to the astonishment of the officers and other cadets. He then requested to be allowed to reenter active service to defend his school with his life. To redeem himself for his youthful transgression, regain his honor, and preserve the family name (his father had died in the country's service when he had been young), he once again put on his dress uniform on Wednesday September 8, 1847, after his unauthorized absence from the academy. At last, Cadet Melgar had come home.

On this day, Cadet Melgar had rejoined his comrades to face the upcoming attack on September 13 that was destined to cost him his life (less than a week after having rejoined his comrades) and five other cadets, who were likewise fated to be fatally cut down that morning. The young men of the cadet corps demonstrated to the nation and the world that they had learned their lessons well about the importance of duty and honor.

With growing sense of apprehension about what this September day might bring from a resourceful enemy who had yet to lose a battle during their relentless advance all the way to Mexico City, the cadets knew that this day would be decisive. A blazing sun was about to illuminate the drama that was being played out near the capital of the once-crown jewel of New Spain long before the English colonies were settled on the eastern seaboard far to the north.

The hill of Chapultepec was surrounded by low terrain filled mostly with a broad expanse of cornfields that had long given life to the people of the Mexico City. But this was not just another ordinary late summer day in the great Valley of Mexico that had served as the home of the Aztec people in centuries past. On this fateful morning just southwest of Mexico City, the weak, ill-prepared garrison of Chapultepec, which guarded two vital roads that led to the capital, was targeted for destruction by the Yankee war machine that seemed invincible.

Indeed, this Monday morning was a decisive one for the young Republic of Mexico, which was now reeling from a series of past defeats. The fragile nation and its often-defeated army now faced their greatest crisis. The norteamericano invaders, the so-called hated Yankees, now threatened to capture Mexico City and emerge victorious in this war.

Shimmering in the September heat of the most crucial summer, now on the verge of fading away into the first hints of a soothing cool of an early fall's arrival, in the history of the Republic of Mexico, Chapultepec stood ominously as the last high ground defensive position before the Americans' great goal of capturing Mexico City. Even now, the whitish domes and church spires of the capital were viewed by the lustful eyes of a good many United States officers, who looked upon the city as the Promised Land.

Like their countrymen, including leading politicians, back home, many of these invaders of the ancient land of the Aztec already dreamed of possessing all of Mexico. Fated to die in an 1863 battle during the Civil War, Ohio-born William Haines Lytle, who was enchanted by the beauty of Mexico and its people, penned in a letter how, "I was wholly unprepared to meet with so rich and fertile a country [and] We ought to get it."

These enterprising Yanquis had fought extremely well since the army had performed a masterful ambitious landing of around 11,000 men at Vera Cruz, known as "the Gibraltar of Mexico," in March 1847. They had then laid siege to the important port city and forced its surrender, after a merciless bombardment of Vera Cruz.

This amazing success had partly resulted because most American soldiers, especially the unsophisticated farm boys (mostly Protestants), who faithfully read their Holy Bibles like the cadets, sincerely believed that they were engaged in a holy war sanctioned by God. Also like the young students of the Military College, these American fighting men were also highly-motivated and committed to fighting to the end. These United States soldiers were consumed by the fever of a divinely-inspired Manifest Destiny that called for expanding the republic to the Pacific (President Polk's dream), but entirely at Mexico's expense.

Nevertheless, the invaders recognized that they faced a devout and moral people, who loved Catholicism and God. As he penned in a letter, William Haines Lytle described how: "You have often heard me admire the eminent—the pre-eminent devotion, or rather devoutness, of the Catholic people, particularly manifested in their houses of worship and during the performance of religious exercises."

Envisioning the ending of this far more lengthy than expected war so deep in the heart of Mexico, the American soldiers were now inspired to launch an all-out offensive bid to capture the celebrated "Halls of Montezuma" (America's battle-cry in 1846-1847) at Chapultepec to achieve decisive victory. Montezuma had ruled a vast Aztec empire from this commanding hilltop that overlooked the swampy lowlands and five lakes, before the fateful arrival of the Spanish Conquistadors had forever changed the Aztec world in the most ruthless way possible.

The same pervasive racism and sense of mission that had fueled the Spanish Conquistadors to brutally vanquish the Aztec also played a part in motivating these new invaders, who saw themselves as the new Conquistadors. Many of these young men and boys in blue uniforms so far from home identified with the racist words of an editor of one Illinois newspaper. Although an educated man, this journalist nevertheless emphasized that the Mexicans "are reptiles in the path of progressive democracy" that was now being spread by American bullets, cannonballs, and bayonets deep in Mexico.

Ironically, the Military College had prepared some of Mexico's best and brightest for future leadership role so that the republic would never be seriously threatened like at this time when Mexico City was on the verge of capture. The fighting men of Mexico, especially the finest cavalrymen in the world, had proved brave and resilient in every previous battle, but nothing could compensate for the dismal failures of military and political leadership at the highest levels. If the seemingly ill-fated soldados had only possessed capable leaders to match their own courage displayed on one battlefield after another, then the republic and Mexico City would never be conquered.

Perhaps war between the two neighboring republics—a largely Anglo-Saxon nation versus an Aztec, or Mexica-based mestizo nation—had been inevitable from the beginning, because no two countries could have been more different in regard to race, culture, philosophy, and religion. Both countries had chosen the magnificent eagle, one of God's most majestic creatures, as their national symbols that were now proudly displayed on the battle-flags of the respective armies: the ultimate irony of this cruel war.

Even the respective concepts about the meaning of freedom of these two neighboring republics were radically different, and this was most readily evident in regard to slavery. What has been most forgotten by Americans today was that while Mexico had abolished slavery in September 1829 by a mixed-race hero of the independence struggle, President Vincente Guerrero, the United States contained the largest number of slaves than any republic on the face of the earth at this time.

Clearly, the upcoming showdown for possession of the strategic ground of Chapultepec was about much more than has been long generally assumed, entailing more complex meanings. Entirely unknown and unimagined by this band of dedicated cadets poised on the high ground overlooking Mexico City, they were shortly destined to become forever known as "Los Niños Héroes" to the nation that they loved and were determined to defend with their young lives.

Chapter I

Lost Golden Land of Texas Leads to War

The bountiful and beautiful land of Texas was the primary cause of the tragic conflict in which Mexico was fated to lose half of the nation's fairest territory. Texas had been lost by Mexico forever, although its leaders still refused more than a decade later to acknowledge its disastrous 1836 loss.

Unfortunately for Mexico, its elitist president and commander-in-chief Antonio Lopéz de Santa Anna had led his army north into Texas in early 1836 with the ambition of crushing the uprising of the Protestant Anglo-Celtic settlers. The Anglo-Celtic rebels and their allies (volunteers—private citizens—from the United States) had captured the center of imperial power at San Antonio de Béxar, Texas, in mid-December 1835 and expelled all Mexican soldados from Texas.

Because of the aggressiveness of the feisty Anglo-Celtic rebels and massive interference (arms—including cannon—hefty loans, munitions, and thousands of well-armed American volunteers who had crossed the border to fight against Mexico) from the United States, Santa Anna had no choice but to resort to the most drastic means to regain Texas and keep his internally divided nation intact.

After all, the Texas insurrection (actually part of a larger Mexican civil war of liberals versus conservatives) threatened to spark a series of federalist uprisings of liberal-minded Mexican leaders, who embraced states' rights in opposition to Santa Anna's hard-line centralism to lead to the republic's disintegration, if victory was not won in Texas.

However, Santa Anna's string of relatively easy successes in Texas, starting at the Alamo which fell on March 6, 1836, played a role in ensuring the loss of the fertile lands of Texas by paving to his gross tactical errors and hubris—he thought the war had already been won—that led to disaster at San Jacinto on the decisive afternoon of April 21, 1836.Because of his loss and capture by the Texians (as they called themselves) and their United States allies at San Jacinto, a captured Santa Anna had been forced to recognize the independence of the Texas Republic (declared on March 2, 1836) upon signing treaties to save his life from vengeful Texans.

Ironically, and as a strange fate would have it, the young cadets of the Military College at Chapultepec were now ready to defend Mexico City because of the past folly of their own army's commander, Santa Anna. Now in charge of Mexico City's defense, he had committed his greatest errors (losing Texas by a disastrous tactical performance at San Jacinto because of overconfidence), when the cadets had been only boys playing with toys and living in the bosom of their loving families.

Of course, neither the statesmen of the Mexican Congress or people had agreed to his treaties because they had been signed by Santa Anna to gain his release. Therefore, the Mexican Congress never acknowledged the loss of Texas or recognized the newly-declared Republic of Texas, because Santa Anna had been pressured in signing at the risk of his life.

In fact, to rally his people to support the Mexican-American War and striking an emotional cord, Santa Anna had relied upon the painful (still an old wound to the troubled nation) memory of Texas' loss. He boldly promised the people of Mexico that he would "drive the Yankee invaders to the banks of the Sabine River": the former Mexican-United States border that flowed lazily between Texas and Louisiana during its sluggish southward journey to the Gulf of Mexico.

But Santa Anna was fighting against the strong currents of history that seemed to have a will of its own, because Texas lay squarely in the path of the great migrations in human history: the relentless march of Americans ever-westward in the search of greater opportunities and ever-more land. To these settlers, especially the Scotch-Irish, boundary lines and borders made absolutely no difference and failed to slow their relentless push west. Consequently, in the end, nothing could stop this irresistible tide of Anglo-Celtic settlers pushing toward the setting sun and beautiful places like Texas, and certainly not Santa Anna, as he had discovered to his shock in April 1836.

Greatly complicating matters for Mexico which had long warned officials in Washington, D.C., that this much-feared step of a blatant acquisition would result in war, the United States officially recognized Texas on December 29, 1845. Texas became the 28th state admitted to the Union. Even more distressing for Mexico, the United States even accepted the Texans' bogus claim that its expansive territory extended farther south and all the way to the Río Grande River!

Such an outrageous claim, based weakly on the alleged southern boundary of the Louisiana Territory when sold by Napoleon to the United States in 1803, set the stage for the Mexican-American War. Indeed, open conflict then became all but inevitable in April 1846, after President Polk dispatched an army into Mexico's lands and all the way to the Río Grande opposite Matamoros. These arid lands of the Republic of Mexico had been falsely claimed as part of Texas by greedy expansionists.

Because of this obvious falsehood about what was legitimate and who really owned Mexican territory, President Polk then made the false claim that American blood had been shed on American soil— on the Río Grande's north side—after a roving United States cavalry patrol was attacked by Mexican troops. Of course, the so-called aggressors were merely defending their own national soil on the north bank of the Río Bravo (Río Grande) and performing the same duty as any soldiers of any nation, when their homeland was violated by invaders and sought by illegitimate means.

Nevertheless, the American president's dishonesty and almost laughable fiction about the true ownership of this land located just north of the Río Bravo convinced the opportunistic members of the United States Congress to issue a declaration of war. America now had its artificially manufactured excuse to invade a neighboring republic in an unjust war declared for entirely illegitimate reasons. Because this was America's most unjust war against a peaceful neighbor, most Americans today would rather forget about the conflict, especially its moral contradictions and implications, that was so costly to Mexico.

But Mexico and her people never forgot about their national nightmare that stretched from 1846-1848, because this tragic period was one of their greatest national traumas and heartaches. To this day, America's naked and self-righteous aggression has left a deep scar on the psyche of a proud nation and remarkable people, who had the misfortune of living much too close to a dynamic, strong, and ruthless neighbor, who would not be denied.

Unprepared for the Greatest Challenge

Indeed, Mexico was too weak and divided to adequately defend its vast expanse of territory against a far more powerful opponent. Then, unfortunately for Mexico, Santa Anna's penchant for losing ways on the battlefield continued unabated, after his return from exile in Havana, Cuba. Ironically, he had returned with United States assistance because of his promise to United States officials that he would sell-out Mexico and relinquish covert territories.

Despite his mostly Indian and mestizo soldados having fought fiercely in the hope of keeping additional territory out of the hands of the norteamericanos to avoid Texas' dismal fate, the generalissimo continued to demonstrate that his dismal tactical performance at San Jacinto was no fluke.

The brave sons of Mexico had fought courageously but in vain from 1846-1847. But as noted, the fault for these defeats lay elsewhere. The repeated failures of top military and political leadership, especially Santa Anna, ensured consecutive and costly defeats of the first magnitude. All the while, the American Army had advanced ever-closer to the great prize of Mexico City. As a sad fate would have it, Mexico's political and military leadership were at odds even in regard to how properly wage this most tragic of wars, failing the common people and the nation during their greatest crisis: the antithesis of the strength of the invaders who benefitted immensely from unity and conviction of purpose.

Indeed, highly-motivated American troops had steadily advanced under the "Stars and Stripes" ever-closer to Mexico City to additionally fuel the intoxicating nationalistic dream of Manifest Destiny—the nation's alleged divine right and sanction of expanding to the Pacific—, while singing "Yankee Doodle" and other patriotic songs. Only a relatively few invaders felt a sense of remorse about a stronger power taking full advantage of a weaker one in the name of God and country. Young Lieutenant Ulysses S. Grant, who was destined to play a leading role in saving the Union and a future president, was sickened by the war's grotesque unjustness.

Mexico's ruling elite—descendants of the Spanish—still clung to aristocratic European life-styles in dominating a feudal land at the expense of the masses of a darker-hue, who were the lower working class of mostly Indians and mestizos. Consequently, the republic's highest egalitarian aspirations had never been fully realized for most people, which helped to erode the already fragile fabric of Mexican nationalism. Unlike in the United States because of the blessings of geography (a well-watered and fertile land) and mild climate, a middle class had never developed in Mexico. This gapping divide exposed the wide gap between Mexico's rich and poor to deny any possibilities for true equality.

Consequently, facing such extensive disadvantages to greater social or economic advancement, the great mass of the common people, Indians and mestizos alike, could only once again place their faith in the Virgin of Guadalupe (the dark-skinned Indian Madonna, who had long inspire the dark-skinned people of the lower classes) to save themselves and Mexico during the decisive summer of 1847.

After all, throughout the nation's troubled past, the Virgin of Guadalupe had always served as the faithful protector of the common people, because her purity, love, and goodness shined brightly in an evil world. She had long served as the true mother figure of the Mexican people during times of crisis throughout the past. Consequently, only the Virgin of Guadalupe could save a reeling Mexico now on the verge of decisive defeat like the Aztec people so long ago.

Father Miguel Hidalgo y Costilla, the inspirational parish priest who hailed from the small town of Dolores, had led the first uprising against the autocratic Spanish rulers in 1810.Then, a dark-skinned Father José María Morelos, an inspirational mestizo priest of the common people, continued the legacy of spirited revolutionary leadership of Father Hidalgo, who was executed by the Spanish. These revered religious leaders of the lower classes carried the sacred banner of Our Lady of Guadalupe to inspire the Indian, mestizo, and black masses to greater resistance efforts.

Most significantly, these diehard and devout revolutionaries fought not only to secure their own freedom, but also to destroy slavery that had long generated revenues for Spain's ruling elite. Both on and off the battlefield, the Virgin of Guadalupe served as a beloved national icon for a people and nation born out of severe adversity and pain.

In part because the harsh lessons of history were never lost to the long-suffering Mexican people, they viewed the looming prospect of defeat by American invaders as little more than a nightmarish repeat of the conquest of the Aztec (or the Mexica who were the first Mexicans) by the ruthless Spanish Conquistadors: ironically, an analogy that paradoxically fueled the motivations of many Americans to march all the way to Mexico City with high hopes. The Spanish Conquistadors had destroyed a mighty empire with a combination of superior weaponry (swords of Toledo steel) and lengthy lances with steel tips, while riding their big war horses, revenge-seeking Indian allies with old scores to settle with the Aztec, and the ravages of European diseases for which the Aztec possessed no natural immunity.

Because the American Army had proved unstoppable during this spring and summer campaign, the very life of the Republic of Mexico was at stake during this September of 1847, after the rainy season had passed and the dry days of early autumn had descended the land with swiftness. In a bitter irony for the nation that had long cherished a rich and distinctive history, September had always been a festive time for the Mexican people. The gaining of a hard-won independence had been celebrated in that month since 1821. But now after the arrival of mid-September and General Winfield Scott's Army close to the capital, there was no longer time to celebrate or allow festivities in a serious crisis situation.

Representing the last hope for the beleaguered Mexico, Santa Anna had ordered the withdrawal of his forces west and back into the defenses of Mexico City. The creole general had suffered repeated defeats in attempting to halt the march of the American army, which consisted of barely 10,000 men, during in its relentless push west along the dusty National Road that led to Mexico City. Santa Anna had precious little time to reflect on a fast-paced campaign that had brought the republic to the brink of ruin.

After having crossed the high mountains of the continental divide before mid-August 1847 and descending into the green, bowl-shaped valley of Central Mexico, Scott had continued his unstoppable advance that had pushed aside all opposition since departing Vera Cruz. General Scott was determined to "conquer a peace": winning a sufficient number of victories to force the Mexican government to capitulate and sign a peace treaty. But Mexico's leader and people were fiercely proud and independent, refusing to give up the struggle. And now General Scott and his army were on the very doorstep of Mexico City.

The Americans discovered to their surprise that the area around Mexico City was situated at a high elevation (7,300 feet above sea level, while Chapultepec stood at more than 7,500 feet above sea level). This region provided a refreshing and more moderate climate (subtropical highland) to the invaders than in the humid lowlands around Vera Cruz, which had been almost unbearable to the norteamericanos, even soldiers from the Deep South, unfamiliar with *la tierracaliente*.

General Scott and his troops had arrived at the best time of year to descend upon Mexico City, because the valley's hottest month of May had long since passed. But to Scott's men, the vicinity around Mexico City was sufficiently hot to sap their strength and energy. All the while, the hot rays of the golden summer sun beat down upon the American soldiers, mostly middle-class farm boys, so far from home.

Located around 250 miles west of Vera Cruz, Mexico City, the home of more than 200,000 people, was situated in a low basin that consisted of mostly marshy ground and grassy savannahs. Five lakes (the northern three lakes were salty, while the southern two lakes were freshwater) had long sustained the daily life of the Aztec people. Because of not only the placid lakes but also the marshy terrain of these sun-baked lowlands, a number of causeways now led to the European-like metropolis.

Repeated battlefield successes had made General Scott and his men even more confident and eager "to push on to the 'Halls'" of Montezuma to secure decisive victory, in the words of Lieutenant

John James Peck, 2nd United States Artillery, from a letter. Santa Anna had made a wise decision to make a defensive stand to maximize his superior numbers (outnumbering the invaders by at least three to one) in a well-constructed array of strong defenses that protected the capital city, especially on the east side toward where the American Army had marched from Puebla. However, many leading military observers on both sides of the Atlantic still feared disaster for the audacious invaders, because Scott's relatively small army had pushed so deep into the heart of Mexico.

A religious-minded Mississippi officer, who faithfully read his Holy Bible and hated the non-religious behavior of the United States soldiers (more the case of unruly volunteers rather than highly-disciplined regulars) in Mexico, feared the worst. Captain Franklin Smith, 1st Mississippi Volunteers, made an analogy to Napoleon's disastrous invasion of Russia: "I would not be surprised yet if the army found a [1812] *Moscow in Mexico* instead of the 'Halls of Montezuma.'" God delights in humbling the proud and exalting the weak—and never was there a prouder [and] more confident and vain glorious arm than this—or one that looks less to God and more to themselves."

Indeed, General Scott faced a host of problems and a great dilemma in his plans to capture Mexico City. Santa Anna had wisely strengthened not only the eastern, but also the southern defensive sectors before the city in preparation for forthcoming American attacks. To avoid the marshy land, the heaviest defenses, the largest concentration of defenders, and the three lakes—Texcoco (northeast of Mexico City), Chalco and Xochimilco (the last two were located southeast of Mexico City)—that limited American maneuverability, and the easily-defended narrow causeways that crossed over swampy ground and led to the capital, General Scott had maneuvered with prudent care. Throughout this campaign, he immensely benefited from a group of highly-capable young engineering officers, who had graduated from West Point: a confidence and trust for which Scott was well-rewarded by their magnificent performances in this decisive campaign.

Equally impressive, the Mexican Army also possessed an elite corps of brilliant engineers—more unsung than the American engineers--who served with skill under the capable Lieutenant

Colonel Manuel Robles Pezuela. These talented military engineers were among Mexico's best and brightest. Most importantly, they greatly assisted Santa Anna by enhancing the strength of his defenses around Mexico City.

Scott positioned his troops for an attack where Santa Anna least expected a blow. Here, just below Mexico City, the wide natural barrier of an extensive lava formation, known as the Pedregal, lay directly south of the capital and west of Lake Xochimilco, which was situated just northwest of Lake Chalco.

United States Army engineers, led by West Point-trained Captain Robert Edward Lee (the army's highly-capable senior engineer), found a narrow passage way through the vast lava field. This path provided the way for the Americans to ease into a good position to out-flank Santa Anna's units of a defending army positioned below Mexico City. Indeed, hard-working soldiers had created a makeshift road wide enough for the passage of artillery, through the Pedregal. Santa Anna had considered the Pedregal impassible: a dangerous assumption when so much was at stake.

Consequently, the Americans not only out-flanked, but also eased behind Mexican forces that were caught them completely by surprise by a sudden attack on the morning of August 20. Like Santa Anna, they had counted on the Pedregal's natural protection for safety.

Initiating the battle of Contreras, Scott's attackers, shouting and cheering, charged into the Mexican force's rear, causing a panic from the unexpected assault. A large number of Mexicans were killed, wounded, and taken prisoners, including 94 officers (their American captors were shocked by the overall youth of the captive officers, which equated to inexperience), in the swift surprise attack on their seemingly safe encampment, which was located just west of the Pedregal. Artillery pieces and stockpiles of ammunition were also captured after only a short fight: the gaining of a much-needed resupply for Scott's Army, because Mexican guns and ammunition could now be used to bolster capabilities during the final drive upon Mexico City.

This brilliant maneuver forced the troops under one of Santa Anna's best lieutenants, General Gabriel Valencia, to hastily retire northeast to an excellent defensive position at Churubusco that stood just north of San Antonio and the Pedregal to the southwest.

Confident of winning still another victory thanks in part to superiority of training and weaponry (firearms and artillery), Scott's troops marched north along the San Antonio Road toward the capital.

After the most recent success won at Contreras, the way was now open for a direct approach on Mexico City. In a desperate bid to halt the relentless advance of the seemingly unstoppable Americans, Santa Anna ordered a defensive stand to be made at the defensive complex at Churubusco. Here, Santa Anna hoped to buy precious time to make defensive improvements and adjustments along the city's inner defensive line. Most importantly, the well-positioned defenders of Churubusco also protected the evacuation route of the defeated troops and their withdrawal north and closer to Mexico City. Santa Anna's tactical plan was basically sound, but it was still insufficient to stop such a confident and resourceful opponent.

As on past battlefields where victories had been reaped, General Scott unleashed frontal assaults on the powerful defenses of Churubusco. Protecting the road leading to north, the Franciscan Convento de San Mateo and church of San Diego at Churubusco were located just north of the lava bed and two miles north of the town of San Antonio. Not even the desperate fighting of the elite fighting men, the United States Army deserters of the San Patricio Battalion (St. Patrick's Battalion) of artillery, on August 20 was enough to stop the hard-charging Yankees on the war's bloodiest day.

The Americans lost more than 1,000 men in the bitter fighting at Churubusco. A shocked Santa Anna was reeling after the strong defensive positions at Churubusco were carried by storm, because the old monastery compound had seemed impregnable. One disheartened Mexican soldier penned in a letter about the disheartening disaster: "We trusted for safety in our numbers, but our enemy sleeps not and knows no fear."

A Smart and Timely Truce

After additional hard fighting and maneuvering to ease closer to the capital, Scott's troops took positions only three miles from Mexico City. After successive defeats, the capital was consumed with panic by the enemy's relentless approach. After consistently defying the odds and scoring one success after another that seemed impossible to win, the Americans had advanced almost to the gates of one of the beautiful cities in the New World.

Nothing seemingly could stop the relentless Yankees, who wore light blue coats and white cross belts, while their officers were donned in wool uniforms a darker navy blue. A shrewd politician and crass opportunist (his greatest skills were political rather than tactical) who knew that he now needed to buy additional time because the capital lay virtually defenseless and his forces were disorganized, Santa Anna had no choice but to slow the enemy's momentum by any means possible.

He, therefore, cleverly proposed a truce. A naïve General Scott mistakenly accepted the ruse because the negotiations were nothing more than a farce to stall for time. The respite allowed Santa Anna, well known for his wily ways long before the Texas Revolution, to gain precious time to reorganize and strengthen his defenses during the armistice that lasted nearly two weeks.

Most importantly immediately after Churubusco's fall, the Americans had missed their best opportunity to seize the high ground of Chapultepec before its defenses were strengthened and reinforced with additional troops by Santa Anna. Knowing little about the Mexican republic's government or laws, General Scott and his top officers had not realized that Santa Anna possessed no authority to conclude a permanent peace settlement, which could only be decided by the Mexican Congress.

Once General Scott, a War of 1812 veteran, realized his serious mistake in judgment, he ended the armistice on September 8. Scott then took action, compensating for having been so easily duped. Despite less than 8,000 men available for unleashing the tactical offensive on the city's strong array of defenses, he was determined to capture Mexico City and bring an end to his bloody war as soon as possible. Consequently, Scott's offensive was resumed with an uncharacteristic recklessness that proved costly to the men in the ranks, especially after the extra time that had been granted to Santa Anna: a certain guarantee of future heavy American losses in assaulting newly-strengthened defenses manned by more troops than had been previously in position.

With an ever-increasing sense of concern, Sergeant Thomas Barclay, Company E, 2nd Pennsylvania Infantry, penned in his journal how "Santa Anna made the most active preparations for the defense of the Capitol [and] The military academy at Chapultepec, a commanding military position, was strongly garrisoned." Many men in General Scott's ranks, including officers, began to lose faith in their commander who had been fooled by the wily Santa Anna. All in all, the resourceful Santa Anna had employed a clever ploy, and reaped considerable dividends.

Bloody Molino del Rey

Consequently, the next obstacle facing Scott's Army on the road to Mexico City was the complex of stone buildings known as Molino del Rey (or the King's Mill) and the Casa Mata. The Casa Mata was an old munitions factory located around 500 yards west of the looming heights of Chapultepec. Behind the low, white-washed buildings of the Molino complex and situated just to the east stood the forest of towering Mexican Bald Cypress trees that covered the base of Chapultepec like a dark-green shroud.

During the phony peace negotiations, Santa Anna had smartly reinforced the Molino del Rey complex, making the defensive position more formidable in timely fashion in anticipation of the inevitable assault. A good many young soldiers from across America were about to pay a high price for General Scott's mistake of unleashing frontal assaults in a reckless fashion, as if to win a decisive victory to mask his foolishness in having agreed to a truce.

Here, southwest of Mexico City on the morning of September 8, General William Worth's Division of regulars surged forward with flags flying in three columns. They charged over "an open prairie" that was an ideal killing ground. Overconfident from his past successes, Scott unleashed a direct frontal assault with more than 3,000 men, anticipating another sparkling victory.

However, when close to their tactical objective that Scott mistakenly believed (still another error in judgment) was not manned by large numbers of troops because hundreds of soldados remained hidden from view, the attackers were rudely greeted with a devastating fire. Even the artillery pieces of Chapultepec added their wrath from the commanding high ground, sending shot and shell into the surging blue ranks that were entirely exposed in the open. General Scott's assault formations were cut to pieces by well-positioned defenders in strong positions.

Ironically, General Scott's offensive effort was entirely unnecessary because no cannon were being manufacturing factory at Molino del Rey as believed: an ill-founded rumor that revealed a failure in American intelligence-gathering. Indeed, the rumor that church bells were being melted to cast cannon barrels was untrue. Even without this intelligence failure, frontal assaults over a wide stretch of open ground and against determined defenders were simply too risky for an already outnumbered army hampered by an over-extended logistical supply line, after having advanced so deep in hostile territory.

However in the end but at a fearful cost, these strong defensive positions, located just west of the hill of Chapultepec, were carried by storm, after exceptionally hard fighting. But success came at a frightfully high cost, which had been paid in full. Scott lost nearly 800 men in the assault that dampened the American army's spirits.

The fortunate survivors of the attack were nagged by the realization that their over-confident commander had committed still another grave mistake in attacking the strong Molino del Rey defensive complex. The already-small American Army had suffered casualties that it could ill-afford to lose, because there were no available replacements or reinforcements, after having advanced around 250 miles inland from Vera Cruz.

Meanwhile, the Mexicans also suffered heavily (around 2,000 men), including nearly 700 prisoners. Saddened by the heavy losses, like the Mexican troops whose morale also had been severely damaged by still another reversal, many American soldiers were increasingly angry. Survivors correctly blamed General Scott for having foolishly thrown away the lives of so many men by attacking the formidable defenses of Molino del Rey.

Even more, some United States officers believed that the assault should have continued in pursuit of the Mexican retreat from Molino del Rey (the King's Mill) in a bid to overrun nearby Chapultepec, before it was strengthened by Santa Anna. As mentioned, the cannon of Chapultepec, served by well-trained gunners, had played a part in deterring additional aggressiveness of Scott's troops. Served by experienced gunners, these cannon had severely raked the advancing American formations stretched across the fields to increase the casualty lists.

Feeling a sense of admiration for the veteran Mexican gunners of Chapultepec, Sergeant Thomas Barclay paid a compliment to the defenders of the ancient hill of Montezuma when he penned in his journal how: "The Castle of Chapultepec opened upon the victors [of Molino del Rey] and covered the retreat of the vanquished."

However, in overall strategic terms, Santa Anna still based his tactical thinking upon a fundamental miscalculation of the first order. He expected the main American attack on the city from the south, believing that the previous attacks southwest of Mexico City were nothing more than tactical feints, despite the fall of Molino del Rey. Santa Anna, therefore, still expected a main attack five miles east of Chapultepec at Candelaria. He was entirely wrong in his attempts to ascertain the depths of Scott's tactical thinking. After the high losses suffered at Molino del Rey, General Scott was now more careful in regard to making his next tactical decision.

A Vital Conference in an Obscure House of Worship

How had General Scott finally made the correct decision that sealed the doom Chapultepec and how had Santa Anna made the wrong decision in the complex tactical chess game of maneuvers for possession of Mexico City? How had Scott outwitted Santa Anna who commanded three times as many fighting men and possessed all of the advantages of strong defenses that protected Mexico City? How and when was on the most important decision of the war derived to ensure American success when the life of Mexico City was at stake?

Again, the brilliance of Scott's highly-capable West Point-trained engineers (the kind of talented men that Mexico hoped to create for its military establishment from engineer graduates at the Military College) had risen to the fore by having provided the astute tactical analysis that led to the bold decision to attack from the southwest. These gifted men of Scott's Army were members of the so-called Engineer Company.

That all-important decision to advance on Mexico City from the southwest to seal Mexico City's fate and catch Santa Anna by surprise had been agreed upon at a high-level conference held by General Scott. This officers' meeting occurred at the church and convent of Piedad on September 11.Not eager to assault the imposing heights of Chapultepec that appeared so ominous, General Scott had made enough tactical mistakes and errors in judgment in this bloody campaign to have finally gained a measure of hard-earned the wisdom to request second opinions from his top officers. By this time, the sight of Chapultepec was unnerving to his experienced men and officers, who knew that high losses would result if Scott ordered assaults on the formidable defensive position.

Consequently, the commander-in-chief, concerned over the obvious strength of the city's southern defenses and initially inclined to attack from the west despite Chapultepec's height and network of well-conceived fortifications, held his officers' conference on this hot Saturday. The express purpose of this meeting was to determine the best plan of attacking Mexico City to ensure its fall as soon as possible. Naturally, General Scott was focused on developing a well-conceived tactical plan that ensured the greatest chances for success with the lightest losses, especially after the awful bloodletting at Molino del Rey.

September 11, therefore, witnessed the most important commanders' conference of the entire war, because so much was a stake at this time. General Scott most of all wanted to end the war with one masterful stroke and capture of Mexico City, and desired tactical insights from the army's brightest minds.

Revealing a general consensus at this crucial meeting, the army's best leaders and engineers presented their almost universal opinion in advocating for the unleashing on the main attack on the capital from San Antonio to the south. Then, young Pierre Gustave Toutant Beauregard, who had been invited to the high-level conference despite his low rank of only a junior lieutenant, was about to play a prominent role. Ironically and according to army protocol, he was not expected to present his opinion before a meeting of his superiors.

However, in a surprise development, Beauregard suddenly stood up when General Scott asked for his opinion, after noticing the noise of a discussion among a small group of officers near the back of the room. He had previously remained silent, while listening to the tactical views of his articulate and bright senior officers, including the revered Captain Robert E. Lee, and the army's most respected leaders, to present their tactical views about the wisdom of attacking from the south. The young, proud French Creole, who had challenged a fellow officer to a duel with shotguns at close range only last April and often quoted the wise words of Napoleon and Caesar with an effortless ease to his disbelieving men, revealed to the surprise of one and all that the gifted Louisiana-born engineer and tactician was nothing short of brilliant.

Having grown up reading and speaking French on the plantation, where he had been suckled by a black slave nurse from St. Domingue (Haiti), in St. Bernard Parish that was located just below New Orleans, Beauregard had closely studied the tactical brilliance of Napoleon's campaigns and learned a great deal.

Before the assembled audience of officers sitting inside the church, young Engineer Beauregard delivered a masterful Napoleonic-influenced lecture about the importance of the element of surprise, which now called for striking where the enemy least expected. He shocked everyone (higher ranking officers like General Gideon Pillow—President Polk's former law partner—and especially the talented engineers, who were the army's elite) at the conference by his contrarian tactical views .Like a savvy lawyer arguing a case while standing before a council, he advocated against all previous opinions expressed by some of the best and brightest in the United States Army—his own superiors!

Swarthy and dark-featured which was a distinctive look that he had inherited from his Gallic ancestors of south Louisiana, Beauregard's arguments emphasized the wisdom of attacking Mexico City from the southwest and not the south. During this detailed lecture to the crowd of senior officers, who had emphasized that attacking from the south was the key to victory, the insightfulness of the young officer's novel tactical views were well-founded. After a series of past careful reconnaissance missions south of Mexico City since September 7 in which he had watched Santa

Anna's steady build-up of strength on the south almost on an hourly basis, Beauregard had seen the Mexican southern defensive positions gradually become stronger until it was impregnable.

Therefore, to the well-educated Louisianan of the upper class, it was now clear that the generalissimo, who hailed from the beautiful mountain town of Jalapa, expected the main attack from the south. Ever-the-gambler, Santa Anna had indeed placed his high stakes bet with his usual confidence, mustering a massive concentration of strength to defend the southern approach to the city.

Therefore, Lieutenant Beauregard correctly concluded that the southern defensive front was even more powerful defensively than at the powerful Churubusco (a corruption of the word Huitzilipochco) defensive complex, which had recently cost so many attackers' lives. Beauregard was not daunted by the fact that the commanding hill of Chapultepec stood tall, representing the last stronghold before the outer defenses of Mexico City and looming up from the flat terrain like guardian of the capital.

Quite simply, if the Americans could not be stopped at Chapultepec, then they could never be halted by the Mexican Army. Consequently, this defensive high ground represented Mexico's best and last hope for preserving the fast-fading life of its capital city, because the lofty perch seemed impregnable.

Long a devotee of the timeless tactical lessons of Napoleon's campaigns that partly reflected an early interest stemming from his own French Creole heritage of Louisiana, which had been owned by France before its sale to the United States in the 1803 Louisiana Purchase, Beauregard emphasized the importance of capturing this highest ground position that stood so prominently and seemed impregnable.

Beauregard's detailed and analytical lecture about the wisdom of unleashing an assault to overwhelm the most formidable high ground position before Mexico City by an outnumbered army seemed almost insane, until the clarity of the depth of the French Creole's careful reasoning was stated loud and clear at the crowded conference of the army's top leaders. From cosmopolitan New Orleans (America's most ethnic metropolis because of the Gallic influences) where French was still spoken more frequently in the streets than English, darkly-handsome Lieutenant Beauregard emphasized that precisely because of Chapultepec seemed so strong and impossible to overcome, then that was the very reason why it should be attacked, especially because Santa Anna had already sensibly concluded the same.

Gambling that he had successfully ascertained Scott's tactical thinking for attacking the powerful southern defenses, Santa Anna had left Chapultepec relatively lightly defended by comparison. This tactical decision allowed him the luxury of concentrating his troops and artillery on the south instead of the southwest, because he was convinced that Scott would never dare to attack Chapultepec.

In conclusion, Beauregard had presented the true tactical formula for achieving decisive success below Mexico City: a clever feint from the south toward the city's southern gates to reinforce Santa Anna's thinking that Scott's main attack was coming from that direction as he hoped (a case of wishful thinking).Such an adroit feint would keep Santa Anna securely in place and from reinforcing the small garrison at Chapultepec, while unleashing the main assault on Chapultepec from the southwest.

Then and most importantly, after capturing Chapultepec when so near the city's western gates, the American Army could then pivot toward any part of Mexico City to hit the weakest point of its inner defensive line. Lieutenant Beauregard's masterful presentation about the tactical wisdom of attacking Chapultepec won over the council, including generals and even Captain Lee, who had previously thought differently, at the little church at Piedad.

To his great credit and after having learned his lesson from having suffered heavy losses in his attacks at Molino del Rey, General Scott possessed the wisdom to accept young Lieutenant Beauregard's tactical analysis in full. Therefore, the army's commander loudly announced his final decision to conclude the all-important commanders' conference at the house of worship: "Gentlemen, we will attack by the Western gates!"

Chapter II

The Looming Heights of Chapultepec

With the dying summer revealing the first subtle hints that autumn was on its way to the Central Valley of Mexico and far from his lavish Jalapa hacienda nestled in the picturesque highlands bordering the east coast, General Santa Anna failed to fully realize that Chapultepec was the true key to Mexico City, despite the fact that the defensive bastion guarded the two strategic roads that led to Mexico City.

Therefore, the fortress of Chapultepec, situated atop the flat summit of the 200-high hill (actually an east-west running narrow rock ridge) located just southwest of Mexico City, now became the primary target of General Scott. As mentioned, it still seemed to Santa Anna that the Americans would naturally avoid such a strong high ground position at all costs. Again, Santa Anna was wrong in his tactical thinking despite sound reasoning, believing that Chapultepec was not Scott's main objective.

But as envisioned by General Scott and thanks to Lieutenant Beauregard's astute tactical analysis that has been presented at the Piedad church, the attack on Chapultepec was about winning it all in one bold offensive gamble. Scott emphasized to his commanders that immediately after Chapultepec's fall, the attack then should be continued unabated: a classic case of maintaining the initiative and exploiting the momentum in an all-out attempt to capture Mexico City, before Santa Anna realized what was happening and hurriedly shifted troops to reinforce Chapultepec. Therefore, time was now of the essence and not to be wasted by the attackers as so often in the past, when Scott's forces were now so close to Mexico City.

Clearly, Lieutenant Beauregard was not only a brilliant tactical thinker but also every inch of a fighter. On the climactic day, September 13, of the attack on Chapultepec, the ambitious Louisiana

Creole from St. Barnard Parish boasted of his determination to be the first American soldier to charge inside the Castle of Chapultepec "to tear down the Mexican flag," which now waved proudly from the summit in all its splendor. After the bloody combat and high losses in attacking Molino de Rey, the most formidable defensive position before Mexico City now stood as the last natural high ground obstacle before the invaders: the towering hill that seemed almost to touch the clear Mexican skies of blue and seemingly had been created by Montezuma himself for his personal pleasure.

Most importantly in psychological terms, Chapultepec was now seen as the symbolic heart and soul of Mexico, representing the nation's past, present and future. The Military College and the colonial viceroy's residence, which had been constructed during the previous century, composed what was collectively called the Castle of Chapultepec. The school was located in the southeastern corner of the Castle, and now stood in harm's way.

Indeed, for safety against the aggressiveness of the warlike native lake people, whose rich agricultural lands they had invaded from the north around 1245, the Aztec had taken wise precautions. They had found initial safety on this high ground defensive position, fortified with rocks, that they called "grasshopper hill," Chapultepec. Therefore, with history coming full circle, the descendants of the Aztec now prepared to defend the same high ground perch with the same courage and spirit of brave Aztec warriors against the upcoming assault of their hatred enemies from the United States.

The Beautiful Cypress Forest of Chapultepec

Chapultepec and the dark forest of Mexican Bald Cypress (Taxodium Mucronatum) that lay at the base of the 200-foot hill were considered sacred ground by the people of Mexico, because of its spiritual connection to the past. This distinctive forest of stately giants was a magical and mysterious place, where the memories of the Aztec past and legacy never died.

These magnificent trees, known as ahuehuetes and Montezuma bald cypress, grew to imposing heights in this well-watered and sunny place. They had provided the shade that had once cooled the regal majesty of Montezuma, before the arrival of the ruthless professional killers from far-away Spain, Cortéz and his Conquistadors. The width of these virgin trees at the hill's base was truly a sight to behold, nearly resembling the giant redwoods (virgin coastal trees known as sequoias) of northern California that was destined to be shortly lost to Mexico forever, because President Polk was so determined to fulfill his great nationalistic and imperialistic dream.

Compared to other trees that grew around Mexico City, the long-living Mexican Bald Cypress was an impressive tree in girth and height. Some of the cypress had already reached ages of 1,000 years. These giant trees seemed ideally suited in pointing the way for Scott's attackers in their upcoming surge toward the western slope of the hill topped by the Castle complex. This place seemed magical in the relaxed atmosphere of peacetime days which were no more.

But more visible reminders of the ancient Aztec presence were now seen by the defenders of Chapultepec, including atop the summit that commanded such a wide area. Aztec craftsmen and stonemasons had carved an eagle in solid rock on the stony crest of Chapultepec, after Aztec royalty had decided to live at Chapultepec around 1428. Ironically, Spain's colonial viceroy eventually did the same, finding solace and peach atop Chapultepec.

In September 1847, members of the diminutive Mexican garrison, including the cadets, knew of the carved rock's presence that told of a distinctive cultural heritage and sacred memory that they were determined to protect with their lives. Indeed, Aztec royalty had spent hot summer days in comfort under the giant trees of the cool forest. Compared to the swampy lowlands among the five broad lakes that had long given life and protection to the rich civilization that the Aztecs called Anahuac, or "by the water," the comfortable surroundings of Chapultepec had been long literally a breath of fresh air.

The sheer beauty of the Mexican Bald Cypress forest of virgin timber was about to become a bloody killing ground partly because of the excessive pride and arrogance of the leaders of both nations. As if to frame the high ground that rose so suddenly from the vast expanse of level fields, the picturesque grove of Mexican Bald Cypress was situated on relatively level ground at the base of the hill's western edge. The stately trees appeared eerie and even surreal, because of their unusual natural beauty that seemed somewhat out-of-place.

This picturesque cypress forest extended to the hill's western slope, before Castle's western end that loomed 200-feet above the low-lying terrain that stretched for miles on each side of Chapultepec. While the forest of cypress promised a degree of shelter for the attackers from the fire of Chapultepec's guns, the benefits of terrain and vegetation were negated because the western slope guaranteed a difficult climb. During this descent, the norteamericanos were sure to become exhausted, especially after a lengthy advance on another hot day when a hot sun baked the lush Central Valley.

After successive defeats, many soldados (ironically, like many of Scott's men who now questioned their commander's tactical skills and wisdom) were losing faith in their leaders, especially the aristocratic Santa Anna who more often behaved like a feudal lord instead of a true leader of the people. Santa Anna proved unable to sufficiently inspire the troops and lead them to victory, because it seemed as if nothing could stop the Yankees.

Meanwhile, garrison members who held the lofty perch of Chapultepec, defended by ten cannon atop the hill, watched the lengthy formations of disciplined troops in blue uniforms maneuver with precision across the broad meadows and cornfields situated below the commanding heights that once had been considered sacred to the Aztecs. In a letter, Lieutenant John James Peck, the promising West Pointer who had learned of war's ugly realities while serving deep in Mexico, admitted feeling the stress of now facing "the threatening castle of Chapultepec" that seemed impregnable to almost everyone in the ranks.

Talented American engineers, led by the incomparable Captain Lee, who had graduated near the top of their classes at West Point (the engineers were both armies were considered the nation's elite soldiers) began to select good firing positions for the placement of batteries to fulfill General Scott's hope of pounding Chapultepec, including the Military College, in submission.

After the costly assaults on Molina del Rey and to his credit, General Scott now demonstrated greater wisdom out of necessary because his small army had dwindled in size with each bloody battle during the drive ever-closer to Mexico City. Scott, therefore, hoped that the upcoming bombardment would be sufficient to force the surrender of Chapultepec's garrison, so that he could avoid a costly assault.

Among the garrison poised atop the ancient Aztec hill that they had solemnly pledged to defend with their lives, around 200 young men and boys (mostly teenagers) of the prestigious Military College silently watched developments below: the skillful maneuvering of the battle-hardened Americans, who were determined to succeed at any cost. Incredibly, these highly-motivated fighting men had still not lost a single battle on the long march to the outskirts of Mexico City.

Engineer Beauregard, the gifted Gallic-American and West Pointer, who still thought so fondly of his French Creole heritage and Napoleon's enduring legacy that still made Frenchmen proud, this Creole (like Santa Anna) had presented the convincing arguments that would bestow decisive victory for the Anglo-Celtic and Anglo-Saxon soldiers of Scott's Army.

Ironically, Lieutenant Beauregard, who had been raised as a French Creole to believe that his native Latin culture was vastly superior to a less sophisticated American culture, had laid the foundation for decisive victory over a people, who had also long embraced their own concepts of cultural and racial superiority to Americans.

All the while, garrison members, including the young cadets, saw that a good many American cannon began to be aligned in rows and placed in excellent firing positions amid the humid lowlands. The dark barrels of these ominous-looking guns, including mortars, now pointed at the summit of Chapultepec and the Military College.

Deep Divisions Compromise Chapultepec's Defense

The Boy Cadets and Chapultepec's enlisted men and their officers, mostly of Spanish ancestry like Santa Anna, had been astounded by the rapid course of developments and series of sharp reversals during the 1847 Campaign. One dismal Mexican defeat after another had resulted primarily because of failed leadership decisions at the highest levels and the lack of a vibrant sense of nationalism of an intoxicating kind that had made the Americans more effective fighting men, who also benefitted from excellent leaders, especially the West Pointers.

Unfortunately for the brave soldados who fought and died without any real chance for victory in this one-sided war (a David versus Goliath conflict), Mexico was a poor nation without industrial might like the United States. Long before the war began, the fragile republic was extremely vulnerable to conquest by a more united opponent unhampered by the inherent toxic brew of deep political, racial, and ethnic divisions.

Ironically, these confident Yanquis wore the design of an American bald eagle—the ironic national symbol—on their brass buttons, belt buckles, and on cap insignias. At the same time, the Mexican Golden Eagle was likewise displayed proudly on buttons, belt buckles, and cap insignias of the Latino republic's fighting men. A strange destiny had brought two neighboring republics at each other's throats in a dramatic showdown that was about to be played out in full at Chapultepec.

Behind the nationalist facade of a fierce patriotism, righteous indignation, and xenophobia, a vulnerable Republic of Mexico had long been a badly divided between federalists (regionalism or states' rights) and centralists (the government at Mexico City): a recipe for disaster in wartime because of the inherent weaknesses of a divided government at the height of a national emergency. As a sad fate would have it, the Boy Cadets were about to pay a high price for the repeated failures of their government, army, and leaders, especially Santa Anna.

Unfortunately when national unity was most needed for survival as an independent nation, Mexico was also sharply divided by race because this was mostly a mestizo and Indian nation ruled by wealthy and white leaders of Spanish heritage. Even worse, the army consisted largely of Indians or mixed-race men who were under-trained and lacked discipline, because of the lack of proper training and qualified officers. The vast majority of Santa Anna's soldados had been conscripted from rural areas.

Consequently, many soldados felt more loyalty to their local regions than distant Mexico City and a dysfunctional nation dominated by the wealthy elites. Hardy and durable as fighting men on the march and on the battlefield, the Indians of Santa Anna's Army consisted mostly of descendants of the Aztecs. They had lived their lower class lives as peons, or peasants, who worked the land of the landowning elite like lowly serfs in Medieval Europe.

For their entire lives, the native people of Mexico had labored in the seeming endless fields of the vast rural estates and haciendas, which were owned by the wealthy elite of mostly Spanish blood. The Indians' entire world had been systematically destroyed by the Spanish conquest in brutal fashion. They had lost their heritage, Gods (including those of war and the sun), and their ancestral lands, which they endlessly worked to enrich the elite. These former Indian lands were now owned by the Spanish and Creoles, or Spaniards born in the New World.

Trapped by an oppressive peonage and debt peonage system (basically debt slavery) from the advancement of essential goods, including food, to them on credit at the hacienda store that indebted the Indians forever to exploitative hacienda owners, these impoverished native people thereafter spent their entire lives laboring in the vast cornfields of misery. Unfortunately for them, debts were sufficiently inflated so that these sums could never be paid back to ensure a cheap labor supply for the wealthy class.

Without this cheap source of endless labor, the large corn crops could not be planted or harvested to generate the massive production of the hacienda system that was essential to Mexico's economy. Mexico's economic profits from its agricultural products were based on the endless toil and sweat of this oppressed class of a conquered people, who thereafter served a permanent source of cheap labor.

With loyalties devoted primarily to their people and tribal leaders, the Indians possessed relatively little interest in sacrificing their lives in this war for the continued dominance of the ruling class which had vanquished their ancestors and long oppressed them as society's lowest order. In fact, many Indians in uniform were unable to speak Spanish, and instead faithfully maintained the tribal customs and values of their ancestors.

However, they now served in the enlisted ranks in overwhelming numbers, after having been conscripted by the central government. For ample good reason, these poorly-motivated fighting men were not eager to die for Mexico because of society's abuses and inequities that were certain to provide no relief in the future. After all, the ruling elite had lorded over the Indians for generations as a natural right.

Consequently and in general, the Indian soldado was an unwilling fighting man in this brutal war, but nevertheless fought with courage and determination. In the end, nevertheless, it was not as much of the failure of Indian soldiery that led to Mexico's decisive defeat as it was from leadership failures of the privileged elite. Like in the United States, the Indians had been culturally and economically cut-off from the mainstream of society, but they were still forced through conscription to fight to save exactly what had long oppressed them.

They, consequently, still kept faith with their own Gods to worship as they pleased, which limited the formation of a sense of Mexican nationalism, even during a foreign invasion: the antithesis of the case of the Military College cadets, who were highly-motivated to defend their homeland with their lives. Even worse to negate their overall combat capabilities for confronting the advancing Americans(the common man in the ranks had been raised in the use of muskets and shotguns), Indians had long been outlawed by Mexico City from owning firearms. Not surprisingly, these men were anything but good marksmen in the heat of battle, when firing British-made "Brown Bess" muskets. The "Brown Bess" was a large caliber smoothbore that packed a hefty kick, minimizing the accuracy of even a trained soldado.

But to Mexico's credit and thanks to the past humanitarian efforts of the Catholic Church, the Indians were now full citizens of the republic and equal to the mestizos according to the law. The Indians, toughened by difficult agrarian lives, were good soldiers in terms of overall endurance and displaying courage on the battlefield, and they played key roles in Mexico City's defense.

To the war's end, the Indian soldado demonstrated heroism on the battlefield and died by the hundreds in one miserable defeat after another in this savage war that had turned so cruelly against Mexico by September 1847.

The Tragedy of Failed Leadership

The Indians, or peasants, who made-up the enlisted ranks were led by lighter-skinned leaders (that equated to higher social status instead of military qualifications, which were the Mexican Army's greatest overall internal weakness), who lacked proper qualifications. Therefore, this unfortunate situation minimized the strengths and potential of the Indians as fighting men.

As mentioned, Santa Anna was responsible for failing to live-up to the stern challenge of defending the capital, demonstrating relatively little tactical skill in a true crisis situation. In addition, Santa Anna was not a moral leader with inspirational ways when needed by the men in the ranks, when Mexico and its people now needed such an effective leader than ever before.

Unfortunately for Mexico, Santa Anna was the epitome of a self-serving leader whose deep-seated corrupt ways and aristocratic aloofness were legendary across the breath of Mexico for an extended period. But in truth, he was a very able army organizer and administrator that Mexico had initially needed to gather the forces necessary meet the invaders. But defending the capital was another matter.

Indeed, to be entirely fair to Santa Anna, he had succeeded in this key mission of having created a fighting force to defend the capital. While exiled in Havana, Cuba, after the war began along the Rio Grande, Santa Anna had made his most cynical deal: if the Americans returned him to Mexico, then the former president would resume leadership over the nation and negotiate a favorable peace with the United States, which included allowing an annexation of a large part of the Mexican nation.

To a much-surprised President Polk and other naive American leaders, Santa Anna had then suddenly become a patriot after having been allowed to safely land at Vera Cruz. He had then taken over leadership of the republic's army in the north just before General Scott's march on Mexico City. Clearly, Santa Anna had duped the Yankees, including President Polk and then General Scott, who were made to look like fools by the savvy general's double-dealing ways.

Like most Mexican Creoles with a higher skin tone than the majority of Mexico's citizens of Indian and mestizo heritage, the wealthy Santa Anna held his Indian soldiers (the army's vast majority of fighting men) with the usual upper class contempt. The generalissimo lamented the history of his country's extensive racial intermixing that he believed had weakened the basic fabric of the Mexican nation. Of course, this was a biased and race-based perspective stemming from his elevated Creole status and lighter skin color.

But in truth, Mexico had only inherited the class, race (based on skin color), and caste systems that had been long established in Spain. In this sense, racism was not an original sin of Mexico, but a tragic legacy of the past that was a core determinant of history of the mother country. Unfortunately, such deeply-entrenched racial attitudes limited the Mexican nation's overall effectiveness in waging war when a strong sense of nationalism was now needed to guarantee a united front against the invaders from the north. Therefore, from the beginning, Mexico was simply not prepared to meet the many formidable challenges of the demanding Campaign of 1847, especially in defending Mexico City.

For such pressing concerns that needed to be addressed for the republic's overall welfare, the Military College housed in the southeast section of the Castle (the summer home, or palace, of the Viceroy during Spain's colonial days) atop the heights had been established in 1833 partly to address a host of deep-seated inherent weaknesses of the Mexican Army, especially in regard to leadership. The young cadets were not from the lower class of the Indian peasant class. Because of their higher social backgrounds than the Indians of the army's enlisted ranks, the young men of the Military College were never seen embracing Indian customs, such as consuming the Indians' favorite drink, pulque. This popular drink had so often drowned out the sorrows of the miserable existence of the most oppressed people in Mexico.

The members of the Cadet Corps were either of Spanish or mixed-blood, and most of their fathers had served as officers of the Mexican military in the past: the distinguished military service that played a key role in their successful entry into the Military College. They naturally possessed a great deal of pride in their military academy and republic, which likewise looked with pride upon these young men.

It was these highly-motivated youths, among the nation's most promising young men of a new generation, upon which Mexico depended in the future to lead Mexico's troops to victory and perhaps even save the republic, whenever a new crisis called for well-educated and talented leadership.

Dramatic Showdown Looming

All the while, the dramatic showdown for possession of Chapultepec was drawing ever-closer, and the capital's fate hung in the balance on this warm September. The unleashing of the massive American assault was now only a matter of time, and the Military College's cadets realized as much. Indeed, the future destiny of not only the capital city, but also the Mexican nation would be shortly decided.

As fate would have it, the mood atop Chapultepec was one of misplaced confidence, because no one realized that that General Scott had embraced a clever plan to gain the last high ground before Mexico City. However, some of the more experienced defenders wondered if they would live to see another fair September like this one in the heart of Mexico.

Ironically, throughout the past and as mentioned, the more balmy days of past Septembers in the Central Valley had long been the month of celebration for the people Mexico. This historically festive month celebrated the winning of Mexico's independence from Spain in 1821, after a decade of bitter struggle of mostly darker-skin freedom fighters against the hated royalists. But now in a tense Mexico City and in the army's ranks, the usual mood of celebration was now noticeably absent during the second week of September 1847, because so much was at stake.

Another new red dawn shined over a threatened Mexico City and illuminated the thick foliage of late summer, including the natural beauty of the Mexican Bald Cypress forest on September 13: a harbinger for the blood-letting that was about to come, because the Americans were shortly to unleash the full weight of their attack on

Chapultepec. This lofty high ground position was not only symbolic, but also strategic. The hill overlooked and guarded the western approaches to Mexico City less than two miles distant to the northeast. This resilient American army, which included highly-disciplined regular United States regiments, was formidable, despite its recent heavy losses and relatively small size.

Lieutenant John James Peck, a well-educated New Yorker and West Point graduate at age eighteen (Class of 1843 that included Lieutenant Ulysses S. Grant, 4th United States Infantry), had penned in February 1847 letter of a situation that especially applied to the overall tactical situation now that Scott's Army was poised before Mexico City: "'The Halls of Montezuma' seem no longer a mere byword or an effort of the imagination, but assume form and shape and may at no distant day dazzle our eyes with their splendor," with the magnificent church spires of Mexico City now within sight. Representing Catholicism's powerful influence over the land and its hard-working people, these stately church spires now loomed before the invaders like a New World Mecca or Medina, which served as the center of the world's other major religion, Islam, after the faiths of Catholicism and Protestantism that were at war deep in Mexico.

Broad Fields of Plenty

The soft light of another September morning (Monday September 13) revealed a broad expanse of bright green cornfields that filled the broad plain that was spread below the imposing heights, some 7,628 feet above sea level, of Chapultepec.

Like some silent guardian that had been specifically created by the ancient Aztec Corn God to scare off the omnipresent flocks of Mexican crows (smaller than the common crows in the United States) from raiding the great abundance provided by the ripe cornfields, this was the dominant high ground for miles around.

The legendary hill of Chapultepec stood high above the green rows of corn in the heat-hazed lowlands that seemed to stretch forever to the distant horizon. This luxurious expanse of cornfields had grown on this same fertile ground for centuries. These golden maize fields of plenty were part of Mexico's most fertile valley, the vast central plateau (the Mesa Central, which the Yankee invaders had marched through with a confident arrogance despite far from home) was the cradle of Mexican civilization. These broad fields of ripe ears of corn, already displaying yellow tassels of silk on the tall green stalks, had long bestowed life to people of this beautiful valley.

Symbolically, like in September 1847, the Aztec people had long depended on a corn-based diet, thanks to the Sun God's blessings and gifts, like the Mexican people (Indian and mestizo alike), almost as if nothing had changed over the centuries.

As far as the eye could see, the nearly-ripe cornfields filled the low-lying plain (former marshlands that had been drained by the advanced engineering skills of the Aztec, who also created a well-designed irrigation system) and the sprawling basin, covering the dark, rich soil like a soft blanket.

This vast basin of fertile soil was distinguished by five large, shallow likes, formed millions of years ago by volcanic activity, which surrounded Mexico City. All in all, the lush Central Valley was an agricultural Garden of Eden (but not of course to the exploited Indian slaves who had not been freed by the Spanish until 1542) compared to Mexico's northern part that was mostly arid lands, mountains. Meanwhile, dense jungles covered other parts of Mexico, like the Yucatán peninsula—the tropical land of another ancient people blessed with a rich heritage and culture, the Maya.

The Legacy of an Eagle and Snake

During this decisive September, the young students at the Military College were ready to defend their beloved homeland with their lives. As the soldados of Chapultepec, including the Boy Cadets, realized at this time because it had been a storied part of their history, these life-giving bodies of water (originally five, but only three—Lakes Texcoco, Xochimilco and Chalco—by 1847) had long served as the center of the ancient Aztec civilization.

According to the enduring ancient legend, the leader of the Aztec and his Tenochca (People of the Sun) followers had first migrated south from war-torn northwestern Mexico (Aztlan). He had been inspired by a prophetic dream from the chief god (Huitzilipochtli who had taken the form of a War Eagle), who had told him to lead his people south and then search for a beautiful lake in a new far-away land. During their lengthy trek south, the People of the Sun finally reached the Promised Land of five lakes around 1325, when they saw a rare sight in the world of nature as prophetically promised by the faithful words of Huitzilipochtli.

Therefore, as they had been advised by their wise chief god, the Aztec had finally settled on two islands in the middle of S-shaped Lake Texcoco, situated just northeast of Mexico City. This strategic location proved ideal for defensive purposes. Here, they reestablished their village at this prophetic point because of the predicted sight of a majestic Mexican Golden Eagle perched atop a large cactus plant (a tenochtl or sun plant known today as a prickly pear) with a writhing snake (a tasty dinner of high protein) in its peak. This sight of an example of survival of the fittest in the natural world provided the long-awaited sign stemming from the omen that had been bestowed to the Aztec leader by the vivid dream from their god.

Significantly, the Mexica, or Aztec, had learned their lessons well. These placid lakes—that served as ideal natural moats—provided excellent natural barriers to hordes of attackers, unlike when they had been driven by their enemies from their more arid native homeland of Aztlan to the northwest.

Symbolically, the red, white and green national flags now flying from atop the highest perches of Chapultepec Castle were painted with the colorful designs of the magnificent Mexican Golden Eagle sitting majestically atop the prickly pear (as had been first foreseen by Huitzilipochtli) with a snake in its lethal grasp: an iconic and cherished national symbol that provided an invigorating source of inspiration to the young cadets.

Mexico City's Life at Stake

Despite the long summer in which each steamy day seemed hotter than the previous one, the wide fields of maize located just outside Mexico City were especially lush by the arrival of September's second week. Row upon row of Indian corn stood above head level.

The length and thickness of the golden yellow silk that grew at the top of the large ears of ripe corn revealed that the ears of corn were ripe. To the delight of wealthy landowners, this crop of corn, already well into the silking and tasseling stage before the arrival of mid-September, was a very good one.

One of the most important annual events for the Mexican people and upon which their general prosperity had long depended, the corn was now ready for harvest when the life of Chapultepec was threatened as never before. The first light breeze of the September morning ruffled the leafy green stalks of the bounty that covered the wide plain. This magnificent bounty had once fed the Aztec people to sustain life, before the Spaniards' arrival with their horses, protective armor, Toledo steel swords, and long lances of the lethal cavalrymen. Under the shadow of Chapultepec, these same high-yielding fields of maize had long feed the indigenous people of the largest population center of Mexico for centuries, and the people had long given thanks to their God in consequence.

The clear skies of late summer, with not a cloud in sight that hinted of rain, promised another scorching day, as realized by the anxious defenders stationed atop Chapultepec. Amid the seemingly endless stretch of cornfields that flowed to the horizon, all that was seen in the skies were occasional solitary mourning doves in swift flight. In gracefully chasing mosquitoes for their nourishment rather than for sport, some darting black swallows swept low and fast in the early morning's half-light. The swallows flew just above the gold tassels--a delicate silk-like topping--that brought a bright color to the rows the darker corn stalks. However, no so-called Indio citizen of the young republic was now working in the fields or harvesting those precious ears of corn to feed the people of nearby Mexico City.

Long known as Metzlipan, or the "Navel of the Moon," this green-colored island situated amid the placid waters of Lake Texcoco, situated just northeast of Mexico City, had long served as the ancient capital of a vast Aztec, or Mexica as the people of Mexico-Tenochtitlan (a name that honored the god Tenoch) proudly called themselves and their sophisticated civilization of infinite richness.

But the Spanish Conquistadors had brought disease, death, and fire, including to the sacred Aztec Temples, to forever change the

Aztec's world that had quickly crumbled before their eyes. This fateful clash of cultures had resulted in the fall of the vast and prosperous Mexico-Tenochtitlan Empire. Now in September 1847, the main Cathedral in Mexico City stood in all of its magnificence atop what was left of the ruins of ancient temples of the Sun God, eliminating the religious and cultural symbols of a defeated people, who had lacked the superior weaponry and powerful war horses of the heavily-armed interlopers.

Heroic Last Stand at Chapultepec

Meanwhile, Chapultepec's defenders continued to nervously await developments. In stoic silence, they stood beside their cannon and held loaded muskets, while the large Mexican national flag waved from the top of the tower near the Castle's eastern edge. After Santa Anna had suffered so many disastrous losses in 1847, the young men and boys of the Military College might have been more optimistic than the battle-hardened soldados about the final outcome of the upcoming battle. Clearly, something was seriously internally wrong with the Mexican Army, because humiliating defeats had come one after another.

The young men and boys of Chapultepec wondered why so many brave Mexican soldiers, who had been trained and drilled in Napoleonic tactics, had been seemingly always defeated by the norteamericanos of a heretical nation? How and why had a merciful God seemingly turned against Mexico in her darkest hour and greatest time of need? Had their own vanquished Aztec ancestors placed a terrible curse on Mexico for having been so thoroughly vanquished by the Spanish Conquistadors, since so many of Mexico's sons possessed Spanish blood? Such thoughts might have raced through the minds of the young men and boys of the Military College on this haunting September.

However, in truth, so many past defeats on hard-fought battlefields across the invaded homeland could only mean that these sharp reversals stemmed from the gross failures stemming from the incompetence of military leadership. After all, Mexican soldiers had fought bravely and died in large numbers on every battlefield in defense of sacred Mexico soil, but now thousands of Yankees were positioned before Chapultepec and almost within sight of Mexico City.

Ironically, and unknown to the Boy Cadets at this time, Chapultepec was actually weaker than it appeared at first glance, despite ten pieces of artillery placed in good defensive positions across the high ground. And no one in the Mexican military and government had been more to blame than General Santa Anna. Thanks to Santa Anna's growing list of miscalculations and tactical mistakes, the defense of Chapultepec had already been severely compromised.

As mentioned, he had gambled that General Scott dared not attempt to assault such a high ground position that certainly looked impregnable. Indeed, this had been the general consensus of leading American officers, until Engineer Beauregard had skillfully presented his insightful arguments at the officers' conference that revealed otherwise.

Therefore, Santa Anna had placed most of his troops and best commanders in excellent defensive positions on the city's south, where he still fully expected General Scott to strike. In this regard, Santa Anna had outsmarted himself by making an ill-founded calculation that he was destined to lose in the end. Unfortunately, Santa Anna would not personally lose anything in his high stakes gamble, because a frightful price would only have to be paid in killed, wounded, and captured (46 men or more than 25 percent of the student body) by the young men and boys, including the Military School cadets, at Chapultepec.

Consequently, in overall relative terms and despite towering above the surrounding plain, Chapultepec was very much of a paper tiger, although this fact was still not realized by General Scott and his men. Because of Santa Anna's tactical misjudgments, Chapultepec's defenses were still inadequate and incomplete. Here, Major General Nicholás Bravo Rueda possessed only 832 soldados, including around 200 cadets, to defend the expansive grounds of Chapultepec from the base of the hill to the commanding summit. And unfortunately for the overall chances of a successful defense, Major General Bravo now commanded mostly National Guard troops, who were poorly trained and inefficiently led for the most part, with the notable exception of the determined fighting men of the San Blas Battalion.

One historian estimated that Major General Bravo required at least 2,000 men to defend all of the ground of this defensive complex. But in fact, this was a significant underestimation of what was actually required for a successful defense of Chapultepec. In truth, General Bravo actually needed more than three times (at least 2,500 men) as many troops to adequately defend Chapultepec. Although a brave and determined commander, who was able to inspire his men to do their best, Bravo was already past his prime at age seventy-one.

At this time, he was more of a high-level politician than a general. Clearly Santa Anna had kept his best troops and most experienced commanders to the east and the south of Mexico City, where he still expected the Americans to launch their main attack. The consummate gambler of the gaming tables and cockfight pits—from Mexico City to Jalapa--had gambled once too often, but now the stakes had never been higher and he could ill-afford to lose.

A Noble and Courageous Act in the Face of Danger

In a noble act that bolstered the admiration and respect of the Boy Cadets, Major General Bravo had earlier gained additional volunteers to defend the hilltop when least expected. Around 200 cadets (the entire student body) had boldly volunteered to defend Chapultepec to the last, after the Military College's commandant, General José Marino Monterde, had recommended that they depart Chapultepec and return to their homes to preserve the lives of these young men with promising futures.

Impressed by the degree of the cadets' patriotism and sense of self-sacrifice that was often lacking among the troops and even including some of the army's top leaders, General Monterde had accepted their bold suggestion to rescind his initial desire. What was significant was that the cadets' decision had come at a time when Santa Anna had even contemplated surrender. Worst of all, he stubbornly remained focused primarily on facing the threat from the south, where he still felt the main assault would be launched.

The heartfelt, if not sacrificial, act of the Boy Cadets in volunteering to stay with the inadequate number of garrison members and share their fate—not a bright one—encouraged other defenders, who were simply too few to stem the American tide once unleashed. General Monterde and Major General Bravo, who lamented that Santa Anna had still dispatched no reinforcements to Chapultepec as he had so smugly promised, realized that Mexico City would not be captured, if a good many more fighting men possessed the same determination as the young cadets.

A Forgotten Cruel Retribution

Knowing that a great assault from the best units of Scott's Army was inevitable, some cadets might have prepared for the worst. But given their youth and inexperience, a sense of optimism remained high among most students of the Military College at this time. As young idealists who had much to learn about life and war, they still believed in the abilities of the army's commanders, including Santa Anna.

But these young men did not know that their own countrymen (fellow soldiers and seasoned veterans compared to themselves) had made their own personal situations and future fates far more precarious by what had occurred on September 8 just west of Chapultepec. Here, on the bloody field of Molino del Rey, initially because Mexican defenders had been hidden in good defensive positions until the last moment when they had suddenly risen up as one to blast away at close range with a murderous fire, the American attackers had been initially repulsed at the strong defensive complex of Molino del Rey, including a foundry made of stone.

The 8th Infantry (one of General Scott's excellent regular regiments that served him so well throughout the campaign) attackers on the foundry under General George Wright (part of the 1st Brigade, under Lieutenant Colonel Thomas Staniford, of Brigadier General William J. Worth's 2nd Division of regulars) were cut to pieces. Stunned by the punishment, they were forced to retreat before the blazing fire, leaving clumps of their dead and wounded behind them.

Then, the awful slaughter had taken place on the open fields of destruction before the stone foundry. Some defenders of the Molino de Rey complex began the slaughter by opening a hot fire from their defensive positions to kill wounded Americans lying in clumps in the open fields. But this firing on helpless men was not enough to eliminate all of the injured 8th Infantry regulars, after the crack regiment had been forced to retreat. Infantrymen and lancers, the Mexican Army's most lethal men, dashed forward to eliminate the large number of wounded Americans, who had only recently believed that they were about to become the conquers of Mexico City.

In one of the horrors of the Mexican-American War, the finely-uniform lancers galloped over the field to spear the bodies of fallen Americans, including some of the army's most respected officers, while these helpless men had pleaded for water and mercy. These last wishes of the wounded Americans were not granted. To finish the cruel job not fully completed by the thrusts from the long wooden lances topped with lengthy steel points (irony a legacy bestowed by the Spanish Conquistadors), the lancers then dismounted to cut the throats of the last injured Americans, who still showed signs of life.

Perhaps these soldados thought that eliminating these men might deter the Americans from additional attacks or strike fear into their comrades, but such was not the case. But clearly, these killers felt a great hatred for the invaders and despoilers of their beautiful country. In fact, the slaughter had the opposite effort of what was intended, instilling a greater resolve among the United States troops to succeed. Consequently, these seasonal fighting men, including soldiers like Lieutenants George Edward Pickett and James Longstreet, of the 8th Infantry, would shortly lead the way in the upcoming assault on Chapultepec with old scores to settle with garrison members.

Indeed, the disciplined regulars of the 8th Infantry and other troops had watched in horror at the grisly sight of the massacre of their wounded comrades in the open fields (a grassy prairie) of slaughter. Thereafter, angry Americans swore no-quarter warfare upon any Mexican soldiers who they encountered on the battlefield in the future.

As a sad fate would have it and as mentioned, the Boy Cadets were destined to pay a fearful price for the atrocities committed by the Mexican infantrymen and mounted lancers in the killing of the large number of wounded Americans who lay before Molino del Rey. Clearly, with the invaders now so close to Mexico City, the war was degenerating to new levels of brutality and barbarity on both sides.

But, of course, the rage that had fueled the slaughter of the fallen Americans was partly justified. In overall terms, what the invaders now continued unabated was one of the oldest and ugliest chapters of America's saga that existed even before the American Revolution of 1775-1783: the systematic vanquishing and pushing aside of Native American people, most recently in the wars against their Seminole and the Black Seminole (former slaves who had assimilated in the tribe of Creek roots) people in what once had been Spanish Florida, in the quest of expanding its territory by military might. And America was now in the process of defeating Mexico in still another giant land grab (far larger than any previous stealing of other people's lands) that eventually resulted in the acquisition of half of Mexico's territory, including all the way to the Pacific's shores. Significantly, this aggressive and greedy imperialism was a race-based Manifest Destiny that had propelled the young republic deep into Mexico during the first foreign war in the nation's history.

Symbolically, the conquest of one Native American tribe after another and the gaining of even more territory that had brought the tide of settlers across the Mississippi and ever-farther west in a relentless migration had set the stage for the invasion of Mexico. At this time, the traditionally xenophobic Anglo-Saxons, who had inherited the core racial concepts from the insular island of England, looked at Mexicans as little more than Native Americans, because of their darker hues.

Consequently, according to the perverted racial reasoning of the day, because Mexicans were deemed by so many Americans to be inferior in regard to race, culture, and society, they allegedly were undeserving of owning their own ancestral lands! In this sense and according to this racist premise, the Mexican-American War was a mere extension of the Indian Wars and for some of the same principal reasons that were largely race-based. The seemingly countless bloody battles and slaughters that resulted from an aggressive national expansion largely because of race had begun in America during the colonial period. Therefore, in this sense, the cadets were simply on the wrong end of his brutal historical equation and continuum fueled in part by Anglo-Saxon racism that boded ill for the Cadet Corps in the upcoming battle to decide Mexico City's fate.

As noted, these ugly realities and grim developments of America's bloody past were largely unknown to the cadets of the Military College, but what cannot be denied was the fact that they were now on the wrong end of the course of history and America's relentless expansionism. They had not even seen the slaughter (of course, no race or culture has been immune to committing atrocities in wartime) on the killing fields before the defenses of Molino del Rey, which was located about a half mile west of Chapultepec.

Consequently, in their youthful innocence, the students of the Military College felt no fear from any repercussions for what others, non-cadets in this case, had done on bloody September 8. In this savage war that continued to degenerate, both sides had been guilty of committing atrocities in the name of fighting for their country.

Almost certainly and like members of the Mexican regular army, the young men of the Cadet Corps had almost certainly heard about the American atrocities committed mostly by undisciplined volunteers against unfortunate Mexican civilians, who were victims of murder and rape, in northern Mexico and to a lesser extent during the march from Vera Cruz. For a variety of reasons, consequently, the cadets were highly motivated to hold firm at Chapultepec in part to save the civilians, especially the helpless women and children, of Mexico City from the grasp of the invader, as Mexican propaganda had long emphasized with considerable enthusiasm.

An Ancient Hill of Destiny

In his journal that revealed how the location of the Military College, situated atop the high hill before them, was common knowledge among the Americans, Sergeant Thomas Barclay, 2nd Pennsylvania Volunteers, described how: "The Castle of Chapultepec is built upon a knob or mound which rises high and abrupt from the plain. The Castle is approached by a road that winds around the mound. On all sides the hill is steep and in many places inaccessible. The main building [Castle] intended for an [military] academy is converted into a regular fortress which formidable by its position is rendered still more so by the defences and outworks which surround it." For a host of reasons, Scott's men now wondered what kind of fighting men they would encounter upon meeting Mexico's Cadet Corps on the battlefield.

Surrounding the rocky elevation of Chapultepec that seemed to rise up out of the vast expanse of cornfields that had long nourished the capital city's populace, these broad fields of plenty were now entirely empty of the usual large numbers of Indian pickers, who always wore their traditional white cotton peasant garb. Known to the Aztec as Grasshopper Hill when a glorious sun had once shined brightly on the future of the Aztec Empire during its glory days that they had believed would never end, Chapultepec had now become the primary bone of contention in the latest struggle for possession of this golden land of the eagle and the snake.

As the cadets knew from having heard stories from childhood days, they now realized that they defended sacred soil. Indeed, the ancient capital of the Aztec had been first built where Huitzilopochtli, after transforming himself into a Mexican Golden Eagle, had perched atop a cactus plant to eat a recently caught snake: the long-awaited prophetic sign had revealed the right location for the people to settle, after the people's long trek from the north. Known as Tenochtitlan that was situated in a low-lying, marshy region of five lakes that dominated this section of the green valley, the ancient Aztec capital had been supplied with cold and clear drinking water that flowed from a stone aqueduct running from the fresh water springs of Chapultepec.

From the most humble of beginnings, the Mexica (Aztec) people had conquered their neighbors in this fertile valley to create a great empire that had lasted for centuries. Tenochtitlan had grown into a sprawling city, thanks in part to the creation of artificial islands and a maze of irrigation ditches constructed by skilled Aztec engineers, who also strengthened their defenses against enemies.

But unfortunately for the internally-weakened Republic of Mexico, a new day had dawned because an even stronger conqueror, who was likewise inspired by a majestic eagle (American bald eagle that now symbolized the lofty ambitions that had been achieved by the race-based faith of Manifest Destiny), had descended upon the nation with a crusading mission that was considered holy. Wearing his finest dark blue uniform that was immaculate as if reviewing a lengthy row of cadets at West Point, General Scott had thousands of his finest troops now poised on the southwestern side of the capital.

A student of history, including the narrative of Hernándo Cortéz's bloody campaign of the most brutal of conquests, General Scott knew that the great capital city and its beautiful National Cathedral had been erected upon the ruins of the ancient Aztec capital. Born in Virginia, Scott fully embraced the analogy that he now led the advance of modern-day Conquistadors, who were mostly Anglo-Saxons and Anglo-Celts imbued with the heady vision of Manifest Destiny.

Clearly, history had come full circle for the unfortunate people of Mexico, became an old tragedy was now in the process of being reborn with devastating national consequences by these aggressors, causing a deep sense of fatalism among Mexico's disillusioned soldados, after having suffered so many recent defeats.

In an earlier letter that captured the reflective mood among some of the Yankees situated before Mexico City and proved prophetic in the end, Lieutenant John James Peck, whose father had served in the War of 1812 in which Scott won distinction for his leadership abilities, described how: "I have great confidence in the success of our arms, and trust I shall be spared to announce in my friends [in a future letter] that the American flag floats over the 'Halls'."

Of course, these young United States soldiers only reflected the spirit of their tactically-astute commander. General Scott was confident of success. He now coveted Mexico City as never before, and almost as much as the unstoppable Spanish Conquistadors, who had worn armor unlike the Aztec warriors, including the legendary Eagle Warriors (the "Eagle Knight").Instead of lowly peasant workers laboring in the green sea of life-giving fields of maize in the lowlands situated below Chapultepec, thousands of young men and boys from the far-away United States were now aligned in lengthy lines in preparation for receiving the final orders to advance against this hill of destiny, when everything was at stake for both nations.

Unlike the Americans who possessed modern firearms, Mexican troops now carried old "Brown Bess" muskets manufactured in England, castoffs from the Napoleonic War, when most of Europe, except England, had been conquered by Napoleon. A reality that foretold who would be the eventual winner in this 1847 war, Mexico was too impoverished and backward to possess the industrial capabilities to manufacture its own firearms unlike in the United States, which had emerged as an industrial power.

At this time, the cadets carried a cut-down version of the "Brown Bess." Although it could still blow a hole in an attacker's mid-section at close range, this weapon was lighter and shorter to facilitate drill and practice for the young men of the Cadet Corps in loading on the parade ground situated atop the summit before the main entrance of the Military College.

After having endured all of the extensive training by the cadets, the greater ease of more quickly loading their smooth-bore muskets was about to pay dividends for the cadets in the close-range combat during the Military College's defense on September 13. All the while, large numbers of American soldiers waited patiently in advanced positions for their orders on this early Monday morning to begin their attack Chapultepec. General Scott viewed the assault on the commanding hill as only the first phase of the final push to capture Mexico City and finally end America's first foreign war that had been fueled by a lust for more land.

However, it would not be an easy undertaking for the Americans, who were still haunted by the awful memories of the bloody lessons of Molino del Rey, which were still fresh in mind of survivors. The imposing defensive obstacle of Lomas de Chapultepec (the heights of Chapultepec that stood defiant and proud with colorful Mexican flags waving atop the wind-swept summit) now had to be captured at all costs, before American troops could gain the two roads that led to the strategic capital city.

Major General Bravo's Outnumbered But Resolute Defenders

Meanwhile, atop the commanding eminence of Chapultepec, rising up more than 200 feet from the level plain that surrounded the hill on all sides, Mexico City's determined defenders, including members of the Cadet Corps, had waited for days under the scorching sun that might have now reminded them of the blessings of the legendary Aztec Sun God. With loaded muskets nearby, even the cadets, although this was their first battle, might have even looked forward to meeting the upcoming assault to prove their worth in a crisis situation.

Among the school's defenders on the same hallowed ground of what had been the summer retreat Aztec leaders were around 200 cadets, who were prepared for whatever challenge might come. This prestigious institution was simply known as the Military College to the people of Mexico, and they felt a sense of pride in the institution.

Juan Baptist Pascasio Escutia was one of the youngest cadets in this class of promising youths from across Mexico. He was also the newest member of the Cadet Corps, having been admitted on September 8, 1847. As a sad fate would have it and in total, Escutia was destined to serve his country for only six days, before he was killed on fatal September 13.

He had been admitted to the academy on the same day (September 8) as Cadet Agustín Melgar, who more unconventional than the other youths in uniform. Melgar had been expelled from the school for having missed a May 4, 1847 review on the parade ground, which was situated on the wide terrace before the front of the Military College, for some unknown reason. Like his fellow cadets who were wearing their field gray uniforms, Melgar was now more than ready to defend the republic and the Military College.

Juan was only age sixteen, but he was tall for his age and in overall good health. Slim but still athletic and agile, Cadet Escutia felt older partly because of the burden of a sense of responsibility of knowing that the cadets, including even younger ones, were now assigned to defending the capital with their lives. Haunted throughout the previous nights by the nagging realization that a great storm was about to break upon the ancient hilltop with a fury, Juan and his fellow cadets instinctively knew that General Scott's long-awaited assault on Chapultepec was about to come at long last. Perhaps some young cadets now wondered if they would survive the approaching clash of arms and survive to see their families once again.

God's Sacred Temple in Mexico City

One disillusioned invader of Mexico, the ever-curious Captain Franklin Smith, who possessed a distinctive intellectual and philosophical side, wrote of a truism in his journal on a Sunday that could not be denied by the cadets at this time: "there are no Sabbaths in war—war like the grave levels everything—Christian people fight each other on that day which the founder of their faith consecrated to the reign of peace and universal love!"

Lieutenant Juan de la Barrera, a native son of Mexico City and like the other five cadets who were fated to be killed (Cadet Melgar was destined to be mortally wounded and die the following day) at Chapultepec on September 13, had not been granted a leave of absence to worship at the beautiful National Cathedral now that the Americans were about to strike.

On this early morning Sunday when the thoughts of devout Catholics turned away from the nightmare of war to the blessings and mercies of God, the young cadet named Escutia no doubt had wanted nothing more than to have visited the great National Cathedral of Mexico City to reinforce the strong devotion to his faith on Sunday September 12, because he knew that his life might be ending shortly, if the Americans decided to attack.

In the most magnificent church that he had ever seen in his life and like other cadets, Juan Escutia might have now wanted nothing more than one last opportunity to observe Mass and pray to God in the most sacred place in all Mexico City. If Juan and other cadets now desired for a final opportunity to ask for forgiveness and the Lord's mercy in the hope of increasing their chances to survive the upcoming assault that they knew was inevitable, these young men would never have that last opportunity.

A smooth-faced, well-liked youth who never had any need to shave and like other members of the Cadet Corps, Escutia understood why this most beautiful of Cathedrals in Mexico had taken centuries to build into the most breath-taking of all houses of worship. The cadets believed that the city's main Cathedral, the pride and joy of not only Mexico City but also Mexico, had to be protected from the heretical invaders—unsavory heretics—at all costs. Hence, the cadets viewed their upcoming roles in defending Chapultepec as all-important in not only national but also in spiritual terms. Mexico City and its many splendors held a tight grip on the hearts and minds of many young cadets, especially those who called the capital home.

Leaving behind a treasured architectural heritage, the Spanish had enthusiastically transformed Mexico City into what was essentially an European city that brought a measure of Old World sophistication to the New World, becoming one of the seven wonders of the modern world in regard to its sheer beauty. However, the Spanish had become too complacent by the sheer magnitude of the easy riches (stealing Mexico's great natural wealth in gold and silver) that partly caused them to foolishly squander the fantastic wealth of the New World on luxury and extravagance. However, the most enduring physical legacy in the New World had been the Spaniard's creation of magnificent cathedrals, which were built from the sweat and pain of generations of Indian laborers, who worked overtime and extremely hard to meet the exact specifications of ambitious Spanish and Creole architects.

In a great city distinguished by beautiful churches, the National Cathedral situated on the main plaza of Mexico City was the most unforgettable house of worship in a land that had long revered and loved Catholicism. More than a full city block in length, the expansive National Cathedral was flanked by two magnificent bell towers that touched the blue skies over the capital city. In strolling through the immense open expanse of Constitution Plaza and toward the Cathedral's exquisitely-decorated facade, Escutia and other cadets had often felt a deep sense of awe combined with a holy reverence, which increased their religious and patriotic fervor to safeguard Catholicism and defend Chapultepec with their lives.

On past Sundays when this murderous war was not on Mexico City's doorstep and standing out from the crowd of solemn worshipers saying silent prayers, the cadets had often walked through the great doorway with a deep sense of reverence. They had then entered the holy silence of the most awe-inspiring church in Mexico, while wearing their neat dress uniforms of dark blue.

The great Cathedral's heavily-decorated interior, splashed in gold and distinguished by the splendor of dazzling architecture, was absolutely breath-taking to worshipers who entered Mexico's most sacred house of worship in respectful silence. Unlike Protestant churches in America, including Catholic Cathedrals located mostly in the cities, there were no benches, seats, or pews. Consequently, devout worshipers in the National Cathedral knelt on the smooth stone floor and prayed in reverent devotion for extended periods of time. Here, they prayed longer than members of a typical Protestant church in the United States.

While overwhelmed by the Cathedral's holy interior beauty of gold, stained glass, and colorful religious artwork that was awe-inspiring, the boyish cadets had prayed on past peaceful Sundays that were so unlike September 12.Here, at Chapultepec, cadets from towns like Puebla, Tepic, Chihuahua City, and other communities made their confessions to respected priests, who bestowed upon them the comforting feeling of a serene and calm solace to soothe their souls. The priests, who led humble and modest lives devoted to the glory of God, had also bestowed future guidance to the young men of the Cadet Corps. After all, they were away from home for the first time in the lives and about to face their first battle with the Protestant heretics.

Like other cadets, Juan Baptist Pascasio Escutia fulfilled the promise that he had made to his beloved mother, María Dolores Martínez, before he departed home to serve in Mexico City's defense and joined the garrison on September 8.Juan perhaps felt that he had sinned for not writing home more often; losing his composure, perhaps even temper, when he perhaps dropped his musket inspection on the parade ground of the Military College, or failed to have every brass military button properly shined to the academy's exacting standards. Of course, these were violations of the rules angered his drill sergeant and officers of the Cadet Corps.

Most important for the final showdown at Chapultepec, the spiritual beauty of the Holy Mass had long recharged the cadets' faith in themselves and their hopes for a brighter future, while renewing their love of God. Religious faith was important because some of the youngest cadets felt like orphans at the Military College, while they were so far from home and parents for the first time in their lives. With large numbers of American troops now situated so close to Mexico City during this crucial late summer, Cadet Juan Escutia and other cadets now defending Chapultepec must have wondered if they would ever again see Mexico City's grandest Cathedral.

They naturally hoped that the Virgin of Guadalupe, whose righteous symbolism had long inspired and led the Mexican people of all colors to the winning of dramatic victories during the bloody struggle for liberty until independence had been gained in 1821, would protect them in their first battle that was about to shortly erupt at Chapultepec.

Above all else, the young cadets early realized that they would need as much spiritual protection as possible once the fighting erupted in full fury at Chapultepec. No doubt, some of these young men and boys wore crucifixes of gold or silver as symbolic of their religious devotion. However, the cadets were novices at war. Members of the Cadet Corps still did not know about war's harsh realities that were destined to soon descend upon the isolated hilltop in full fury. Indeed, it was now only a matter of time before General Scott ordered thousands of his veteran troops forward in a desperate offensive effort to overcome the last high ground and the final natural barrier that protected the capital. Therefore, tension and nervous anticipation remained high among the cadets atop the commanding summit of Chapultepec, while General Scott and his top lieutenants for the unleashing of a massive assault.

However, the cadets could not quite understand why Mexico City, with a population of around 200,000 citizens, was still full of people, who seemed to be entirely unaffected by the war, at such a crucial time. As if no war existed at all, the city's residents continued to stroll along the popular tree-lined known as the Alameda, located just west of the National Cathedral and near the Garita (Gate) de San Cosme on the city's northwest side, and the wide *avenidas*, especially Avenida Montezuma. Even the tables of the popular *cantinas* and restaurants were crowed with patrons, almost as if the war did not exist.

But yet relatively few soldiers were assigned to defending Chapultepec, and not enough troops to successfully defend this high ground perch. And they continued to wonder how General Santa Anna, who commanded Mexico's National Army, could possibly have lost every battle, including in northern Mexico before Scott's invasion. This was a grim reality that haunted the cadets, especially when they were now about to face their first attack.

Unfortunately, Santa Anna had proved to be a curse to Mexico, extending back to his disastrous loss of Texas, which had led to the outbreak of this terrible war that had brought so much misery and suffering. And now the people and government of Mexico had placed all their faith in Santa Anna's ability to stop the Americans from capturing Chapultepec and Mexico City. But as a sad fate would have it, he was simply not up the stiff challenge—all but impossible under the circumstances—of saving Mexico in her darkest hour.

Sad Reflections

Clearly, the overall faltering strategic situation in regard to Mexico City's defense raised a host of questions in the minds of the cadets that they could not answer. But such were the mysterious ways of war not yet understood by these young men who had yet to engage in a raging battle. Since the war's beginning, Juan and other cadets now thought differently about a good many things before General Scott's Army had advanced so close to threaten the life of Mexico City.

Ever since the Americans had marched inland from Vera Cruz, this conflict between vastly different races, cultures, and religions had steadily evolved from what had been initially considered a glorious adventure by the men on both sides into something that was cruel and bestial to a degree imaginable at the war's beginning: an cruel reality most recently demonstrated during the savagery displayed by enraged *soldados* killing injured Americans in the open fields lying before the defenses of Molino del Rey. As had been fully revealed in the 1847 Campaign, both sides had proved equally capable of violating the accepted rules of civilized warfare and dictates of Christianity.

Because of this vicious war in which all of the once quaint notions of chivalry and glory for both sides had been proven to be hopelessly out of date, the cadets had already lost some of their innocence by September 1847.These promising youths of the Cadet Corps no longer basked in the smug comfort of their former youthful idealism that were actually departures from the ugly truths about the war's harsh realities: romantic concepts about war that had faded away by this time, and especially now with the Americans at the gates of Mexico City.

With their once-bright futures darkened by the war's savagery that seemed to have no end, the cadets had matured during the tragic course of events during this bitter conflict that had turned so sharply against Mexico, becoming more cynical and world-wise. Indeed, by this time, the war had evolved from little more than a romantic tournament of finely-uniformed rivals into something very hard and cold: the brutality of what had evolved into a total war with all its accompanying horrors that had gradually intensified with each passing month.

Unlike previously and probably only to themselves because they were members of the Cadet Corps, perhaps the most free-thinking cadets now began to question the wisdom of the highest-ranking authorities because the overall war effort was going so badly on Mexico's own soil. Like so many others, they gradually began to understand that Santa Anna was essentially leading the army and nation to utter ruin.

Despite mostly teenagers and like so many other members of the often-defeated Mexican military, some of the more questioning cadets were slowly but surely becoming more fatalistic about this war by this time. Even the youthful eyes of these young men, who had yet to shave or to make love for the first time, in gray service uniforms became more questioning of the highest ranking and most respected leaders, especially Santa Anna, and their nation's military and strategic policies not previously understood by them, while growing up in home towns like Chihuahua City, Puebla, and Tepic.

A Beloved Surrogate Home

Especially during the fateful summer of 1847, their experiences at the Military College had already begun to significantly change these cadets in profound ways, since the unforgettable day when they had kissed their mothers good-bye just before leaving home. The cadets' departure from homes and families now seemed like a lifetime ago to these youths, who now faced the prospect of death for the first time, whenever General Scott ordered his assault that had been calculated to carry everything before it.

Mexico's leading center for the military education of its most gifted and promising young men made this hilltop complex, now collectively known as Chapultepec Castle, especially important because of what it symbolized to both sides. The Military College had become not only a safe and secure refuge, but also a home for the students of the Cadet Corps.

The popular name of Chapultepec Castle had been bestowed because of the nature of the commanding terrain of Lomas de Chapultepec and the well-constructed buildings, including the Military College. As mentioned, this extensive palace and summer residence had been created by considerable expense by the Spanish Viceroy Bernardo de Galvez, when he had ordered construction on the residence to begin in 1785, not long after reaching his new home of Mexico City in June of that year.

Born in Spain, Galvez was a highly-capable leader of the American Revolution. Although mostly forgotten by Americans today, Galvez had played a key role in helping America win its independence, emerging as a true hero of the struggle for liberty. He conquered British Florida for Spain, after his capture of the strategic port of Pensacola, Florida, on the northern edge of Gulf of Mexico east of New Orleans. Ironically, General Scott's soldiers, especially the less educated men of the enlisted ranks, had no knowledge that Galvez had played a key role in the winning of American independence.

Symbolically, to the cadets, the Military College now represented the past, present, and the future. Now housed in the southeastern section of the overall Chapultepec Castle complex that towered about the surrounding plain, the military school was the pride and joy of its dedicated students. Standing high above the humid lowlands, the large complex was situated on the flat summit that lay along as east-west axis.

As the cadets realized, Chapultepec had once served as the summer residence of the Aztec leaders, reminding them of their nation's rich Indian roots and legacies. Members of the Cadet Corps had basked in the cool of the shade of the cypress forest and the refreshing breezes that swept the summit, before the arrival of General Scott's conquering army that seemingly could not be beaten. Chapultepec had been only recently transformed into a defensive bastion, taking on an entirely new appearance from the more innocent days in the past.

During the War of Independence and for whatever reason, the Spanish rulers, military or civilian, had never taken the wise precaution of fortifying the hilltop. Most importantly, the belated steps to make adequate defensive preparations on this high ground perch only indicated how not even the capital was safe from this determined invaders. But these defensive efforts had not been enough to transform the hill into an impregnable position by this time. And now thousands of the invaders stood before Chapultepec with fixed bayonets and grim resolution to carry the high ground at all costs in an overpowering advance.

The Castle was protected by two high, white-washed walls of stone that were around four feet in thickness: first, the outer wall located at the foot of the hill to enclose the forested grounds bordering the fields of the surrounding lowlands, and, second, the second set of high walls—twelve feet high—that enclosed the summit and the Castle—the formidable inner wall.

But despite these defensive strengths and advantages, the chances of Major General Bravo's defenses holding firm against thousands of Scott's veteran attackers were significantly reduced by Santa Anna's own arrogance. He had failed to reverse his prior misplaced judgment that Chapultepec was not the main target. Santa Anna, therefore, continued to believe that the main attack was about to come from the south. However, to be fair to Santa Anna, he had been fooled by tactical trickery from a savvy opponent. Scott had smartly ordered a series of convincing demonstrations before the southern sector for the express purpose of deceiving the over-confident general. These demonstrations had proven successful in fooling Santa Anna to ensure that Chapultepec's defenders were now on their own and without any reinforcements when needed.

During the night, large numbers of American troops who had demonstrated aggressively before the southern sector on September 12 had marched quietly west to take advanced positions in front of Chapultepec before the sunrise of September 13: a stealthy tactical movement unseen and unknown to Santa Anna.

Therefore, Chapultepec continued to be manned by far too few soldados to adequately defend a sprawling defensive complex that covered a wide area of a quarter of a mile wide and three-quarters of a mile long. Meanwhile, Santa Anna continued to withhold the reinforcements that should have been urgently dispatched to the isolated bastion and its isolated defenders, who were on its own.

Rendezvous with a Tragic Destiny

September 13 was a day that the cadets never forgot. Cadet Juan Baptist Pascasio Escutia and other cadets had been awakened on the early morning of September 13 by the brass trumpet that played Reveille. The early morning darkness was already becoming gradually warmer, while providing a reminder that the late summer heat had not faded away even when the cooler air of autumn drew ever-closer.

Ironically, the tune echoing over Chapultepec's summit early on September 13 was heard and recognized by the Americans, who had learned a great deal about the Mexican Army during this bloody campaign. The fighting men of a far-away nation instantly recognized the distinctive bugle call. Sergeant Thomas Barley noted in his journal that the Mexican trumpeter on the distant hilltop played the Mexican Army's wake-up call that early rang across the summit. This was described by one American soldier as a "shrill music"—more "shrill" than the Americans' Reveille.

The sergeant readily recognized the martial tune because it was the same call that had been used by the Vera Cruz garrison at Fort San Juan de Ulúa, a massive rectangular masonry fortress located just off the gulf coast, when it had been besieged in March 1847 and pounded into submission by the big American guns. Ironically, captured Mexican cannon now made Scott's Army even more formidable. General Juan Baptisto Morales, a former colonel who had led the predawn attack on the Alamo's south wall, where the main entrance was located, on the morning of March 6, 1836, had surrendered Vera Cruz, after a devastating bombardment.

As mentioned, the cadets had not been able to attend Holy Mass on Sunday, and now realized that they also would not have that opportunity on this Monday, September 13.The sharp notes of the bugle slanting over the hilltop and the rapid beating drums of the green-uniform drummer boys of the Military College told the cadets to prepare for action as soon as possible.

Although many cadets preferred to think about God and the National Cathedral's splendor rather than the nightmare of war, they had leaped from their bunks of their barracks to answer the call. Then, the cadets then hurriedly grabbed weapons in preparation for meeting the stern challenges on early September 13.Unlike the thousands of American troops who had rested relatively well during the night, the young men and boys of Chapultepec was weary and tired. Atop the commanding summit that overlooked such a wide area, they had spent a restless and vigilant night in anticipation of a possible assault being unleashed at any moment, especially after the intense bombardment of the previous day that had begun at daylight.

After having been awakened to a harsh reality and sense of added responsibility, Juan Escutia and his fellow cadets had early realized that this was a day of destiny. Surely the long-awaited American assault was about to come, because none had been forthcoming on September 12. Indeed, they knew that September 13 would ultimately decide the fate of not only Mexico City, but also all of Mexico.

After realizing that his intense artillery bombardment had been unleashed on Chapultepec for the entire day of September 12 had not been enough to force the garrison's surrender when no white flag was raised, Scott had become frustrated. Inside the comfort of his Tacubaya headquarters, therefore, General Scott had then made plans that evening for the unleashing of an all-out assault early on September 13.

Like the determined stand of the brave American defenders who stood firm in the brick masonry bastion of Fort McHenry that protected the inner harbor of the port of Baltimore, Maryland, where the United States gained its national anthem because the outsized American flag had not been lowered during a fierce artillery bombardment from British warships during the War of 1812, so the large Mexican flag now waved in majesty and defiance from the summit played a comparable role.

Indeed, the national colors of green, red, and white proudly waved atop the tower on the summit's east side: an infuriating sight which told General Scott that Chapultepec would never surrender, regardless of how many projectiles pounded on the summit. All the while, the garrison's spirited defiance now inspired the cadets, fortifying their resolve to fight to the bitter end, if and when American troops charged up the hill. Already, garrison members took great pride in the fact that no defenders had raised a white flag, as so smugly expected by General Scott from the beginning.

To inspire confidence early on September 13, General Scott boasted to his top commanders that "We will conquer Mexico City today!" Scott's ambitious plan now called for a massive assault that would overpower Chapultepec and then propel the attackers northeast in a continued surge northeastward to capture Mexico City. According to this plan, the attackers would then follow on the heels of the retreating Mexicans to storm the inner, or last, defensive line of the city, before Santa Anna had time to rush reinforcements west to these threatened points.

Meanwhile, seemingly everyone among the Chapultepec garrison now knew that the very life of Mexico City was at stake and everything was about to be determined. As could be expected before their first battle, some cadets had been unable to sleep well during the nerve-wracking night of September 12-13, knowing that all hell would break loose with the first light of day. At some point this morning, the cadets evidently hastily gobbled down a hasty meal of most likely slices of bread (perhaps tortillas), or maybe even the far less tasty hardtack like American soldiers, because the attack might come at any time.

Most of all, there had been no time on this early morning of September 13—the most fateful Monday of their lives—to eat at the mess hall of the Cadet Corps, after the buglers had sounded Reveille to awake the garrison in the predawn darkness. Such formalities and niceties were things of the past, because the first American gunners aligned in the lowlands below were about to open fire in the hazy, faint light of dawn. To inflict as much damage as possible, General Scott had issued orders for a continuation of the bombardment from the day before.

After the Military College's two young buglers and four drummer boys, dressed in natty uniforms of green, had sounded the assembly, the cadets had aligned in a tight formation on the stone-lined terrace fronting the military academy. On the wide parade ground of the Military College, the young musicians beat their drums that were decorated with beautiful hand-painted Mexican Golden Eagles and other national emblems, with frantic energy.

Finely-uniformed cadets had then raced down the stairs and departed the academy's halls on the double with their weapons in hand. As they had practiced many times in the past, the members of the Cadet Corps then spilled out into the wide parade ground on the flat terrace before the front of the Military College to form in proper alignment. With a natural degree of nervousness and anxiousness when about to engage in their first battle, they hurriedly took their assigned positions in the early morning darkness just before the dawn. At some point, the cadets then might well have received a hasty blessing from a military chaplain or civilian priest, because the great attack was shortly expected.

Wearing their new service uniforms of gray, the cadets were then released from their formations of assembly, and given their final defensive assignments. In a hurry, they had taken their assigned defensive positions to resist the norteamericano's inevitable onslaught, which was now only a matter of time. A bastion that must be defended at all costs and as mentioned, Chapultepec occupied a most strategic position because it guarded two key roads that were open avenues which led to the capital city. The nearby Tacubaya Road, on Chapultepec's east side, led to two causeways (the Belén Causeway and the La Verónica Causeway) that pointed the way into Mexico City from the southwest. The Belén Causeway proceeded all the way to the Garita (Gate) de Belén at the city's southwestern side.

The darkness of the lowlands on the early morning of September 13 had been eerily still and hauntingly quiet, until the sun finally rose on the most eventful day in the cadets' lives: an ominous silence before a great eruption of pent-up furies that were about to be unleashed by the Gods of War. More than during the previous night, the night of September 12-13 had been a bit cooler than usual, but the heat increased with the rising sun.

Most of all, something foreboding seemed to hang heavy in the late summer air and over the lonely hilltop of defenders, who would receive no reinforcements on this day of destiny. For ample good reasons, many questions still persisted and were unanswered in the minds of the most inquisitive cadets. Was this the day when the Yankees finally launched their attack, after having been restrained from attacking on the previous day? Or would General Scott only rely upon artillery to pound Chapultepec into submission in an attempt to force the garrison's surrender, hurling tons of shot and shell to rake the summit as throughout September 12? The most naive soldiers, especially the youngest cadets, believed that Scott dared not attack such a high ground perch that was brimming of troops and cannon, while older defenders now expected the worst. After not having lost a battle, Scott's feisty and hard-fighting army had no intention of turning back, especially now when on the doorstep of the greatest prize of all, Mexico City.

Rows of Booming American Artillery

Ironically, because of so many past successes, the experienced United States artillerymen now possessed a good many captured Mexican artillery pieces, including old Spanish guns, and ample supplies of ammunition to thoroughly pound Chapultepec's defenses in preparation of the great assault. In fact, the number of large American cannon, invaluable siege guns, had been tripled in number by the early morning of September 13, thanks to so many past American victories, such as at Cerro Gordo, which had been won on the long road to Mexico City.

A good many field pieces, including large siege guns, of four batteries had been first brought up under the protective cover of darkness on September 11. Then, these cannon had been set-up in the best firing positions as designated by the hard-working engineers, whose expertise gained at West Point continued to shine brightly, and within easy range of Chapultepec.

As noted, guns from several batteries aligned in the lowlands had unleashed a heavy barrage beginning at daylight September 12, and they were now ready to resume their fire on the early morning of September 13.In the final insult and most bitter irony that was not realized by the cadets, they had been bombarded throughout the previous day by a number of Mexican guns and ammunition that had captured at the battles of Contreras and most recently at Churubusco.

Because of the bombardment's fury on Sunday to ensure that there had been no opportunity or time to go to Mass, the cadets now looked at the debris and rubble scattered all around them. Chapultepec had been bombarded by four batteries of brass American cannon for more than fourteen hours from daybreak to sunset on Sunday September 12.

As mentioned, General Scott had hoped to pound the bastion into submission to avoid the heavy losses like he had suffered at Molino del Rey. He also realized that he had made the mistake of only unleashing a brief pre-assault artillery bombardment on this strong defensive position because of the high losses resulting from the attack. Therefore, Chapultepec and the Military College were destined to pay a high price in compensation for Scott's errors at Molino del Rey, because he had adjusted his tactics.

Therefore, the punishment had been severe on September 12. Lieutenant John James Peck, 2nd United States Artillery, described in a letter how: "All are at work for the taking of the castle of Chapultepec [after the] Batteries opened this morning with shells and shot and have played all day," in the hope of forcing a surrender of the garrison, including the cadets.

One of the most effective guns that had pounded Chapultepec on September 12 was a 10.5 inch mortar. This large mortar lobbed iron projectiles that plunged through the thin roofs of the Castle and the Military College with thundering crashes. As proven during the bombardment, the roofs were light and more decorative than solidly built. Clearly, they had never been constructed for military purposes, especially to withstand a bombardment from the concentrated fire of heavy artillery.

A terror to the defenders because they had no proper shelter—such as bomb-proofs to protect them from projectiles—against the intense artillery bombardment, this mortar had lobbed a seemingly endless number of big shells onto the top of the strategic hill, inflicting considerable damage and heavy losses.

A hero of the struggle for Mexican Independence, Major General Bravo feared the worst for the future and for ample good reason. Most of all, he required urgent reinforcements from Santa Anna, who promised that they would be dispatched to bolster Chapultepec's weak garrison in the nick of time, if an attack seemed about to be launched: still another false promise never fulfilled by Santa Anna. As could be expected, General Santa Anna remained safely far away to the east from the deadly bombardment that killed a good many defenders and severely damaged the Military College.

Some faint-hearted defenders of Chapultepec had slipped away and deserted during the furious bombardment of September 12, fearing for their lives under the relentless pounding of the big guns. As if knowing that Santa Anna would not keep his promise about sending reinforcements to the west, these faint-of-heart soldados sensed correctly that Chapultepec possessed far too few defenders, and that the belated attempts to strengthen the inadequate defenses were incomplete partly because efforts to strengthen the works had begun much too late.

These deserters, mostly from generally unreliable (compared to regulars) National Guard units whose members lacked proper training and discipline, wanted to escape the upcoming American attack. Nevertheless and in a testament to their determination, the around 200 cadets had not left their assigned defensive positions. Therefore, they now waited for the inevitable storm to break loose in full fury in the half-light of the morning of September 13.

This Monday was almost certainly the day that the massive assault would become a terrible reality for the defenders, because the Americans had not attacked Chapultepec on Sunday when expected by Major General Bravo and his men. Instead, Chapultepec had been pounded by artillery for more than 14 hours on September 12.Shells had burst over the Military College and crashed through the roof to explode inside. Solid shot (cannonballs) had also caused extensive damage to the Castle complex. This was the generally forgotten siege of Chapultepec in which the defenders, including the cadets, withstood a terrible bombardment.

On September 12, handsome Private Richard Coulter, 2nd Pennsylvania Volunteers, described in his journal how the blazing cannon "did most terrible execution, every round shot boring through the building [Castle that included the Military College] and our shells bursting immediately over their guns" to kill and wound artillerymen, and despite the fact that the "Castle was considerably elevated above our battery."

He also described how the well-trained United States gunners made "some brag shots," and the 10.5-inch mortar "did great execution, throwing every shell into the very center of the works." Besides inflicting considerable havoc to the Military College and the Castle, the intense bombardment also damaged the earthen parapets and punched holes in the high, white-washed stone wall (the inner wall) that enclosed the summit. Worst of all for the infantry defenders, including the cadets, at least 5 of the 10 cannon of Chapultepec were knocked-out by the accurate bombardment, which boded ill for a successful defense on the following day.

Despite the cannonade that had raked the hilltop all of Sunday with a vengeance, Bravo and his men had defiantly refused to even contemplate the possibly of surrendering Chapultepec on September 12.The major general's defiance under the heavy artillery bombardment set the stage for the final showdown early on the morning of September 13.

Clearly, it would now be far easier for the Americans to overrun the high ground with half of the defending cannon disabled from the accurate bombardment that had already significantly weakened defensive capabilities. Major General Bravo and his men were determined to hold out to the bitter end. This determination was because they considered Chapultepec not only a strategic, but also a sacred place that was well worth fighting and dying for if necessary. While the projectiles had rained down throughout a nerve-wracking September 12 when a good many defenders were killed and horribly maimed, they had refused to relinquish their tenacious grip on the ancient hilltop of the Aztecs. General Scott had fully expected the garrison to surrender, but such was only wishful thinking. Therefore, Chapultepec would have to be carried by the assault of thousands of battle-hardened troops on this early Monday morning, because the garrison had refused to give up.

A Napoleonic type with lofty ambitions and an outsized ego from his past successes, General Scott had already decided to unleash a September 13 assault on the previous evening, because the Mexican flag still flew with pride from the top of the exquisite stone tower situated on the east side of the Chapultepec Castle complex. Not even the relentless bombardment on Sunday—not observed as a day of rest and worship by the opportunistic Americans—had knocked down the beautiful Mexican flag waving high atop the smoke-wreathed summit. The riddle that existed among the Chapultepec's defenders of what would happen next and exactly when on this early Monday morning was soon decisively answered in the most convincing fashion.

Throughout Santa Anna's Army, spirits were relatively low (ironically, like American spirits after the terrible bloodletting at Molino del Rey, especially after the killing of Scott's wounded men) among the soldados, after having suffered the crushing defeat at Churubusco (a powerful defensive bastion that could not stop the Americans) on August 20. After all, the Churubusco defensive complex had been manned by Santa Anna's best troops and commanders.

The hard-luck and seemingly ill-fated Mexican Army had lost nearly 40 artillery pieces and hundreds of prisoners, despite a tenacious defensive stand and magnificent fighting demonstrated by tough soldados at Churubusco. Here, Mexican valor and that of the Irish and other immigrants of the San Patricio Battalion (St. Patrick's Battalion—named after the patron saint of Ireland—that consisted mostly of deserters from the United States Army) had shined on this bloody day.

Most ominously, not even the heavy losses among the attackers at Churubusco were sufficient to deter the Yankees' resolve to gain their great prize of Mexico City with additional aggressiveness. But the faith and spirits of the cadets remained high on the early morning of September 13, despite the previous day's bombardment that had caused extensive damage and losses.

If Chapultepec fell to the invaders and as noted, then the Yankees planned to continue their attack. After overwhelming the last high ground situated before the city, the Americans then planned to follow the length of the Belén Causeway (which ran northeast over a wide expanse of swamps and led to the city's southwestern edge) and the stone aqueduct (a cultural, architectural, and engineering legacies of the ancient Romans, who had conquered Spain, transferred to the New World) that stood on the northern edge of Chapultepec's grounds that led from the rocky hill's clear springs straight to the Belén Gate (Garita de Belén) of Mexico City.

Confidence among the hilltop's defenders was bolstered by Mexico's largest and most powerful cannon. Ten guns (now reduced to only five by the bombardment), including a 16-pounder, had been aligned atop Chapultepec. Even more, a high, but incomplete, stone wall of around 15-20 feet in height stood at the hill's base on the east and the south. This wall's length was in the shape of rectangle that extended nearly three-quarters of a mile in length and a quarter mile wide.

For security concerns, the grounds of the colonial viceroy's palace had been walled in the tradition of the extensive haciendas of wealthy noblemen from Andalusia and other regions in rural Spain. Outside the walls flowed the seemingly endless expanse of fields of cornfields, while inside the walls stood clumps of tall timber, including the ancient forest of Mexican Bald Cypress, that were part of Chapultepec's expansive grounds.

In addition, a defensive network of concealed explosive mines of black powder had been planted along the slope to protect the strategic summit. Located at the slope's western base, a small redan, a two-sided (half of a triangle) earthen defensive work, had been built to command the approach through the open fields. Situated farther up the slope past the mine fields, a circular redoubt anchored the second defensive line that stood on the southern slope to protect the road. This dusty road led up the steep hill to the entrance of the terrace and parade ground that lay before the front of the Military College that faced south.

Then, still another wall (the parapet, or inner, wall that was 12-feet high) protected by a deep ditch, surrounded the hill's crest. This innermost wall, also known to the soldados as the parapet wall, at the plateau's edge protected the crest, the Military College, and Castle atop the flat summit, where a courageous last stand against the odds had been made to defy the norteamericanos.

Consequently, a good many defenders on this hill of destiny were still confident of successfully defending the key high ground, after having endured the severe bombardment throughout the previous day. Having no thoughts of surrendering, Major General Bravo and his men felt that they could hold firm and hurl back the Yankees to save the people of Mexico City from the hated invaders of a different race, culture, and religion.

Therefore, the overall motivations of the young cadets remained sky high on the early morning of September 13, and even more than the majority of the regular soldados of Santa Anna's often-defeated army, because of the recent setbacks. Chapultepec's defenders were determined to hold firm and never surrender, regardless of how many shells and cannonballs that were hurled at them.

Most of all, the defenders knew that if strategic Chapultepec fell, then the Yankee army would have gained two open avenues to advance along the dual causeways, which passed over the swampy lowlands, that led to Mexico City. Therefore, Major General Bravo's troops, including the cadets, realized that this special place called Chapultepec had to be held at all costs this morning. After all, the Yankees would have an unopposed march into the very heart of Mexico City, if the cadets and garrison were either ordered to surrender or were pushed aside by the attackers.

However, Chapultepec was relatively remote in its isolated position nearly two miles southwest of Mexico City, increasing its overall vulnerability. This distance ensured that even if Santa Anna ascertained Scott's correct strategy to striking from the southwest and finally dispatched reinforcements to reinforce the lonely hilltop position, then they would probably not arrive in time to assist the outnumbered defenders. Therefore, the Chapultepec garrison continued to be on their own.

As General Scott had hoped and planned, Santa Anna fell for the clever tactical feint to the south, however. Santa Anna believed that this southern point was the true point of attack in part because Scott had made sure that the generalissimo saw the build-up of American troops south of the city in daylight hours. Santa Anna, consequently, saw the September 12 bombardment and movements before Chapultepec as nothing more than a feint. To be fair to Santa Anna, he was attempting to protect the approaches to three city gates simultaneously, which limited his tactical options and hampered his decision-making process.

And now in the lingering cool of the early morning of September 13, a lengthy row of American cannon were about to open fire on Santa Anna's southern positions to additionally convince him that the main attack was about to come his way, which was certainly not the case.

Therefore, as a cruel fate would have it, the outnumbered and isolated men of Chapultepec were guaranteed to be on their own for all of fateful September 13: a situation that ultimately decided the capital city's fate. This was the long-awaited day of destiny that General Scott had envisioned, when "he would be met with a white flag" from Mexico City in a formal surrender, after capturing the strategic high ground of Chapultepec.

Hellish Bombardment Continued Unabated

The sunrise of September 13 came slowly when the red ball ascended into a cloudless sky, promising to bake the dry land. American cannon, including the deadly mortar, located in the lowlands of the fields suddenly opened-up a heavy fire on Chapultepec with the first light of day. In a letter, Lieutenant John James Peck, 2nd United States Artillery, described how the "Bombardment began at dawn and was kept up vigorously until . . . all was readiness for the assault" on Chapultepec.

The experienced American gunners shortly gained the exact range on the commanding summit, thanks to what they had learned the previous day in pounding the hilltop. Shot and shells cascaded into the Chapultepec complex, inflicting additional damage among the defenses and the garrison. Sergeant Thomas Barclay, 2nd Pennsylvania Volunteers, penned in his journal how the morning was "beautiful," but this was not the case for Chapultepec's beleaguered defenders, who severely suffered in the hellish bombardment. While the projectiles plowed into their Military College for the second day in a row, the cadets held firm under the intense barrage at their assigned defensive positions as ordered by thei8r officers. Food and ammunition among the garrison were already low because Santa Anna had not planned for a siege. However, the fighting spirits among the defenders remained high, while the shells and cannonballs rained down and they held firm.

Like his Military College comrades who gamely withstood the artillery pounding, Cadet Juan Escutia and his fellow cadets had never before experienced such a devastating cannonade. The noisy row of American guns, which almost seemed without end to the nervous cadets, continued to steadily hammer away. From the smoke-wreathed summit, members of the Cadet Corps watched the fast-working American gunners in action, while shells and cannonballs shrieked overhead.

Iron projectiles, including from the large 16-pounders of Captain Simon H. Drum's 4th United States Artillery, smashed into the buildings and defenses of the Castle, now torn with holes from multiple direct hits. Meanwhile, the spirits among the Americans in blue uniforms soared higher, when they saw projectiles crashing into targets and causing even more damage, including the systemic elimination of additional defenders who were cut down.

As penned in his journal, Sergeant Barclay described the destruction from one direct hit after another: "Every ball and bomb fell with the greatest accuracy and clouds of dust told where they had taken effect." Also fueling confidence among Scott's men was the fact that the return fire from Chapultepec's guns was largely ineffective in part because the assault forces were well-positioned on the lower ground, including lying under good cover for concealment.

Also because the cannon of the fortress were located so high on the summit, Mexican artillerymen encountered difficulty in depressing barrels sufficiently to get the exact range. Therefore, most Mexican cannon-fire roared too high, sailing over the heads of the American artillerymen and infantrymen. In addition, a lengthy, but thin, line of bluecoat men in skirmish formation advanced over the fields and reached a point close to the walls bordering the Castle's grounds near the foot of the hill. After exchanging hot fires with Scott's long line of skirmishers, the Mexican skirmishers had been gradually pushed back toward the high ground and the Mexican Bald

Cypress forest that offered shelter from Yankee bullets and the wrath of the Protestants.

Most of all, General Scott hoped to significantly reduce the strength of the defensive network in preparation for the unleashing of a massive infantry assault that he had decided upon the previous evening. But the men and boys of Chapultepec still raised no white flags on the morning of September 13, despite suffering greater loses under the extensive pounding of the big guns. When an opportunity had existed, Santa Anna had earlier offered no terms for surrender. At this time, many Mexicans believed was the only hope of preserving Mexico City--instead of sharing Vera Cruz's tragic fate--lay in a humiliating capitulation.

Meanwhile, the defiant men of Chapultepec, including the Boy Cadets, still refused to contemplate the nauseating notion of surrender to the interlopers. No one on the projective-swept hilltop was going to take down the large red-white-green flag that was waving majestically in the breeze from the main tower at the summit. Major General Bravo had been ordered to hold Chapultepec, and he took Santa Anna's directives most seriously. And he was the kind of man who obeyed orders to the end. Scott knew that the upcoming assault by thousands of his best infantrymen would prove costly, but he had no choice with the defiant defenders remaining firm to mock his intense cannonade and soaring ambitions, despite the intense bombardment's accuracy.

Like during the previous day's bombardment, the rain of projectiles continued to tear through the unprotected rooftop of the Military College, which was located in the viceroy's old palace, raising clouds of dust that lifted high over the battered summit. As mentioned, damage from the barrage of solid shot was extensive, because the Castle—the comfortable summer palace of the Viceroy—was not built to withstand a steady bombardment from the fire from a row of modern cannon.

Indeed, like on the day before, General Bravo ordered his engineers and work parties to hurriedly repair the damage caused by each direct hit from a hurled projectile. But even these frantic efforts to make emergency repairs were simply not enough to strengthen the weak defenses. As on the previous day, the most damage was inflicted by the 10.5-inch mortar, which continued to lob heavy cannonballs into the midst of the Castle complex. Quite simply, Chapultepec's defenders were completely at the mercy of the murderous cannon that roared unabated.

Infuriating the cadets and additionally fueling their determination to hold firm under the severe punishment, the military academy, in the Castle's southeastern section, had been extensively damaged by the rain of shot and shell on a terrible Sunday that violated the sacredness of the holy day. Despite its location atop imposing Lomas de Chapultepec, the entire complex of Chapultepec Castle, including the Military College, was in overall bad shape by this time, after the lengthy bombardment on the sacred Sabbath.

And now on this equally harrowing Monday morning, the Military College continued to take a beating from the hail of projectiles. Lengthy rows of American cannon continued to blaze away at the complex atop the hill, as if there was no tomorrow. But still Chapultepec's brave defenders held firm in stubborn defiance, enduring the deadly storm.

All the while, the sizeable Mexico flag still proudly waved from atop the tower and over the hard-hit garrison, while Bravo's men suffered the ever-increasing losses without abandoning their defensive positions. But despite running low on ammunition, food, and manpower, garrison members still refused to even think about surrendering to the hated Yankees, sabotaging General Scott's tactical plan of forcing an early surrender by their determination.

To Juan Escutia and his fellow cadets, the roar of the big guns, especially the angry 16-pounders of Captain Drum's battery and the duller booms from the 10.5-inch mortar that fired incessantly from near Molina del Rey, sounded like the thunder of a summer storm sweeping across the lush, green valley under the shadow of the ancient volcanoes, snow-capped Iztaccihuatl and Popocatépetl.

Now that Mexico City was threatened as never before, Escutia and other cadets might have recalled reading the story of the conquest of Mexico and the decimation to the proud Aztec. If so, then they might have felt a greater sense of unease when remembering that the great killer Cortéz had first reached Mexico City from the south, before committing slaughter and genocide upon the unfortunate Aztec, whose Sun God could no longer save them. And, then one of the great civilizations of the ancient world fell to the light-skinned Conquistadors, whose strength had been significantly bolstered by thousands of Aztec-hating Indian allies. In the process, the Spanish had committed unspeakable atrocities in the name of God.

On this day of destiny (Monday September 13), this promising youth from the town of Tepic and other cadets perhaps even briefly thought about Homer's *Iliad*(first published in Spain during the 1500s), and how the ancient city of Troy had fallen to the determined Greek warriors, including the fabled Achilles. Could Mexico City, the beloved home of Lieutenant Juan de la Barrera, suffer a comparable tragic fate of not only conquest, but also even total destruction from these new invaders? Would the struggle for possession of Mexico City be as bloody and horrible as that brutal conflict described by the ancient Trojans and Greeks in the immortal pages of the *Iliad*?

Of course, no one today knows the exact thoughts that swirled through the cadets' troubled minds, while they remained at their defensive positions in the early morning hours of September 13 and the shells exploded nearby, including direct hits on the Military College. What was clear to the cadets was that the ancient Aztec war god Huitzilopochtli (like the god of war Mars who had inspired the warrior ways of the ancient Greeks) was especially angry this morning, and it seemed that his terrible wrath had spilled over the ancient hill of Chapultepec.

In the words of Sergeant Barclay, "the firing between the [American] batteries and the Castle was kept up with great spirit." Additional damage was inflicted on the Military College with each passing minute, while the cadets looked on helplessly and could do nothing to protect or save their battered school.

Meanwhile, the determination, but not a blind confidence based on arrogance or xenophobia that held the Americans in contempt and vice versa, began to sink among the garrison at Chapultepec under the relentless artillery pounding and spiraling losses of additional good fighting men.

Santa Anna's False Facade

Unfortunately for the defenders, Chapultepec appeared far stronger and more formidable than was actually the case. Nevertheless, the top Mexican leaders, including Santa Anna, continued to believe that Chapultepec was an impregnable position and could withstand the approaching storm.

But this belief was ill-founded and nothing more than an illusion. However, Santa Anna's faith in Chapultepec's impregnability continued to cause him not to order forth what was now most needed for the young men and boys waiting atop this sacred hill of the Aztecs: the ordering of large numbers of reinforcements to bolster the outnumbered garrison, before it was too late.

Clearly, time was now running out for Chapultepec's defenders, whose numbers continued to decline with each direct hit from an exploding shell. As mentioned, they now possessed only five working cannon after that same number of guns had been knocked-out by the devastating cannonade. Worst of all, however, Santa Anna continued to believe that Scott's main attack was coming on the south side of Mexico City and not from the southwest.

As mentioned and besides half of its guns disabled, Chapultepec was also vulnerable because of its isolated position, with no adjoining high ground or troops to protect its vulnerable flanks on the east and west. It seemed to stand solitary amid the sea of cornfields, as if this sharp elevation had been dropped in the middle of the level plain by the hand of God, who had not completed his creation work of forming adjacent high ground of the lonely hill.

Therefore, this isolated high ground perch of the ancient Aztec, whose warrior society had once joyously celebrated their festival of Huitzilopochtli, could also be easily surrounded by attacking Americans, because no natural barriers existed on either side of Chapultepec for protection. Chapultepec's outnumbered garrison, which had relatively little, if any, chance of winning the upcoming fight, was destined to face the full weight of the Americans' wrath.

Standing proudly like the regal Montezuma when he had ruled a mighty empire before the arrival of Cortez and his armor-clad murderers, who had been hardened by brutal wars against the Islamic

Moors, after having pushed them back into north Africa, "Grasshopper Hill" continued to be vulnerable. The hill rising up from the plain seemed almost like a single sailing ship, which was journeying all alone on the ocean's wide expanse and amid hostile waters.

As the Aztec had fully appreciated not long after their arrival in this fertile valley of seemingly endless bounty, this elevation dominated a wide expanse of flat, marshy ground. This place was called "Grasshopper Hill" because it had had long provided safety to large numbers of grasshoppers fleeing the encroachment of flood waters during torrential rains and periodic flooding. But on the morning of September 13, nothing in the world could protect the hill's most recent residents—garrison members, including the cadets—from the full force of the inevitable assault.

In a strange, if not paradoxical, way, the hill's natural strength was also proving to be its extreme vulnerability. Indeed, Chapultepec's natural strength was largely a facade that blinded Santa Anna to its vulnerabilities. But almost certainly, this commanding high ground perch brought a measure of comfort to the naive cadets, who still believed that the Yankee soldiers could not scale the steep slope and capture their beloved Military College and the ancient home of the Aztec rulers.

After all, it was believed that not only a Christian God but also the ancient Gods of the Aztecs were on the side of the optimistic members of the Cadet Corps. Like other garrison members, they must have been convinced that these collective deities of divergent civilizations would never allow the northern heretics now positioned below them to desecrate the holy ground of ancient Chapultepec, which now symbolized all of Mexico, including its very soul.

Worst of all for the outnumbered defenders, Chapultepec's slopes, especially the eastern slope, were rocky and steep, except on its west side that provided a good natural approach for attackers to ascend all the way up to the imposing summit. A gradual slope that led through the forest of towering Mexican Bald Cypress trees offered an avenue for the attackers to outflank the defenses at the foot of the hill.

Indeed, this natural avenue was the Achilles Heel of Chapultepec, an ancient Aztec word that meant something very special to the

Mexican people who never forgot their distinguished past, because the forest would offer protection to the attackers, once they reached this point. Here, among the tall cypress trees, worn American soldiers would be able to catch their breath and suck water from canteens from behind the good cover provided by the large trees on this hot morning, before a final surge up the hill.

Thanks to Lieutenant Beauregard's tactical insights, General Scott was correct in his belief that Chapultepec was actually weaker and more vulnerable than the southern approaches to Mexico City, where Santa Anna had massed a powerful defensive array, including rows of cannon. Scott's overall tactical plan of unleashed two assault columns was a good one. The cypress trees of the picturesque forest located at the western slope's base would provide good cover for the attackers rather than if they attempted to charge solely down the elevated causeway of the Tacubaya Road, which led to the southwest gate, Garita de Belén, of Mexico City.

The sight of so many National Guard troops—instead of regular troops of Mexican line regiments—did nothing to increase the defenders' confidence, while they were situated in stationary defensive positions on the hill's crest. Even more, the defenders of the hill, from its base to its top and including in the cypress forest, had resulted in too few troops having been spread too thin by Major General Bravo because of too many defensive requirements. In attempting to protect too much ground, including the Mexican Cypress Forest at the hill's base and on the lowest part of the slope, Bravo had reduced his chances of successfully defending the crest, because he had no choice under the circumstances.

In truth, Santa Anna had been correct when he voiced his tactical opinions during a meeting between him and Bravo on the night of September 12, when he had emphasized for Bravo to withdraw his troops from the cypress forest to defend the crest proper. But revealing tactical merit, Major General Bravo remained convinced that the extensive cypress grove should be held to keep the onslaught of attackers as far down the hillside and to slow the advance to buy precious time, Bravo knew that relying on the 12-foot inner wall, which surrounded the summit and was lined with defenders, to stop the Yankees was not enough.

The tactical wisdom of Bravo's desire to defend the forest, once cherished by Montezuma and Aztec royalty, to buy additional time had been seemingly confirmed by Santa Anna's promise that troops would be dispatched to reinforce the small garrison: the crucial promise never fulfilled on this day of destiny by the generalissimo, because of a series of highly-effective bluffs, including the opening of artillery-fire on the defensive positions south of the city east of Chapultepec. Therefore, in overall tactical terms, Bravo was wise to establish a defense in depth, especially the deployment of troops in the cypress forest, instead of simply concentrating on a defense of the summit.

Indeed, Santa Anna was now mostly unconcerned about Chapultepec's fate and had no specific plan to reinforce Major General Bravo, because he was far more worried about the possibility of an assault from the south. However, he had earlier, but inadequately, answered Bravo's appeals for assistance, just before the final meeting between him and the major general on the night before the main attack on Chapultepec.

But in a token gesture, Santa Anna had only dispatched a single National Guard battalion (that was promptly deployed by Bravo in the cypress grove) to reinforce the garrison. However, Santa Anna then later decided to recall the unit just before the Americans attacked. Clearly, Scott's clever feint on the south of Mexico City had been most effective in confusing General Santa Anna all the way up to the crucial morning of September 13.

Therefore, a host of nagging doubts continued to increase among the Mexican troops. Could their high ground position be successfully defended, especially after the intense bombardment had succeeded in knocking-out artillery crews and half of the garrison's cannon? Chapultepec's defenders were chilled by the nagging realization that the Americans had not lost a battle in his war since having captured Vera Cruz, despite having suffered heavy losses at bloody field like Molino del Rey.

About to meet the Yankees for the first time, the cadets were troubled about the overall situation. After all, this war had proved to be an absolute disaster for Mexico, because the miserable defeats had continued ever since the war's beginning. The first two hard-fought battles, Palo Alto (May 8, 1846) and Resaca de la Palma (May 9,

1846), in the Lower Río Grande Valley located just north of the Río Grande River, had been humiliating defeats, even before war was officially declared by the United States. Both early reversals just north of Matamoros suffered by Mexico's northern army had resulted from ill-fated attempts to save Matamoros, which was located on the south bank of the mighty river that flowed more swiftly than today.

Indeed, amid the wide prairie lands, now brown and arid in September but green with new life during the spring of 1846, the Americans had won their first victory at Palo Alto during a showdown between dueling artillery. Then, a series of American victories followed on every battlefield in northern Mexico, including in the late summer of 1847 at Buena Vista, where Santa Anna had been thwarted.

All of these defeats revealed the undeniable fact that the young Mexican republic was too weak, undeveloped, and economically poor to successfully resist the invaders' onslaught. From the war's beginning and representing an economically backward nation that was still feudal (a dark legacy inherited from Spain) in many ways, Mexico's Army was ill-prepared for the climactic showdown that was now about to be played-out just outside the gates of Mexico City at Chapultepec.

Barely a decade before, Mexico had lost its beautiful land of Texas to rebellious Anglo-Celtic settlers, who were immensely benefited by a conspiracy of American citizens across the United States, including Washington, D.C., to steal Texas. And now the mighty colossus of the North had turned its greedy eyes to focus on the stealing of even more of Mexico's vast lands that had been first won by the might of the sword (Spanish Conquistadors) and religion (first spread by Franciscan missionaries).Most of all, President Polk lusted to gain California and its golden Pacific shores, having early dispatched any army and naval vessels to take possession of this magnificent land, where gold was destined to be discovered in 1849.

Ironically, Mexico shared a proud egalitarian and revolutionary heritage with the United States of winning its independence from a major European power. But that shared revolutionary heritage, egalitarianism, and republican faith (like Christianity) that should have forged close bonds between the two neighboring republics no longer mattered in an increasingly vicious war in which the winner would take all, because Mexico refused to give up the struggle or surrender, despite facing insurmountable odds.

Young Cadet Agustín Melgar

While the cannonballs from the blazing American guns, including the especially lethal 10.5-inch mortar, continued to smash into the hilltop perch and kill and wound additional defenders, the cadets, including teenagers, continued to lay low or found sheltered positions under the relentless pounding. As much as possible, they attempted to stay out of harm's way, while maintaining their assigned defensive positions.

Gripping their cut-down muskets tightly and sweating in the mounting tension and rising warmth of early morning, Cadet Agustín Melgar, the sixteen-year-old son of an army lieutenant colonel named Esteban Melgar who had died in the faithful service of his country, held his defensive position under the terrible bombardment that seemed to have no end.

Like other cadets and unlike the thousands of fighting men who had been considerably toughened after a lengthy campaign, this was Agustín Melgar's baptismal fire. All the while, American cannon continued to roar and projectiles pounded the hilltop with the same intensity as the previous day. Under the relentless bombardment, Cadet Melgar might have thought about his hometown of Chihuahua and the finest cathedral in northwest Mexico. Never forgetting his roots and family, the young man was the promising son of Lieutenant Colonel Esteban Melgar and his wife María de la Sevilla.

At this time, Cadet Melgar's motivations could not have been higher. The high-spirited teenager had old personal scores to settle with the norteamericanos on the fateful morning of September 13.Indeed, Melgar's hometown of Chihuahua, where he had been born in 1829, was located some 890 miles northwest of Mexico City in a more remote and drier region compared to Mexico's Central Valley, was never far from his mind. After all, this was his beloved home, and one of the most beautiful cities, surrounded by picturesque mountains, in northern Mexico. But this magnificent city, with its Spanish Baroque Cathedral of Chihuahua, had been conquered by Missouri troops, who had advanced south from Santa Fe with flags flying, in the late winter of 1847.

Melgar could never forget that his own hometown had been occupied by the invaders earlier in this war. It is not known, but he might have received disturbing letters from surviving family members, including his mother María, about what had happened to Chihuahua, after falling to the enemy. If so, then he probably had learned of the ill-treatment of Mexico citizens by the victorious norteamericos, who tended to view all Mexicans as hostile.

To be fair to the Americans, the occupation of this proud community in northern Mexico was certainly not nearly as severe as if it had been occupied by a French Napoleonic Army, but it was bad enough. Civilians were abused to a limited degree, usually by way of theft of foodstuffs and verbal harassment. After the death of his father, Cadet Melgar represented the head of the family. He, therefore, now also fought for the future safety and well-being of his sister, Merced, and his mother, María, on the fateful morning of September 13.

For ample good reason, Cadet Melgar felt that his conquered native home town needed to be avenged. Since the city had been captured by Colonel Doniphan and his roughhewn Missouri boys, Melgar might have been even more motivated cadet than others members of the Cadet Corps, whose home towns had not been captured or occupied, because of Chihuahua's fate.

The pent-up anger that had been built-up in the heart of Cadet Melgar was now about to be unleashed at the first opportunity, if the Yankees dared to attack the Military College. But even more, Mexico City was now Melgar's adopted home town, after his father died while serving in a lieutenant colonel's uniform to make his family proud. The fact that his father had given his life for Mexico likewise motivated Agustín to perform well beyond the traditional call of duty on this Monday that was destined to be his second to last day on this earth.

Therefore, this dedicated teenager might well have been extremely eager to set the sights of his musket on the first American who came into gun-shot range. Finally and at long last, Cadet Melgar was finally about to obtain his long-awaited opportunity to redeem the fallen honor of his conquered native hometown by inflicting as much damage as possible upon the tormentors of the people of Chihuahua.

Such a high level of determination ensured that Melgar would fight today to his last breath and to the very end, because the Military College, which he had entered on November 4, 1846 as a bright-eyed fifteen-year-old thanks partly to the efforts of an older brother named Favor and sister Merced, was now his home. To ensure that Agustín had successfully gained entry into the prestigious institution to fulfill a long-envisioned personal dream, Merced had emphasized the traits of her younger brother's sterling character, which helped to create a model cadet, to school officials.

Melgar and his fellow cadets who were also teenagers, like fifteen-year-old Francisco Márquez; Fernando Montes de Oca, who had been born in the village of Atzcapotzalco ("place of the anthills") located just northwest of Mexico City; Juan Escutia; Juan de la Barrera; and Vicente Suárez also stood firm under the cannonade's punishment. On this hellish morning, the young cadets were defending everything that they considered sacred, decent, and honorable: home, family, religion, Mexico City, and the Military College that was situated atop the most picturesque hill for many miles around.

As a sad fate would have it, all six of these teenage cadets were destined to be were fatally cut down on this day. Perhaps these half dozen young men now wondered if they would live to see another dawn over the beautiful Central Valley of Mexico, while the rain of shot and shell continued to hammer the summit without mercy.

Meanwhile, Cadet Juan de la Barrera, age nineteen and a proud member of the crack Zapadores (Sappers or Engineers), might also have been thinking about his hometown like other cadets on the early morning of September 13.But he was not concerned about far-away Chihuahua like Cadet Melgar. Instead, de la Barrera was worried about the fate of his own hometown, Mexico City now that the enemy had advanced to less than two miles from the beautiful city. Juan had been born in Mexico City on June 26, 1828 only seven years after independence had been won.

But to him, the most important day in the life of de la Barrera was on February15, 1841, when he was admitted to the Military College at the tender age of twelve. Then, a promotion was earned by him, because of his outstanding leadership qualities, when Juan de la Barrera became a second lieutenant of the artillery, Fourth Company, First Brigade.

Most of all, the young man was ambitious and forward-thinking. Despite his recent promotion, de la Barrera desired a more elevated position in the army's most prestigious arm, the engineers. Therefore, in 1843, he requested permission to embark upon study for a career as a military engineer at the Military College. A new dream finally came true for young de la Barrera on December 1, 1843, when his request was granted. At that time, he was then allowed to return to study at the Military College. Clearly, as an officer, he had been on the fast-track and his future prospects were bright, until the war suddenly erupted to change his fate and life forever.

Officially, de la Barrera was no longer a member of the Cadet Corps as of August 11, 1847, when he gained a rank of a lieutenant of engineers, which was granted by no less than Santa Anna. He was now no longer officially on the books as a cadet, because he had been assigned to a combat engineer battalion that defended the strategic hilltop of Chapultepec.

However, to avoid confusion and for the purpose of this narrative that has focused on "the Child Heroes" as much as possible, he will to be referred alternately to as both Cadet and Lieutenant Juan de la Barrera, with an emphasis on cadet because that had beeb his designation for almost the entirety of his military career, except for only less than a month that his God had allowed him to live on this earth. By the time of the battle of Chapultepec and like other cadets, de la Barrera was assigned to the defenses of the Castle and the school, although he was now no longer officially member of the Military College. Nevertheless, he defended the summit like the cadets in part because of his deep bond and past ties with the Cadet Corps.

Unlike Cadet Melgar and now under the direct orders of General Monterde, who was still the Military College's commandant, de la Barrera now possessed the opportunity to fight in the hope of saving his hometown from the invaders' clutches and quite unlike fresh-faced cadets from towns like Chihuahua, Perote, and Puebla. While growing up in Mexico City, he had often gazed upon the heights that residents had called "Grasshopper Hill," and as long as he could remember. But in his early boyhood days, Barrera could never have imagined that one day would find him defending the picturesque hilltop with his life in his country's uniform, when Mexico City was threatened by a mighty invader. Today, September 13 and as fate would have it, was that dreaded day when everything would be finally decided.

Whizzing by the cadets and making a thunderous crash upon impact, iron projectiles continued to knock out chunks of masonry and blasted large holes in walls. Manned by the fast-working gun crews, who fired the deadly 10.5 mortar located near Molino del Rey and Captain Drum's big 16-pounders aligned southwest of Chapultepec, these artillery pieces continued to inflict the most damage to the Castle and the Military College.

Expert artillerymen of the lethal mortar were the most effective in sending giant iron balls that smashed into the Castle and Military College, after having carefully measured the exact range to Chapultepec's lofty summit with the use of a gunner's quadrant. Losing some of their innocence in this destructive process that was part of modern war's brutalities, the cadets experienced the horror of mortar rounds landing atop the roof of buildings once thought to have been safely out of range. These large rounds then tore downward through the heavy timbers of cypress, crashing through successive floors of the former viceroy's palace.

The extensive damage inflicted on the Military College infuriated the cadets, who witnessed a systematic destruction that could not be stopped, partly because half of Chapultepec's cannon (five field pieces) had been knocked-out by this time. But the systematic destruction of their beloved academy by the incessant artillery bombardment only fortified the determination of these young men to never retreat or surrender this morning in hell.

Most upsetting to the cadets was in enduring a sense of helplessness, when these large mortal projectiles, lobbed high in the air above to drop down into the Chapultepec complex. This sprawling complex situated atop the summit was too large to miss for well-trained and experienced gunners of the United Sates Artillery. Therefore, almost every shot resulted in a direct hit. Whenever fires were sparked in the Military College by the exploding projectiles, they were then doused and put out by fast-working soldado teams.

All the while, Major General Bravo's engineers and volunteers continued to repair the damage as quickly as possible. But not enough time remained to complete the time-consuming work, because the Yankees would not allow that luxury. At great risk to themselves, soldados exposed in the open continued to dutifully attempt to conduct emergency repairs by piling up sandbags in a race with the clock before the Americans struck. Sandbags, however, were unable to adequately strengthen the battered defenses, because as soon as one makeshift defensive position was created, then another shell dismantled what had been built after so much effort and expenditure of time.

Worst of all, there was simply no adequate defensive measures that could be taken against the steady rain of projectiles, while the men of Mexico withstood their relentless punishment with a brave stoicism. Against the odds, they were determined to hold their lofty defensive positions atop Grasshopper Hill at all costs. If Generals Santa Anna or Bravo (neither were trained artillerymen) had initially believed that artillery projectiles would not be able reach the top of Lomas de Chapultepec, that rose more than 200 feet above the sprawling plain covered in cornfields interspersed with an occasional meadow of high grass, then they were sadly mistaken.

Perhaps the two generals could not believe—with ample justification—that the Americans could have never possibly hauled these large, heavy siege guns, like the cumbersome 16-pounders (each weighing tons), overland from where sailing ships had landed them at Vera Cruz around 250 miles to the east.

Meanwhile, a more nagging concern tortured the young soldiers on this morning at a time when a projectile could land on top of a cadet, who would have never seen it coming. Would Mexico, the sacred motherland to generations of their ancestors, live to see another day, if the Americans launched another great assault like that ones that had proved so successful in the past? Was Mexico once again about to be vanished by another army of splendidly-armed foreign invaders like when the Spanish Conquistadors, under the ruthless Hernándo Cortéz, had conquered Montezuma's vast empire in a more innocent time, after they had first landed at Vera Cruz, like the Americans in early 1847, in 1519?

As the determined defenders of Chapultepec realized, a benevolent God was now needed as never before to save Mexico City from still another unholy conquest. Therefore, the last high ground before the city had to be defended to the last man to save Mexico City and the republic: a solemn duty embraced and long held sacred by the cadets.

While experiencing their first bombardment that was absolutely terrifying, the cadets calmly waited for the inevitable American attack, while the day gradually became hotter, as if this time of year was now June instead of mid-September. Sweat trickled down the faces of the cadets, dropping lightly on light gray service uniforms, while tension and anxiety reached new highs. Fear among the defenders naturally increased whenever a shell exploded overhead or nearby in a great crash that shattered timbered beams, regardless of their width, and masonry of the Castle and the Military College.

Under the punishing cannonade that gradually reduced the defenses, the young men and boys atop Chapultepec wished in vain for a refreshing breeze to bring a breath of cooling comfort to partly ease the increased warmth that had been built-up by nervousness and high anxiety, while additional soldados fell in the fiery explosions. Water was eagerly sucked from cadet canteens, but the mouths of the defenders, including the cadets, remained dry and hearts beat rapidly, while they stoically awaited the massive American assault that was now only a matter of time.

The Curse of Politics Raises Its Ugly Head

All the while, the young men and boys of the Military College refused to waver in a true crisis situation, because they were determined to sacrifice themselves, if necessary, to save Mexico City and the sacred Motherland. However, as a sad fate would have it, General Santa Anna felt differently about the urgency and importance of defending Chapultepec.

Although they were still only novice soldiers who were now enduring their first artillery fire, the cadets, nevertheless, gamely held their defensive positions under the storm of artillery rounds. Still naïve about the ways of war and its harsh realities, the young soldiers, mostly teenagers, withstood the artillery punishment with the steely resolve of hardened veterans of many battles to earn the respect of nearby officers, including Major General Bravo.

However, at this time, the cadets were not aware that Santa Anna was still convinced that the wily General Scott dared not assault the high ground position of Chapultepec, because he could not afford the high losses that had been suffered at Churubusco and Molino del Rey. This casual assumption about the fear of suffering high losses was entirely correct, but, paradoxically, this was exactly the fundamental reason why Scott had decided to attack Chapultepec precisely because of Santa Anna's tactical reasoning that the War of 1812 hero had accurately ascertained.

Quite simply, Santa Anna had been outsmarted and rather badly in overall tactical terms. A meticulous commander who was America's most gifted military leader and as mentioned, Scott had created the illusion of an impending assault by shifting units south of Mexico City to heighten the impression—a brilliant ruse—that the main attack would come east of Chapultepec and directly south of the capital. Proving to be most effective to convincing the general that an assault was about to be unleashed, American artillery had already opened up from the south this early morning to additionally fool Santa Anna. As noted, Santa Anna had swallowed the bait entirely, dooming the boy cadets and others defenders to a miserable defeat, because they received no reinforcements when most needed.

Therefore, Major General Nicolás Bravo, attired in a resplendent dark blue dress uniform and wearing a decorative brass belt buckle decorated with Mexico's coat of arms and national symbol (the Mexico Golden Eagle perched atop the prickly pear with a snake in its sharp beak), continued to be sorely disappointed—to say the least--in not securing the much-needed promised assistance from Santa Anna.

Complicating matters, General Bravo, who had served as the eleventh president of Mexico from 1823-1824, was a political rival of Santa Anna to ensure poor teamwork at the highest level. Consequently, the ever-cynical Santa Anna might have feared that

Bravo might eventually rise to power to replace him, if he achieved a sparkling success in stopping General Scott to save Mexico City.

In fact, Bravo had served as the vice president of Mexico twice in a lengthy career, including as recently as 1845. Unfortunately for the cadets, Santa Anna almost certainly possessed a number of political and personal reasons to deny Bravo the reinforcements that he urgently needed to adequately defend Chapultepec. Cynical Santa Anna, the consummate calculating politician who was excessively crafty, would rather see Mexico decisively defeated than to lose power, prestige, and popularity, which were so dear to him.

Clearly, Bravo's tactical insights and repeated urgent requests for assistance should not have been dismissed by Santa Anna. After all, Bravo was an experienced leader who possessed sound tactical views, especially about what was needed to adequately defend Chapultepec. He had even fought beside the courageous Father José María Morelos against the Spanish in the War of Mexican Independence.

Quite simply, Major General Bravo had not fallen victim to General Scott's clever tactical plan of making it seem that the main attack was coming elsewhere. He had early correctly sensed that Chapultepec was the primary target of the interlopers. Santa Anna would not listen, remaining unconvinced, however. A confident Santa Anna, who remained stubborn to the end, had his own tactical ideas that were considerably off target just as General Scott had hoped with a sense of eager anticipation.

Too Few Defenders

Unlike Santa Anna, this savvy veteran of countless battles for Mexico's liberty and seasoned military man, who had not been part of Santa Anna's disastrous 1836 Campaign, was tactically insightful. He, consequently, had almost instinctively early understood that Chapultepec was the Americans' main target. Most of all, Bravo fully realized how he needed a good many more men for any realistic chance of holding Chapultepec against the impending American onslaught.

Indeed, he now commanded less than 900 men in an over-extended defensive position with a lengthy perimeter, ensuring a wide dispersal of troops, because the Americans might strike all four sides at once: the ultimate tactical nightmare. Major General Bravo now possessed the reliable troops of the 10th Infantry Regiment of the Line (regular troops) that had been placed by him in good defensive positions. However, the less dependable and inadequately-trained men of the National Guard consisted of the majority of Bravo's garrison.

Major General Bravo's National Guard units included the San Blas (400 men), Union (211 men), Mina, Toluca, Patria, and Querétaro (115 soldados in the latter unit) infantry battalions. Consisting of 277 men, the Mina National Guard was an artillery unit that had been assigned to operating the 10 cannon (only five field pieces were now still firing on the morning of September 13 after the other five guns had been disabled in the bombardment) that defended Chapultepec's summit.

Unfortunately for the defenders, the fire from these iron and brass barrels of the remaining five guns were unable to knock-out the fast-firing American artillery pieces, which continued to blast away without interruption from the lowlands. However, these United States guns were about to fall silent whenever the Americans were finally ordered to advance and then nearly reached to the outer walls of the complex at the hill's base, after having fired over the heads of the fast-moving formations of blue.

Demonstrating their mettle in the heat of combat, the 277 men of the Mina National Guard of Artillery had fought well at Molino del Rey. Here, they helped to inflict high losses on the attackers with an accurate fire, before the Americans finally gained the upper hand. The command's colors had been saved at the last minute in the hand-to-hand combat at Molino de Rey by a brave Mexican lieutenant. He had torn the unit's flag from its staff and wrapped it around his body for safekeeping. However, the flag's savior was mortally wounded for his heroics in rescuing the cherished colors.

The 250 regulars of the 10th Infantry Regiment, his only regular army unit, represented Bravo's best trained command in the defense. However, the men of three companies (400 soldados) of Lieutenant Colonel Felipe de Santiago Xicoténcatl's San Blas National Guard

Battalion were destined to rise to the occasion in splendid fashion on September 13. As the most forgotten defenders of Chapultepec, they performed as well as any regular army command in the upcoming tenacious defense of the southwestern and southern slopes of Chapultepec.

But this impressive demonstration of valor came at a fearful price for this hard-fighting unit. Consequently, the San Blas Battalion was fated to suffer devastating losses of around 370 soldados, which meant than only around 30 men were destined to escape the nightmarish combat in the cypress forest and along the slope: a staggering attrition rate that told a sad tale of the unit's systematic destruction.

Because of Santa Anna's stubborn belief that Scott would attack from the south, most of the army's best regular units were positioned elsewhere, especially in protecting the southern sector to seal the fate of Chapultepec's defenders. Less experienced men like the cadets would have to fill in the gap because of the absence of regular troops with experience.

Major General Bravo also possessed the unit known as the Fijo (Fixed) de Mexico. This was a small command like the Toluca Battalion of only around 30 soldados. Clearly, in an irony for defending such an important strategic position situated just before Mexico City, Bravo was handicapped by far too many National Guard units. As mentioned, Santa Anna kept the best units—the better disciplined and more experienced regular infantry of the line—and the best commanders on the south, because he still expected Scott to strike from that direction with his main force.

As revealed once the battle opened in full fury, these three companies of the San Blas battalion were the best National Guard units at Chapultepec in large part because of its determined commander, Felipe de Santiago Xicoténcatl. He was a highly-capable leader who could be counted on to the bitter end. In the upcoming forgotten last stand of Chapultepec, Xicoténcatl was fated to be cut down in the upcoming attack like most of his doomed followers of the San Blas Battalion in defending the hill's base, the cypress forest, and then the slope on the southwest

For good reason, Bravo now expected the worst this morning. He had long watched how Santa Anna had steadily shifted additional troops farther away from Chapultepec to defend the city's southern approaches. Therefore, the major general, disgusted by the tragic betrayal, had early realized that Chapultepec's defense was doomed, despite his best efforts and urgent pleas for assistance. A man of compassion and faith, he had been born on a profit-generating hacienda near Chilancingo in the sugar cane country of southwest Mexico. Despite the host of disadvantages that they faced, Bravo and Monterde made a good leadership team, which functioned smoothly in a stressful and demanding situation, but they could little to save Chapultepec in the end.

As mentioned, General Monterde had already recommended for the around 200 cadets to be removed to the safety of Mexico City to save them (a precious commodity for Mexico and representing its future) from the inevitable artillery bombardment and then full-scale assault. But an official protest had been raised by the feisty cadets, who desired most of all to stay atop the summit to defend what they loved, the Military College and Mexico City.

Lieutenant Juan de la Barrera, the promising son of Lieutenant Colonel Ignacio Mario de la Barrera and Juana Inzarruaga, had spoken on behalf of the cadets in a dignified manner, representing them because he was held in such high esteem. Barrera was destined to play a key role on this bloody morning, and one that was destined not to be forgotten.

As mentioned, Barrera was no longer officially a Military College student since August, because of this crisis situation that required his presence elsewhere. Therefore, he could more freely speak for the cadets outside of the official chain of command and traditional protocol without drawing any negative repercussions to either himself or the cadets: all important considerations in the strict military establishment that always closely followed the strict rules and old traditions, which extended back to Europe and a misty past.

This was another reason why the cadets, including Juan Escutia and Agustín Melgar, not only respected, but also loved de la Barrerra, age nineteen, like an older brother. The Military College experience had forged a deep bond between these young men, and this bond that united members of the Cadet Corps could not be broken. Because of the urgency of defending the strategic summit and as mentioned, de la Barrera had been recently promoted from the Military College to a combat engineer battalion.

Therefore, he was now assigned to the battery of guns positioned near the main gate. But he never wavered in his love and loyalty to his old friends of the Cadet Corps and the Military College. Quite simply, the strong ties of the cadet brotherhood could not be severed by enemy bullets or general's orders: not unlike the situation that has long existed for the elite Marines of the United States Marine Corps, which was revealed in its Latin motto of Semper Fidelis, or "always faithful" and "always loyal."Indeed, in this sense, the Boy Cadets were always faithful and loyal to their country, the Military College, fellow cadets, and, in the very end.

Generals Bravo and Monterde had long been impressed with Lieutenant de la Barrera's dignified and soldiery bearing for one of his young age. They knew that he possessed all the makings of an excellent officer. Indeed, de la Barrera had compiled a sterling record at the Military College, where he had performed at his best. Like a number of leading officers, fellow cadets had long believed that de la Barrera, the oldest cadet at age nineteen (Cadet Francisco Márquez was the youngest at age thirteen) by September 1847, would become a Mexican general one day just like his distinguished father.

Knowing that he needed every soldier because the garrison was much too small for adequately defending Chapultepec with barely 800 men, Major General Bravo knew the impossibility of his key mission. He and General Monterde, nevertheless, had eventually accepted the cadet's collective argument, which had been presented diplomatically by de la Barrera to the commander of the Cadet Corps: the unity of purpose in their desire to remain on the targeted hilltop to defend their school with their young lives.

Of course, the rationale for the cadets to make their last stand and fight at Chapultepec was most fitting and symbolic, representing the nation's youth and the future of Mexico. If Mexico's cadets were ever needed to engage in combat during a crisis situation, then it was now when the country's life and the fate of Mexico City were at stake. In this sense, the cadets, consequently, were actually in the right place and the right time on the early morning of September 13: symbolically defending their beloved Military College that now bore the deep scars of a heavy artillery bombardment during the last two days.

As mentioned and as a cruel fate would have it, the cadets were about to pay a high price for the folly(past and present) of General Santa Anna that extended back for more than a decade. In a battle that had lasted less than twenty minutes on the gulf coastal plain, he had singlehandedly lost Texas on April 21, 1836 at San Jacinto. Here, on a hot afternoon along the brown waters of Buffalo Bayou, where the Gulf or Southern Bald Cypress (a member of the Redwood family like the Mexican Bald Cypress of Chapultepec) lined its banks, and near where the muddy San Jacinto River entered the northwest corner of Galveston Bay, Santa Anna had been asleep at the worst possible moment. He was sleeping in his large headquarters tent when General Sam Houston's Texians and volunteers from the United States (even United States regulars, including expert artillerymen, from a United States military installation in western Louisiana played a key role) attacked when least expected.

The attackers' brutal no-quarter policy at San Jacinto was not entirely without reason to the typical thinking of Houston's men on bloody April 21.Santa Anna had waged an especially brutal campaign on Texas soil, after having marched north to reclaim their bountiful region in early 1836.Desperate to keep Texas within the fragile union of Mexican states in the face of massive economic, logistical, and manpower interference from the United States to fuel the so-called Texian rebellion, Santa Anna had systematically slaughtered Texas and United States volunteers at the Alamo, the old Franciscan mission located on the San Antonio River, and then on a horrible Palm Sunday at Goliad not long thereafter. On this terrible Sunday, Santa Anna had ordered the execution of hundreds of prisoners at Goliad, Texas, on March 27, 1836.

Nevertheless, Santa Anna's life had been spared by his captors in the aftermath of the San Jacinto fiasco at a time when the cadets had been only infants back home, ensuring that half of dozen of them would never live to adulthood, after the showdown at Chapultepec on September 13.The overconfident Santa Anna was once again repeating the same tactical folly that had paved the way to disaster at San Jacinto but now on the very doorstep of Mexico's capital city.

Relying on gut instincts rather than the wisdom of past military experience not yet gained by the cadets, some prophetic students of the Military College almost certainly knew that an attack was coming straight up Chapultepec's hillsides, despite their steepness and the key locations of the redan, the redoubt, and the minefield.

However, at this time, not a small number of soldados allowed their xenophobia (a heightened sense of religious, cultural, and racial superiority that ironically was shared by the Americans in regard to their own civilization and race) to override more rational thought about the existing situation. With undisguised contempt, the men of Mexico had confidently declared that the norteamericanos simply lacked the courage to scale the heights. After all, these Yanquis were considered to be immoral heretics, who lacked the moral resolve of a religious Mexican soldiery in defending their sacred home soil.

Unlike the inexperienced cadets, the intensity of the artillery shelling that raked the summit told Bravo's veterans the undeniable truth about Scott's tactical intentions. They realized that it was now only a matter of time before the Yankees attacked the imposing heights of Chapultepec: a development that Santa Anna, with his typical abandon, had bet heavily against ever happening. After successive defeats and as the bombardment lengthened, the mood among the defenders had grown increasingly glum from the steady pounding on the projectile-raked summit, especially after seeing no arriving reinforcements.

Indeed, fearing the worst on the night of September 12, Colonel Juan Cano, the garrison's senior engineer who survived the bloodletting at Churubusco, had dispatched his brother, Lorenzo Cano, with a message to their uniformed relative, who was assigned to Santa Anna's headquarters, because of a never-darkening situation before Chapultepec that proved most prophetic: "Dear Uncle, I am certain that tomorrow we will die, and because I do not want to give my elderly parents the unbearable bitterness of receiving news of the death of two sons at the same time, I beg you to keep my brother Lorenzo from returning to my side" at Chapultepec.

If this seasoned senior engineer officer, who was Lieutenant de la Barrera's commander and now a member of the army's elite engineering corps, had been overwhelmed by such dark thoughts, then some cadets, who had never before seen a battle, might well have been similarly gloomy about what was about to come. Nevertheless, they were still determined to hold firm and committed to the task of defending their Military College and Chapultepec regardless of what was to come.

Meanwhile, Cadet Juan Baptist Pascasio Escutia (known as Juan Escutia to his friends and fellow esteemed members of the Cadet Corps) and Francisco Márquez, the youngest cadet, were determined to stand firm, regardless of how many screaming norteamericanos, with steel bayonets flashing in the sun, surged up the heights. Despite the punishing artillery bombardment, the cadets continued to be fully, if not fanatically, committed to never allowing the Godless Yankees to ever touch the scared national flag of the Motherland. Like other garrison members, members of the Cadet Corps occasionally looked up in pride to see the Mexican tri-color flying majestically over the shell-torn summit during the intense pounding from the steady bombardment.

While cannonballs, shells, and mortar rounds steadily hammered the hilltop on this crucial morning, the national flag, the large beautiful banner of vertical stripes of green, white, and red and distinguished by a painting of the magnificent Mexican Golden Eagle (the ancient Aztec symbol adopted after Mexico won its independence) in the center, continued to wave through the punishing bombardment to inspire confidence among the ever-dwindling band of defenders. This colorful banner flew from the medieval-looking tower, known as "the tall knight" (Caballero Alto), that dominated the highest point of Chapultepec like a mighty beacon, which now symbolized Mexico City's spirited defense against the odds. Consequently, the cadets looked up and felt a sense of national pride in the invigorating sight of the flapping colors that represented everything that they loved with all their hearts.

Like other cadets, such as Fernando Montes de Oca, from the area around the capital, this upcoming battle was a special one for Cadet Juan Escutia. He had been born in nearby Tepic, founded in 1542 and practically under the shadow of the extinct volcano known as Sanganguey, located in southwest Mexico, on February 22, 1822.

He had been baptized by a revered priest in the holy shrine of Tepic on July 1 of the same year. Tepic was a Nahuatl word, like Chapultepec. The state of Nayarit, in which Tepic served as the state capital, was Cadet Escutia's native homeland. Here, he had worshiped at the Tepic's beautiful neo-Gothic Cathedral, graced with two stately tall twin towers. His strict religious teachings at the Cathedral provided inspiration for him to lead a moral life throughout his formative years.

Escutia had become a cadet at Mexico's only military college only five days before on September 8, when he was officially listed as "an added student," because of the emergency situation, when the Americans were drawing ever-closer to the city. But Cadet Escutia possessed the resolve of the most hardened veteran when it came to defending Mexico City and its people with his life. Escutia was a devout young man, and he had long conducted himself based on his religious teachings and a moral character to make his family proud.

In fact, Escutia had dedicated his life as much to God as to a life in the military to protect his beloved country, which was no contradiction in his intelligent mind. Like other Chapultepec defenders, he knew that Mexico had been created by inspirational legacies of revolutionary priest-warriors. He never forgot how they had led the common people of the lower classes with great bravery against the oppressive and pro-slavery Spanish to create a new nation based on equality, while giving a voice to the long-suffering common people. For such reasons besides spiritual protection, Cadet Escutia now perhaps wore a silver crucifix and carried the small Holy Bible given to him by loving family members, when he had left home for the last time to fight for God and country.

Like Cadets Juan Escutia, Agustín Melgar, Vicente Suárez, and Francisco Márquez, who had entered the Military College in January 1847 like Cadet Fernando Montes de Oca, one other equally ill-fated cadet (Juan de la Barrera) were motivated to stand firm by the impressive sight of the brightly-colored national colors flapping in the early morning breeze sweeping over the ancient hilltop of the Aztec rulers. This glorious banner fluttered in the early morning's light wind before the day's heat intensified and the slight breeze died away like on a hot summer afternoon in the Central Valley.

But these six teenage cadets, now wearing their stylish gray uniforms, were destined not to be fortunate enough to live to feel the cooler and refreshing breeze that later came with the arrival of the evening of September 13. A young man of deep religious faith that was buried deep inside his heart and soul, Escutia might have thought about his devout mother, María Dolores Martínez, while also invoking God to give him comfort and strength in this crisis situation.

However, the cadets were especially now convinced that God was on their side, and that such places like Chapultepec and Mexico City would never fall to the heretics from the North. After all, they were defending a civilized nation with great future potential and one that had bestowed them a righteous mission of preserving the Catholic faith. Even more, Mexico possessed an especially rich culture that was far older and more sophisticated than the United States. Even more, Mexico had abolished slavery unlike in the American South, retaining the moral high ground in this war that was very much about the issue of slavery. Even now, Scott's Army contained a large number of slave-owners, which was not the case in the ranks of the Mexican Army, even among the top generals and aristocrats.

As the cadets had learned while studying day and night at the Military College, the historical lessons and analogies to the present situation were plentiful. Was not the ancient world's greatest civilization destroyed by light-skinned barbarian invaders who had come sweeping down from the north, overwhelming the glory and splendor that was Rome? Was not Mexico's capital of stately European-style buildings, elegant homes, and beautiful churches, which made it look more than Madrid, Spain, than a typical New World capital or a city in the United States, now in a comparable situation in facing another powerful northern invader?

For generations, Spain had sent forth its zealous Franciscans, whose powerful faith brought them to the New World with a crusading zeal, to establish missions along the untamed northern frontier to bring Christianity to the native people: a distinguished religious heritage and spiritual legacy that needed to be preserved by the cadets and the garrison. And now with history having come full circle in the late summer of 1847, the future existence of the Church and Catholicism in this land of plenty were at stake. Therefore, the teenage cadets of the Military College were determined to stand firm against the inevitable onslaught to save a distinctive civilization and rich cultural legacies from the northern horde of modern-day barbarians as they saw it.

In fact, people, including of the leading expansionist politicians in Washington, D.C, and across the United States, now envisioned the annexation (like Texas on December 29, 1845) of all Mexico, if Mexico City could be captured. Then, after a weak Mexico was conquered, which now seemed only a matter of time, many Americans believed that United States occupation and rule would bring the overall process of whitening the race: a truly frightening racial formula of Anglo-Saxons for complete conquest of an entire people of a different face and religion, including the eventual destroying of an existing culture.

The ambitious and insidious plan called for former United States soldiers and immigrants to settle in a vanquished Mexico to begin the process of whitening the race. Of course, this overall whitening process over time called for the taking Mexican women (Creole, Indian, mestizo, and Spanish) by the Anglo-Celts (civilian and military) for either casual relationships or marriages to produce an entirely new Mexican to inhabit the land of the Aztecs. Because of this cynical racial cleansing-based plan based on natural reproduction, the cadets also made their last stand at Chapultepec to save their race from the threat of the process of racial mixing to whiten the population. Such a race-based obsession and policy might perhaps make victims of their own sisters and mothers. Over time, this racial purification policy (almost Nazi-like in the sheer scope of its racial ambitions and objectives) was a diabolical means of destroying the preexisting culture and distinctive civilization, if expansion-minded American politicians in Congress decided to claim all Mexico, as now advocated by many people across the United States.

Clearly, the fighting men of Mexico possessed the moral high ground and advantage on multiple levels. Even the commander of the South Carolina (Palmetto) Regiment of Volunteers, Colonel Pierce M. Butler, the former South Carolina governor (1836-1838) who had been only recently shot in the head and killed in leading the attack on Churubusco on August 20, 1847, had admitted to South Carolina's governor an ugly truth by writing in a letter how this war "is unequal and the service an inglorious one."

Unknown to the cadets, the dashing colonel's honwarly-expressed sentiments echoed the voices of the ever-growing anti-war movement across the United States. This anti-war movement was especially active in the northeast and among America's leading intellectuals, including Henry David Thoreau.

Even a former lawyer and usually tall politician from the Illinois prairies named Abraham Lincoln voiced his opposition to a cruel and unnatural war between two Christian republics. Even Mexican newspapers had been reprinting anti-war editorials and articles that had recently appeared in anti-administration United States newspapers. These highly-critical articles revealed the ever-increasing anti-war mood across the United States, while their boys continued to fight and die deep in far-away Mexico.

Like other cadets, Juan Escutia now lamented the severity of the artillery pounding and the damage suffered by the Military College, which had been authorized in 1831 and much later the United States Military Academy. Situated up the Hudson River just north of New York City, West Point had been founded on March 16, 1802 by President Thomas Jefferson, a large Virginia slave-owner and author of the Declaration of Independence.

At this time, Escutia only possessed the Military College in his life, and it had become his true home and meant everything to him. Therefore, like other cadets, he was determined to perform at his best in defending this special place that he loved so that there would be no discretion of this holy ground of Chapultepec by the hated Yanquis.

In preparation for the desperate bid of overwhelming the commanding high ground, General Scott's men, especially the officers, were about to make very good use of their fine educations that had been gained from the prestigious institution located along the wide Hudson River that cut through the densely-wooded hills of the picturesque Hudson Valley. Compared to West Point that had produced the nation's finest officers, especially the talented young men of the engineering corps, Mexico's Military College was in still its infancy.

All in all, in a dramatic showdown between the men from two premier military colleges of neighboring republics, the cadets had something to prove to themselves and everyone else on the gradually-warming morning of September 13.But as a cruel fate would have it, the fact that the United States Military Academy had been founded more than 20 years before Mexico's Military Academy was destined to play a key role in separating winner for loser not only in the showdown at Chapultepec, but also in this war.

During its first foreign conflict and thanks to its superior might and efficient factories, especially in the northeast, because of the Industrial Revolution, the United States was also able to wage its first truly modern war unlike Mexico that was still fundamentally feudal in many respects. As mentioned, highly-educated West Pointers, some of America's best and brightest, played a large role in paving the way to decisive victory.

Indeed, Mexico had lost every major battle, and a great amount of the republic's territory was now occupied by the invaders, thanks in part to the engineers' significant contributions to the Americans' sweeping success. The Yankees simply could not be stopped, despite all of the valor displayed and the high sacrifice in soldados' lives.

And now, General Scott and his army were determined to eliminate Chapultepec, the Castle, and the Military College in one bold offensive stroke partly because these were all conspicuous national and psychological symbols that represented the prestige of the Mexican military establishment. At this time, the cadets had no idea that they had become not only pawns, but also symbols that had to be eliminated by the invaders for basically non-military purposes.

But as mentioned, the brave men of Chapultepec had already held firm sufficiently long to frustrate General Scott and thwart his original ambitious plan of forcing the outnumbered garrison to surrender under the steady artillery pounding: a glowing source of pride in an exceedingly dark hour, serving to fuel the defenders' resolve to continue to defy the odds and not surrender. General Scott had already been angered by having seen no white flag hoisted atop the highest flagpole on the summit, which revealed the garrison's determination to make a courageous last stand.

This overall situation was not unlike the experience of King Xerxes, the mighty leader of the Persian Empire and military expedition that journeyed from Asia to the edge of Europe. He had fully expected that every Greek city-state would automatically submit to his royal authority without engaging in a futile struggle, because of the army's immense size (the largest ever seen on European soil) and since Greek opposition to the invaders' superior numbers seemed like certain folly. Ironically, in 480 B.C., Xerxes had even expected King Leonidas and his 300 Spartans to flee from the famous pass of Thermopylae, when they saw the great size of his army.

But, of course, such was not the case either at Thermopylae or at Chapultepec, because the defenders courageously stood their ground against the odds. In many ways, Chapultepec defenders, including the around 200 members of the Cadet Corps, had already performed in a manner entirely worthy of praise in previous days, especially during the September 12 bombardment. To one and all, they had impressively demonstrated the full extent of their fierce patriotism and burning sense of duty to God and country.

On this ill-fated morning when they were far from home, "Los Niños Héroes" (Juan Escutia, Agustín Melgar, Vicente Suárez, Fernando Montes, Francisco Márquez, and Juan de la Barrera who were all fated to be fatally cut down) were ready to meet the invaders, while in position at their assigned defensive positions.

Most importantly, they felt secure in the fact that "Vayan Con Dios," (They Go With God) and now found solace in their strong religious faith. Therefore, with an enhanced degree of inner calm and a sense of peace, the young men and boys of the Cadet Corps were now prepared to meet the upcoming assault and do their duty, which called for halting the norteamericanos at all costs to save Mexico City and their beloved republic.

Chapter III

The Great Assault Unleashed

Suddenly, the young cadets heard a deafening silence that was truly haunting. Quite unexpectedly, the American cannon, manned by expert gunners--now sweaty and powder-streaked--ceased to roar at around 8:00 a.m. At long last, these guns finally became quiet, after two hours of a devastating cannonade that had raked the commanding summit without mercy.

By this time, Chapultepec's defenders were in pretty bad shape. Only a feisty fighting spirit remained high among the survivors positioned on the bombarded summit, because crucial supplies, even ammunition, had been reduced to alarming levels. Meanwhile, Major General Bravo's soldados gamely remained in place with fixed bayonets and loaded muskets. Questions about what was inevitably to come this morning raced through the minds of the men of Chapultepec, while the strange silence shrouded the hill and seemed ominous in the morning stillness.

Why had the guns suddenly ceased their intense fire? Was there not going to be still another day-long (14 hours) bombardment like on September 12, as had been fully expected by the defenders? Had General Scott relinquished his plan of forcing the surrender of Chapultepec by an relentless artillery pounding, because no white flags had been raised on the projectile-swept summit? Were the Americans actually foolish enough to launch an attack straight up the highest hill for miles around, as Generals Bravo and Monterde believed and quite unlike Santa Anna? What kind of trickery and cunning was meant by this strange silence from the wily Yanquis, who seemingly always found a way to win a victory when least expected?

All the while, this eerie silence settled over the smoke-wreathed hilltop after the enemy's cannon ceased to roar. Surviving defenders, including the cadets, silently looked at each other and questioned the unknown reason for the sudden descent of the eerie quiet. In their first battle, the cadets did not know what to expect next at this point, unless told by their officers that Scott's troops were about to launch a massive infantry assault. After all, the Americans had not attacked this strategic hilltop, after their heavy bombardment on September 12.

Meanwhile, the damage had been extensive from the incessant fire of the Americans' heavy guns, including the knocking out of half of the Mexican cannon and an even greater loss of defenders, both infantrymen and artillerymen. As planned by General Scott, Chapultepec's defensive capabilities had been significantly reduced by the bombardment's effectiveness, effecting soldado morale as intended. All of the frantic work by soldados and engineers to repair the battered earthen parapets and inner stone wall, which surrounded the flat summit, were insufficient to complete the many repairs, because the damage was too extensive and not enough time remained to finish the reconstruction work.

Equally discouraging to the Boy Cadets, their beloved Military College had been heavily damaged by the stream of projectiles from the siege guns. But more unnerving to these cadets, now mostly stationed in defensive positions to guard the nation's prestigious academy (basically Mexico's West Point), was the fact that the main corridor of the Military College had been transformed into a place of terrible suffering by this time.

Here, hard-working Mexican surgeons, who had been educated in medical colleges on both sides of the Atlantic, attempted to save the many wounded men, who had been cut down during the heavy bombardment. Hour after hour, the flow of wounded men had increased to a flood, filling the main corridor. The sweating, blood-stained surgeons were unable to attend to all the injured soldados, perhaps including some cadets.

By this time, the academy's main hallway had been transformed into a sea of suffering that shocked the naïve cadets, who were still learning about the horrors of war. In the words of one reporter who was sickened by the horror that he saw when he later visited: "In the corridor, converted into a surgical hospital were found mixed up the putrid bodies, the wounded breathing mournful groans, and the young boys of the College." General Scott had hoped that the lengthy bombardment would drive not only the cadets out of the academy building, but also the more seasoned troops from the summit. But instead of fleeing the targeted summit, members of the Cadet Corps were bravely staying at their assigned positions in preparation for defending their school.

While surrounded by the moans and cries of dying and wounded soldados, which grew ever-higher in crowded halls and blood-stained stone floors of the Military College and having never previously known about the extent of war's awful cruelties, the cadets wondered what now lay in store for them on this decisive Monday, after the American batteries had pounded their hilltop position since 5:30 a.m.

Because of the silence, many defenders now expected the worst. Meanwhile, General Scott had correctly judged that the bombardment had significantly damaged the defenses of the Chapultepec Castle complex, including the Military College, and lowered the defenders' morale to make the assault more likely to succeed.

The Military College's thin walls had been smashed by the iron cannonballs from the big guns that had been hauled all the way from the Gulf of Mexico by these enterprising Americans, who the soldados no longer underestimated as so often in the past. All in all, this was no small accomplishment that now paid immense dividends to the resourceful invaders who were proving to be the modern Spanish Conquistadors.

The level, wide stone terrace that served as the cadet's parade ground, fronting the Military College on the south and seemingly located on the top of the world to overlook Mexico City to the northeast, was likewise pocked by direct hits and strewn with debris. Fully aware of West Point's supreme importance in having made his army more formidable during this grueling campaign, General Scott knew of the location of the Military College, which had deemed the academy a legitimate target.

Evidently, a Mexican prisoner or deserter had told him of the exact location of the Military College, which was situated in the southeast section of the Castle complex. Therefore, orders had been early issued to the expert United States gunners to focus their fire to wreck the Military College to reduce morale, especially among the cadets. Scott's seasoned artillerymen had achieved their goal in severely battering the Military College, especially in damaging the thin roof that could not withstand the impact of the heavy iron projectiles.

Surveying the significant amount of destruction inflicted on the Military College and the Chapultepec Castle through binoculars after two hours of bombardment on this clear September morning that was already beginning to heat up, General Scott felt a sense of satisfaction in his belief that the defenses had been sufficiently weakened by the artillery barrage. Consequently, with confidence for achieving success this morning, he knew that it was now time to order thousands of his veteran infantrymen, aligned in formation and ready to charge, forward to overrun the last and most formidable high ground defensive position before Mexico City.

Scott emphasized the extent of the challenge when he was finally ready to unleash his troops in a great assault "to carry Chapultepec, a natural and isolated mound of great elevation, strongly fortified at its base, on its acclivities and heights [and] Besides a numerous [actually relatively small] garrison, here was the military college of the republic, with a large number of sub-lieutenants and other students," in the general's words.

All of a sudden, the cadets and other defenders heard a chorus of wild yells of enemy troops in the lowlands below, sounding like a tribe of Native American warriors, Apache or Comanche, from Mexico's northern frontier. The Americans were cheering the inspiring words of their regimental and company leaders. They had just spoken these encouraging words to fuel the resolve and confidence of their men so far from home. With fixed bayonets, loaded .69 caliber smoothbore muskets, and a determination to carry Chapultepec by storm at the point of the bayonet, the Americans were ready to launch still another attack.

At around 8:00 a.m. and after having marched more than 250 miles since landing at Vera Cruz, it was now time "Los Yankees," more than 7,000 of General Scott's best soldiers, to embark upon their desperate bid to capture the imposing defensive position (thought by both sides to be impregnable) by storm. For ample good reason, many of Scott's troops were understandably nervous in staring up at the dominant heights that had to be overwhelmed at all costs. Indeed, "Chapultepec was regarded as impregnable" wrote

Lieutenant Daniel Harvey Hill, a highly-capable West Pointer (Class of 1842) from the South.

Boding well for the assault's success and as mentioned, General Scott's troops, including a large number of Seminole War veterans, had skillfully demonstrated before the city's southern approaches since September 12. Even more, American artillery positioned south of the city had fired a large number of rounds from an array of artillery, including on this very morning to additionally befuddle Santa Anna.

All of this hectic American activity south of the city continued to convince Santa Anna that was assault was not coming his way east of Chapultepec. Therefore, at the moment of crisis for Chapultepec's defenders, he still persisted in ordering no reinforcements west to bolster Major General Bravo and his small garrison. In consequently, the young men and boys of Chapultepec continued to be now on their own to face Scott's large-scale attack.

Led by an advanced party of around 500 volunteers, who carried wooden scaling ladders, known as the "Forlorn Hope," General Gideon J. Pillow's Third Division, the larger of the two columns, suddenly surged forward from the shelter of the stone buildings of the Molino de Rey complex. With flag flying in the soft summer sun, the troops advanced rapidly with discipline.

All the while, Chapultepec's defenders nervously watched the sweeping formations of blue with a sullen curiosity and a grim resolve. According to his well-designed plan, General Scott ordered two assault columns forward from two different directions: a hard-hitting one-two punch. General Pillow's column of volunteers was the larger assaulting column, and promised to deliver the most powerful blow.

Captain Samuel McKenzie, a skilled North Carolinian of Scotch-Irish descent, a West Pointer who had graduated (Class of 1813) at age sixteen, and a respected member of the 2nd United States Artillery, led the way in the "Forlorn Hope" for Pillow's column. Fated to die of disease in this war like so many of his comrades, he commanded more than 250-men (regulars) of the "Forlorn Hope" that continued to advance at a rapid pace at the head of Pillow's Division in a desperate mission.

Considered to be a suicidal effort, the overall mission of McKenzie's "Forlorn Hope" was to reach the southern wall, and then move along its base until finding an opening (either a gate or a hole blown into it by a shell explosion)through the high outer wall in preparation for opening the way for the main attack from the southwest. Serving as the main attack force, Pillow's troops of the largest force of the main assault advanced from the west in three small columns of considerable strength.

As if nothing could stop them, the troops of Scott's largest column charged straight toward the hill, where the Military College stood in defiance. Before the Pillow's attackers just beyond the defensive complex of Molino del Rey lay marshy ground that was guaranteed to impend the assault's progress and momentum, and then beyond stood the towering trees of the Mexican Bald Cypress forest that lay before the hill's western slope.

Meanwhile, besides General Pillow's column, General John A. Quitman's Fourth Division, consisting of New York, Pennsylvania, and South Carolina regiments and a small group of United States Marines, also attacked around 8:00 a.m. from the southeast. These troops surged up the Tacubaya Road, concealed by "pulque bushes," in one American's words, on each side of the road, which led northeast to the southwest edge of Mexico City. Quitman's attackers headed toward the southeast corner of the Chapultepec complex. General Quitman's troops charged along the dusty road and toward a battery of light artillery, positioned in an excellent location by Major General Bravo, at the crossroads located southeast of the strategic hill.

The guns of this well-positioned battery that blocked the road dropped the first soldiers from the ranks, when "we were now in full view of the Castle and exposed [in an open field, a former cornfield] to their fire, besides being in a convenient range of the cannon and musketry of the battery on the road," wrote Sergeant Thomas Barclay in his journal.

In a surprisingly honest admission, Sergeant Barclay, a highly-capable member of the 2nd Pennsylvania which occupied the division's left (farthest to the west), also wrote how the overall tactical situation and "sight was not very encouraging" for the attackers. Here, in the openness of the grassy meadow that had become a natural killing field, the 2nd Pennsylvania suffered its heaviest loss when raked by multiple fires: from the fast-firing guns of the battery positioned on the Tacubaya Road, Mexican infantrymen firing from "a breastwork" [the redan] at the base of the hill, and from the Castle's parapet at the summit's edge. Quitman's column shifted to the left, or west, to avoid this blistering fire from the battery that had killed and wounded a good many men.

Private Richard Coulter, of the same Pennsylvania regiment, described how: "The Castle of Chapultepec is situated on a rocky knob which rises abruptly from the plain [and] Around the base of this knob was a [high outer] wall which we wished to gain."

Advancing far before Barclay and his Pennsylvania comrades, General Quitman's column was led by the brave men of another "Forlorn Hope" (265 men) under Rhode Island-born Captain Silas Casey (West Point Class of 1826). He was a hard-fighting soldier of Scotch-Irish descent: a tough and resourceful warrior people from the green hills of Ulster Province, north Ireland, who had been long conditioned to adversity, and they were well-known for combativeness. Captain Casey was about to fall seriously wounded in leading the assault toward the hill that stood high above the plain.

Both advanced parties of their respective columns were known as "Forlorn Hopes," whose members (regulars who had volunteered for this hazardous duty from various United States regiments) carried wooden ladders for scaling the high outer wall that surrounded the Castle's grounds. These foremost men served as the spearheads of the two assault columns. To have willingly stepped forward to volunteer for these "Forlorn Hopes" demonstrated considerable courage in leading the assault, especially because these regulars were fully aware of the slaughter at Molino de Rey only four days before.

Symbolically, a number of key players in this attack were destined to rise to the fore in the climactic Confederate assault known as "Pickett's Charge" on July 3, 1863 at the decisive battle of Gettysburg, Pennsylvania, now advanced in Pillow's Division. This fine division consisted of five United States regiments and a regiment of Voltigers, under Colonel Timothy Patrick Andrews. A War of 1812 veteran, Andrews had been born in Ireland in 1794, migrating with his family to America as an infant. Like so many other determined soldiers in this assault that continued to sweep toward the high ground, Andrews was promoted for gallantry for his actions today.

Meanwhile, the troops of Pillow's Division, with the "Forlorn Hope" leading the way, surged toward the dense forest of "magnificent cypress trees," in Engineer Beauregard's admiring words about one of Chapultepec's natural wonders. This forest seemed almost like an enchanted or magical woodland if not for the fact that it was now full of determined troops of the San Blas Battalion. Lieutenant Beauregard's words revealed the impressions of a native resident who hailed from a subtropical land (southern Louisiana), where the American cypress grew in abundance along muddy rivers, creeks, and bayous.

But as fate would have it, the forest shortly became a liability for the defenders. This beautiful grove of Mexican Bald Cypress trees that towered high from the hill's base would provide good cover for the attackers, if they survived the advance to reach this point and pushed aside the lengthy formations of the San Blas Battalion defenders deployed among the tall timber. The base of the hill's eastern and southern sides, outside the ancient woods—including the cypress grove—of the Castle's sprawling grounds, were protected by a stone wall (the outer wall) from 12-15 feet high: a formidable obstacle that was presented even before the attackers reached and ascended the lower slopes of the strategic hill. Therefore, gaining the hill's base was the initial tactical objective of both columns, if the attackers successfully advanced across the open fields swept by fire.

In relative terms, General Pillow's troops had the easiest route of attack in charging straight east because the western slope was more gradual, less steep, and the least rocky compared to the southern and eastern slopes, if they successfully pushed the defenders through the cypress forest that extended from near Molino del Rey to Chapultepec.

But first, Pillow's attackers must overrun the earthen redan situated at the hill's western base and then a circular earthen redoubt, located about mid-way up the southern slope. that contained a single field piece, which was additionally protected by entrenchments on both sides. This small redoubt guarded the elbow of this road that led up the southern slope to the main entrance of the parade ground that stood in front of the Military College. As mentioned, a mine field (that essentially served as an additional line of defensive situated higher up the slope behind the redan, which had been erected at the base of the hill before the redoubt on the southern slope) lay higher up the western slope. This extra defensive line of mines compensated in part for the less steep terrain of the western slope compared to the southern slope and especially the eastern slope.

Now surging ranks pouring over the open fields with a will of their own, George Edward Pickett, James Longstreet, and Lewis A. Armistead were destined to play key roles in a far greater attack in just over a decade and a half. Ironically, the commander of the Army of the Potomac in the future three-day climactic showdown at Gettysburg in far-away Adams County, Pennsylvania, was a young West Point-trained engineer from Pennsylvania, Lieutenant George Gordon Meade.

Like many young Americans from the much colder climates of the north, the native Pennsylvanian had already fallen in love with the mild climate and natural splendor of Mexico that he called "this beautiful country." He wrote with heartfelt sincerity: "were I single, I should be tempted to spend my days in this lovely climate," but no time now existed to admire any of the natural beauty that now surrounded him on the morning of September 13.

But in this sweeping assault of two columns that continued to pour toward the high outer wall, relatively few, if any, attackers were now thinking about living a long life and enjoying a mild tropical climate in their later years. Despite their recent heavy losses at Molino del Rey and the unnerving sight of the imposing heights of Chapultepec, the attackers' motivations remained high, because of having achieved past successes. While under a hot fire, one American officer inspired his men onward over the open fields with the cry, "Drinks in the City of Mexico!"

Meanwhile, the American heavy batteries had reopened their fire by this time, hurling projectiles over the attackers' heads to inflict even more damage on the battered defenses and the shell-torn Military College. Captain MacKenzie's "Forlorn Hope" of Pillow's Division pushed aside the first line of defenders from the southwest wall at the hill's base. With a great cheer, these hardened regulars of Pillow's Division, which were about to gain the lower slope before the troops of Quitman's Division, then surged through the trees of the cypress forest before ascending the southwestern slope, while tenaciously battling the defenders of the San Blas Battalion amid the cypress forest.

General Scott wrote how the troops of both columns rolled onward "with an alacrity that gave assurance of prompt success." A member of Captain Casey's "Forlorn Hope," South Carolina-born Daniel Harvey Hill, a future Confederate general of General Robert E. Lee's Army of Northern Virginia, described in his journal how: "A very strong building used as a Military College placed upon a very rugged, steep hill surrounded by two thick [inner and outer] walls twelve feet high and defended by strong works in front constituted the famous Fortress of Chapultepec."

Meanwhile, the artillerymen of the remaining five guns positioned along the parapet atop the summit continued to blast away, but nothing could stop the steam-rolling of the attackers. Even in the heat of battle, the chivalric Major General Bravo still looked as resplendent and dignified as when he had served as the president of Mexico, while encouraging his men to hold firm against the onslaught.

Like the attackers, the experienced major general knew that the infantry assault now possessed a greater chance for success, after Chapultepec's defenses had been considerably softened up by the artillery barrage. Even before the bombardment had been opened, the defenses along the high ground were already weak, because the Mexican nation had lacked the money, time, and resources to transform Chapultepec into an impregnable fortress to meet the day's high and exacting engineering standards, as realized by the well-trained engineers at the Military College.

To Do or Die

Highly-motivated Mexican officers in fancy uniforms (more decorative than United States officer uniforms in the Napoleonic tradition) passed down the ranks of the grim-faced defenders. They barked out orders and issued directives, while reassuring their cadets to stand firm, while fortifying confidence with well-chosen words and gestures.

Relying on instinct, Lieutenant Juan de la Barrera, age nineteen, knew of Juan Escutia's steely determination that was rare for one so young. Raised by a father-general who had early instilled a distinct military bearing in his youth, de la Barrera now stood beside the artillery pieces of the advanced battery, which was located along the parapet on the edge of the southern summit near the front gate.

The young lieutenant now might have worn the uniform of the crack Zapadores: a dark blue uniform coat with a single epaulette, a distinctive Sapper (Zapadores) insignia patch that had been sown on the lower left shoulder, and gold lace trim on the edges of the high collar of the same dark color as the uniform. But he now might have worn the light gray service uniform like the other members of the Cadet Corps on a day when the fate of Mexico City, de la Barrera's hometown, was destined to be decided.

Now encouraging his fast-working gunners unlike the other cadets who served as infantrymen and had been assigned to good positions to defend the Military College, handsome Lieutenant de la Barrera stood aside the battery of field pieces situated on the flat summit near the main gate. Here, the road entered the parade ground atop the level plateau in front of the Military College on the hill's south side.

All the while, General Bravo's men prepared to meet the attack with fixed bayonets and firm resolve. The proud lieutenant named de la Barrera had descended from a Spanish Conquistador and a distinguished family of Mexico City. He shouted for his gunners, and perhaps some cadets assigned to the battery, to prepare to greet the attackers, when they finally descended upon the Military College in overwhelming numbers, which now seemed inevitable: a grim reality that was now only a matter of time.

Lieutenant Juan de la Barrera hardly looked old enough to give orders to other soldiers, including older men. He appeared almost Nordic (but not in the opinion of American soldiers of Anglo-Saxon descent) compared to the darker-hued fighting men, mostly Indians conscripted from the large haciendas. Like other defenders, the cadets now knew that Santa Anna had ordered Major General Bravo to "preserve the point at all risk," which meant defending the summit to the last ounce of energy.

All the while beyond Lieutenant de la Barrera's advanced defensive position at the gun emplacement along the parapet near the front gate, Cadet Juan Escutia and his comrades at the Military College braced themselves for the inevitable onslaught, whenever the fast-moving Americans gained the summit. But there was now no longer time left for any additional contemplation about destiny or the future during the final frantic preparations to greet the tide of attackers.

As a sad fate would have it, the young cadets had no idea that many Americans were now bent on revenge, after suffering high losses and because of the Molino de Rey atrocities. Meanwhile, the cadets felt the heavy burden of responsibility in defending the sacred symbol of his nation that was waving high from atop the tower and nearby Mexico City.

Significantly, this was no ordinary observation tower in a traditional sense. This elegant tower, with large and tall Palladian-style windows, was a regular architectural feature that fit well into the overall elaborate design of the Chapultepec Castle complex. In fact, this sizeable tower, almost as thick as it was high, was the most distinctive architectural gem situated atop the summit. The garrison's largest Mexican flag waved in all its red-white-green glory, flapping from the top of the tower, which was located on the eastern side of the Castle complex.

In overall terms, the Castle was distinguished by Neo-Gothic, Neo-Romanticism, and Neo-Classical architectural styles that had been popular during the colonial period. These architectural features were familiar to the well-educated cadets because they had studied ancient Greek and Roman civilization and military history at the Military College. The main building that housed the military academy in its southeast section and the Spanish viceroy's old palace and summer residence was separated from the tower by a plaza-like inner courtyard that complimented the wide parade ground situated before the Military College. Clearly, the most distinctive feature of the flat summit was Caballero Alto, or "the Tall Knight." This stately tower rose in magnificent fashion from the eastern part of the Chapultepec Castle complex to serve as an ideal target to guide the attackers onward up the slope.

Like other young soldiers who now wore neat gray uniforms, Cadet Juan Escutia and his comrades realized the supreme importance of defending the Military College to the last. Such a stiff challenge was most daunting because the enemy knew that this elevated vital point was the key to capturing Mexico City. The Boy Cadets were not only defending a precious national flag and this sacred ancient hill of the Aztec, but also symbolically a nation's honor, which had been sullied by its army having suffered one miserable defeat by another.

With their new responsibilities hanging heavier like the rising early morning heat of mid-September, the cadets now possessed a greater sense of seriousness, if not fatal resolution, than any previous time. Without having to be told by officers, the young men and boys of the Cadet Corps had already unscathed their bayonets from the thin leather cases that hug at the sides. To defend their Military College with their lives, the teenagers had fixed their bayonets to the end of the cut-down England-made muskets. Consequently, they were fully prepared to use these steel weapons when the moment came to meet the attackers face-to-face.

As mentioned, these older weapons of the cadets were surplus arms from the Napoleonic Wars. Along with other military equipment, Mexico had imported thousands of these muskets in the 1830s.Mexico was still so underdeveloped that no arms were manufactured in the nation even at this late date—a great disadvantage for this decisive showdown with the United States that had benefited immensely from the efficiency and mass production of the Industrial Revolution.

With grim resolution and without wavering, the cadets continued to stand firm at their assigned defensive positions, including at the windows of the Military College and sentry posts. Fated to be killed today, Vicente Suárez, from the picturesque town of Puebla, was one cadet who now stood at his assigned sentry post. Meanwhile, high from the masonry tower known as Caballero Alto and in magnificent fashion, the flowing colors of the Mexican flag continued to wave in proud defiance to mock America's aggressive dream of Manifest Destiny. Members of the Cadet Corps stood tall and proud at the ready for whatever General Scott threw at them, almost as if General Santa Anna was now conducting a routine morning inspection.

Clearly, the cadets meant business on this morning of decision, despite the fact that this was their first encounter with the light-skinned norteamericanos, who looked on these young men of a darker hue with a racial contempt deeply imbedded in their xenophobic society and culture. For God and country, the cadets remained wholeheartedly determined to defend the Military College at all costs, ignoring the risks and dangers.

At this time, the cadets were distinguished from other troops, both regulars and National Guardsmen, by more than their tender ages. As mentioned, they now wore a light gray service uniform that was distinctive from the uniforms of other Mexican soldiers.

The cadet's wore a neat and tight uniform that fit over their youthfully slim bodies that, in most cases, had still to develop and mature in height and muscularity. This distinctive service uniform (more comfortable wearing compared to the formal blue dress uniform of wool) consisted of a light gray frock coat, high stiff collar with the front trimmed in red, and gray trousers with a wide red stripe for field service. A row of shiny brass Colegio Militar-marked buttons, that were gold-tinted, ran down the length of the cadets' uniform coats.

These stylish uniforms of gray contrasted sharply with the dark blue uniforms of the Mexican regular troops, such as Bravo's 10th Infantry of the Line and the National Guardsmen of the San Blas Battalion. For a number of reasons, including a distinctive uniform, the cadets also possessed a distinctive esprit de corps that set them apart from regulars and guardsmen. Of course, they were too young to have seen the first Spanish missionaries, who had bravely gone forth into the New World to spread the Catholic faith at great risk, while wearing gray habits and silver crosses around necks. But the cadets had inherited the same religious-like zeal and determination of these fearless men of God, which were now fused with a vibrant patriotism.

Here, at the windows of the Military College, located in the southeast section of the Castle, and other assigned defensive positions, the Boy Cadets stood with fixed bayonets and firm resolve for whatever might come. While the lengthy blue formations pushed ever-closer to the summit now wreathed in swirls of sulfurous smoke, the cadets felt a deepening anxiety mixed with a sense of pride in manning their assigned defensive positions.

Just before the Americans struck, these young men awaited the arrival of thousands of swiftly-advancing troops who continued to charge ever-closer. Perhaps some cadets thought back upon the strange, twisting course of their lives. The more reflective cadets might have contemplated their destiny, and how a strange fate had placed them center stage in the dramatic showdown for possession of Chapultepec.

Therefore, perhaps Cadet Fernando Montes de Oca, who had been born in the same year (1829) that President Vincente Guerrera had freed the slaves, now wondered if he would ever again see his beloved mother, Josefa Rodríguez, and father, José María Montes. Likewise, Cadet Francisco Márquez, especially since he was the youngest of the cadets who was destined to die on this morning, might have been thinking about the future welfare and fate of his own parents, Micaela Paniagua and his stepfather Francisco Ortiz, and how they would be devastated if God no longer protected him and he never returned home from this seemingly ill-fated place called Chapultepec.

Irrepressible Cadet Juan Baptist Pascasio Escutia

Like other cadets at Chapultepec, Cadet Juan Escutia might well have promised his mother that he would do his best in his first battle for God and country, just before he had departed home never to return. He almost certainly promised the family that he would never bring shame to the distinguished Escutia family name, especially in regard to the memory of his father and grandfather, who both had fought against the Spanish in the War of Independence.

Yet to shave a face as smooth as that of a pretty woman, Escutia looked even younger than his sixteen years. A handsome youth of promise and ability, Escutia looked more like his attractive mother than his father. Understandably admired by a good many men because of her good looks and feisty spirit, María Dolores Martínez was one of the most beautiful women in Tepic. But unfortunately for them, she was also one of the most Christian. Juan had inherited his mother's good looks, which had always made him popular with the girls as long as he could remember.

María dearly loved her son. She, therefore, had initially attempted to convince Juan not to enter the Military College. Nevertheless, he had succeeded in gaining entry into the prestigious school on September 8, 1847.She had been afraid that Juan's bold decision to fight for this country and cast his uncertain fate with an ill-trained army that too often lost it country's battles on Mexican soil.

Indeed, while María loved Mexico, she loved her son even more. As an infant, she had him baptized at the "Shrine of Tepic" on July 1, 1822.The well-educated godson of the respected president of the commission, whose members had sworn on the Holy Bible at Tepic to uphold Mexico's independence in 1821, was also proud of Juan Escutia.

But as a deeply religious woman, María also desired her son to do his best to defend the faith that she loved against the invading heretics in the name of the holy Virgin of Guadalupe, the beloved patron saint of Mexico. Juan never forgot how his mother had cried when he left home for the final time (never to return) either in late August or early September 1847.Consequently, the innocent cadet felt with all his heart that he was defending her, other family members, and the people of Mexico City on September 13.

On the day of his departure from home, María's tears might have initially caught Juan by some surprise. After all, he had long believed that his mother would have been too filled with patriotic ardor in sending her only son off to war to have any regrets whatsoever. But life and emotions were more complicated than he had imagined, and such was not the case. Like many other people in Mexico, family and blood came first before the troubled and seemingly ill-fated republic in the heart and soul of María.

Therefore, Juan might have reflected upon the central contradiction between what he had expected of his mother and the unvarnished truth when he had departed Tepic for Mexico City and a perhaps tragic fate, based upon his mother's reaction when her tears had flowed like water when he left home. But Juan's young mind had been clouded with romantic illusions about the war at that time, and he expected nothing but a glorious time. Like other youths across

Mexico, he had even fantasized about an upcoming opportunity to reap martial success and recognition.

But perhaps the smiles of the pretty Indian girls, with the long black hair glowing in the sun, along the dusty road to Mexico City made this eager youth forget about his mother's sense of foreboding about her only son marching off to war with an unbridled enthusiasm. Meanwhile, back in Tepic in this September, María Dolores Martínez might well have believed that she would never again see her beloved son, and often cried at night in consequence. If so, then she was entirely correct in her gloomy thoughts. Indeed, dreams of glory for many young soldados often led to the grave in this war, and María had been prophetic about the awful realities that were to come on September 13.

While other cadets held their own defensive positions as had been assigned by their officers, Cadet Escutia remained on his own on the very ground that the most revered Aztec princes and rulers, even the great Montezuma himself, had once walked with dignified authority and majesty, while attired in regal splendor and surrounded by their court.

Nothing would cause Escutia to leave his assigned defensive position and desert his assignment that had been given to him in strict oral directives from his superiors, perhaps by General Monterde, despite that Escutia was still unwell .Like some other soldados, he had caught touches of malaria that had long ravished the swampy lowlands, especially along the coastal regions. Even the opinion of the chief medical officer of Major General Bravo's command had been earlier voiced to allow the sickly Cadet Escutia to be excused from duty.

But on his own initiative and fueled by his own sense of firm resolve, Escutia had defiantly ignored the respected physician's order for medical treatment and off-duty status on Saturday, September 11.He simply refused to go to the hospital, because he was determined not to leave his closest comrades or Chapultepec during their greatest hour of need. Regardless of how he felt physically or how shaky he might be on his feet because of sickness, Cadet Escutia was not about to desert his nation and fellow cadets during a true crisis situation.

The Determined Assault Continues

Thanks to their own commander-in-chief, General Santa Anna, in having decided to shift troops and concentrate them in the wrong sector east of Chapultepec after having been fooled by General Scott's clever tactical diversions, General Bravo and the men, including the cadets, never had a chance to successfully defend Chapultepec, when the American attacks struck on the west (General Pillow's Division) and east (General Quitman's Division) flank of the defenses.

With flags flying, Pillow's men surged through the western edge of the Mexican Bald Cypress forest, defended by the highly-motivated troops of Lieutenant Colonel Felipe de Santiago Xicoténcatl's San Blas Battalion, at the base of the western and southwestern base of the hill .Meanwhile, Quitman's troops continued to advance at a good pace, rapidly surging across the open ground. The regiment (2nd Pennsylvania Volunteers) on the west (on Quitman's left and closest to Pillow's troops) finally gained the high outer wall at the hill's southern base. Most importantly, they then followed the length of the high outer wall to the left, or west.

The fast-moving Pennsylvanians entered a breach in the wall, which had been torn open either by shell-fire or by prying bayonets. They then poured into the Castle's grounds, including the eastern edge of the Mexican Bald Cypress forest, now held by Pillow's New York troops whose attack had stalled, at the hill's base. These two columns (the farthermost troops on Pillow's right and the farthermost men on Quitman's left, the 2nd Pennsylvania) were about to link in the cypress woodlands inside the outer wall to create a pincer movement calculated to catch the San Blas Battalion defenders, aligned on the slopes, and trap them between two fires.

The men of the San Blas Battalion, which had been organized in May 1847 in the State of Jalisco but some soldados had been recruited from the Tepic area, State of Nayarit, fought tenaciously against the onrushing Americans who surged forward with cheers.

In the words of Private Richard Coulter, the cypress "grove at the base of the hill was full of hombres, and for the first time, we had the pleasure of returning the peppering that had given us" on previous fields of strife. Not even the carefully-placed sharpshooters and heavy line of finely-uniformed soldados aligned among the Mexican Bald Cypress trees, with branches festooned with Spanish Moss that hung down to nearly touch the ground, were able to stop Pillow's attackers.

Then, the shouting Americans advanced so far up the slope that they not only outflanked, but also swarmed into advantageous firing positions above (higher ground behind) the ill-fated men of the San Blas Battalion. Uniformed in red pants and blue coats and presenting an impressive appearance, the troops of the San Blas Battalion stood firm as long as possible. Here, they put up a magnificent fight and longer than anyone expected. Loading and firing with accuracy, the Americans literally shot the San Blas Battalion to pieces, with large numbers of soldados falling where the stood in line. In total, around 370 men of the San Blas Battalion were killed, wounded, or taken prisoner on this hellish morning: a heroic and supreme sacrifice at Chapultepec that has been often forgotten.

As mentioned, the fierce artillery bombardment had taken a heavy toll on the garrison's morale and the overall defensive capabilities, including the dismounting of at least five cannon to leave only five that remained firing. Even worse for the defenders, the attack of both columns steadily achieved gains at almost every point. Indeed, the steam-rolling assault secured additional ground with each passing minute, proceeding more swiftly and even better than General Scott had imagined possible.

Indeed, after pouring through the cypress forest from the west and surging up the slope to storm the redoubt situated about half-way up the slope by Pillow's attackers, who had been joined Quitman's left, the 2nd Pennsylvania advanced with speed. In a timely united effort, Pillow's and Quitman's troops had overrun the redoubt, after vicious hand-to-hand combat. Overwhelmed by superior might from two directions and having suffered from two cross-fires, the out-flanked survivors of the San Blas Battalion fled farther up the slope in an attempt to escape the severe punishment. As a sad fate would have it, relatively few members of the hard-fighting battalion survived to fight another day, however.

Demonstrating courage while riding ahead on horseback and bellowing orders, General Pillow had led his troops through the dense woodlands, driving the last of the San Blas Battalion defenders, who wore navy blue uniforms and bright red trousers. As mentioned, the heroic defenders of the San Blas Battalion had held firm for an extended period and as long as possible, but at a far higher cost than other National Guard units defending the hill.

Clearly, Bravo was correct in having repeatedly attempted to convince Santa Anna that he urgently needed reinforcements to bolster the undermanned defenses, especially in the Mexican Bald Cypress forest that he attempted to hold as part of an overall well-designed defense in depth: simply an impossible mission because of his over-extended front and the effectiveness of the pincer movement.

However, the pushing aside of the defenders at the base of the hill and along the lower slopes brought a new peril to the first wave of attackers, when they reached a point higher up the slope—the mine field that was calculated to blow attacking formations to pieces. But "so prompt and resolute [was the attack] that the enemy could not fire any of his mines charged with our destruction," penned Lieutenant John James Page in a letter. General Scott explained in his report after the battle how the Mexicans "retreat allowed not [the] time to fire a single mine without the certainty of blowing up friend and foe. Those who at a distance attempted to apply matches to the long trains were shot down by our men."

Of course, this systematic rout of defenders all along the line was possible because Santa Anna still believed that this powerful offensive effort was still nothing more than a mere feint to mask the main assault that he still expected to emerge from the south. Of course by this time, the defenders of Chapultepec, especially Major General Bravo, knew far better and much differently about the tactical situation than Santa Anna. Incredibly, with eager anticipation, Santa Anna still looked south for the main attack that never came. But Bravo's words of wisdom to Santa Anna had continued to be ignored until it was too late.

The attackers had been successful all along the line. Indeed, on the division's right, Quitman's troops, who had initially attacked toward the southeast corner of Chapultepec, had been equally successful to pushing back resistance. It had all happened with amazing speed: a success that mirrored the gains on the division's left. Indeed and as mentioned, surging Americans on Quitman's left had achieved their objectives, after having departed the road and then poured through the breach at the center of the southern wall just to the right, or east, of where the troops of Captain McKenzie's "Forlorn Hope" had struck. The troops on Quitman's right then raced up the zigzagging man road that led up the southern slope and straight to the Military College, while his troops on the left had surged through the Mexican Bald Cypress forest and then up the steep slope.

In the Captain Casey's "Forlorn Hope," Lieutenant Daniel Harvey Hill described the extent of the success of both surging columns in completing a highly-effective pincer movement in his journal: the troops "dashed forward along the road and drove the Mexicans before us with great slaughter [while] The other storming party [that led Pillow's column] had . . . gained the height from the opposite side" of the hill's western side.

Indeed, Pillow's success had been swift because the vulnerable west side of Chapultepec's sprawling defensive line was the weakest link in the overall defensive position, and Pillow's onrushing attackers poured up the gradual western slope leading to the hilltop, and toward the retaining (inner) wall of the castle's terrace.

Meanwhile, the troops of 2nd Pennsylvania, Quitman's left, "rushed directly up the hill which was very steep," wrote Sergeant Thomas Barclay, after the Pennsylvania boys had charged through the stands of giant cypress: the tactical achievement that had ensured a successful linkage with Pillow's right. Proving to have been an unstoppable tide, the elated troops of Pillow's Division had overwhelmed the defenders, while pouring over protective ditches, earthen works, including trenches, and land mines.

All in all, American successes had been impressive even before they neared the crest. As mentioned, the attackers of Quitman's Division to the right had accomplished the same. The troops of Quitman's Division, the largest force of the two columns, had surged up the slope only a short time later than Pillow's men, but the troops of both columns had united on the slope when the two arms of the pincer met.

The makeshift scaling ladders of the advance parties, the "Forlorn Hope" under Captain McKenzie, assisted the attackers in getting up and across the steepest slopes on the west. Defending the southwest side of the hill to the last man, the last remaining National Guard troops of the San Blas Battalion was "virtually annihilated" by Pillow's attackers during some of the heaviest and most brutal fighting of the day.

Defending the Inner Wall

Guarantying even closer range combat than had been seen among the trees of the cypress forest now swirled like a tempest when the first breathless members of General Pillow's Division gained the edge of the 12-foot high inner wall, which stood several feet lower than the outer wall at the hill's base.

Meanwhile, after having cut down the last withdrawing soldados retiring up the slope now covered with blood-stained bodies, sharp-eyed Americans began to systematically shot down Mexican artillerymen, whose upper torsos and heads were exposed above the parapet on the summit's edge above them.

Just when Pillow's troops were seemingly on the verge of achieving a dramatic success upon nearing the smoke-laced summit, the inevitable suddenly occurred. The advance of Pillow's three regiments was stopped by a formidable defensive obstacle known as the fosse: a 10-foot deep moat or deep ditch situated farther north and just beyond the minefield. This fosse was located just below the Castle and its high inner wall. Therefore, before the fosse, Pillow's men, finding an opportunity to catch their breath, waited for the arrival of wooden ladders to scale the inner wall, while sweating under the blazing Mexican sun and lying low to escape the hail of bullets.

By this time, a good many United States officers had been hit, including brave men who had led by example to inspire their soldiers onward up the slope and through a hot fire. Meanwhile, frantic Mexican gunners on the crest depressed barrels of their cannon to rake the Americans with blasts of canister—a deadly shotgun like blast of projectiles that were larger than musket balls but smaller than cannon balls. General Pillow, President Polk's close friend, had earlier been hit in the left foot by a canister ball, while encouraging his troops onward.

But the Americans, gasping for breath in the suffocating heat, stayed under good cover that existed immediately below the blazing parapet to escape the artillery-fire. Here, they hurriedly reloaded their muskets and then blasted away to cut down additional soldados at the flaming parapet, including exposed artillerymen who were hurriedly working their guns. A desperate General Pillow had earlier requested the assistance of a reserve division of regulars to be hurled forward to reinforce his troops for regaining the momentum, because the attack had stalled at the fosse and in the face of the cannon-fire and musketry pouring down the slope.

At this crucial moment, Lieutenant Juan de la Barrera busily directed a blistering fire of one cannon positioned at the parapet near the main gate, where the road entered the flat plateau upon which stood the Castle complex atop the flat plateau. All the while, those cadets in their most advanced defensive positions exchanged an intense musket-fire with the pinned-down Americans, who hovered under the protection of cover just below the parapet.

In the nick of time, General Quitman, a master politician who owned several cotton plantations and a large number of slaves, answered Pillow's appeal for sending reinforcements, including a small detachment of United States Marines. He rushed these reinforcements west on the double to strengthen the pinned-down attackers to the west. All the while, the cadets continued to blast away, exchanging fire for around fifteen minutes. Sulfurous clouds of smoke filled the shell-battered Military College to choke defenders. Fast-firing cadets, hot and sweaty, felt the ever-increasing thirst from biting off the paper ends of cartridges and dry, parched mouths, while pouring black powder down the barrels in reloading muskets for unleashing additional shots at the enemy.

The scaling ladders finally arrived for Pillow's pinned-down men to launch a final offensive bid to overcome the last obstacles, including the deep ditch and the high inner wall. With typical soldiery resourcefulness, the ladders were planted close together in rows to span the length of the deep ditch. These make-shift bridges were shortly crowded with soldiers, who continued onward toward the high inner wall and through a hail of lead, after performing delicate balancing acts.

Meanwhile, close-range combat also swirled across the slope just below the parapet in Quitman's embattled sector. As if gaining revenge for the earlier decimation of the unfortunate National Guardsmen of the San Blas Battalion, the soldados of the Morelia Battalion had performed heroically. Fighting fiercely, they had cut down clumps of Americans with a blistering fire. Despite poorly trained, the Morelia Battalion men had gamely stood their ground in protecting the five-gun battery located east of Chapultepec, and punished the attackers on Quitman's right that had surged toward Chapultepec's southeast corner. Here, these Guardsmen, under Brigadier General Andres Terres, who had attempted in vain to defend the high south wall in this eastern sector, had swept Quitman's troops on the east with a blistering fire, causing heavy losses that had initially slowed the attack, which, therefore, had been more belated than Pillow's assault, before the arms of the pincers had closed.

Like the Pennsylvanians and South Carolinians, the New Yorkers had also suffered heavily, losing their commander, Lieutenant Colonel Charles Baxter, who had fallen mortally wounded. A continual line of attackers, extending all the way from the west face of the Castle to its south face, had gained advanced positions by this time, after the arrival of additional scaling ladders and the reserve division, under General William Worth, which Pillow had wisely called to assist his stalled offensive effort. To his credit, Pillow had early realized that the assistance of regulars was badly needed for his pinned-down volunteers.

In explaining the rapid ascent of the attackers up the bullet-swept slopes, Pillow's and Quitman's men had raced each other to be the first troops to gain the strategic crest. As mentioned, even the fosse (deep ditch) provided an inadequate barrier to stop the onslaught, because even more Americans continued to cross, after having laid the additional scaling ladders for a successful crossing this deep ditch, and then scampering over the ladders (makeshift foot bridges) that spanned the ten-foot ditch. Then, the ladders were carried forward and planted against the inner wall as solidly as possible, while Mexican bullets whistled by them. To the defenders' disbelief, the bluecoats steadily climbed-up the ladders to get ever-closer to the great goal of reaching the strategic summit.

Out-flanked on two sides (east and west) and with his own casualties skyrocketing, General Bravo knew that the end was near, especially because Santa Anna had failed to send reinforcements. With large numbers of Mexicans, including the San Blas Battalion, routed from the body-strewn slopes, the defenders, including the Boy Cadets, who defended the summit felt increasingly alone and isolated. Indeed, like other defenders atop the summit, members of the Cadet Corps were now on their own to face the surging tide of elated Americans, who already sensed the winning of a great victory, while continuing to advance and leaping over the red-stained bodies of fallen soldados, dead and wounded.

With drawn sword studded with diamonds, ornate and made in Paris, France, and already feeling the anguish of Santa Anna's folly that had doomed Chapultepec even before the first shot had been fired in anger, Major General Bravo now realized that it was far better to retreat to fight another day under more favorable circumstances rather than remaining on the doomed hilltop that was about to be overwhelmed.

In the end, the common belief of Chapultepec's impregnability had proved a myth and a most costly one, because a good many young men and boys from Mexico had to die before this harsh reality was fully realized by Mexican leadership.

The onrushing American soldiers raised a chorus of victory cheers, sensing that still another dramatic success had been seemingly won. The screams of hundreds of charging Americans, now bent on reaping a measure of glory and revenge, additionally unnerved more stunned defenders, who had been shell-shocked by the intense bombardment of Scott's heavy artillery.

Soldiers from across America, including the hard-fighting men of a South Carolina volunteer regiment and a New York volunteer regiment, charged side-by-side on the east. These northerners and southerners from two different cultures (one that was based on slavery and the other based on no slavery) overlooked the gap of considerable sectional differences and jealousies to now unite as one against a common foe.

United States Marines from the Navy Yard on the Anacostia River in Washington, D.C., and who represented some of America's best specialized forces that had been first created to fight against England during the American Revolution, helped to fuel the attack of Pillow's men. Some fast-firing defenders were already stunned by the Americans' audaciousness. One shocked soldado could hardly believe how: "the Yanquis climbed like goats [in] clearing all the rocks" of the bullet-swept southern, eastern, and western slopes, and could not be stopped. Despite a good many Americans had been cut down, they just kept charging and coming up the slopes, as if nothing could stop them.

Finally, the first Americans, after climbing up scaling ladders that had been placed against the high inner wall, began to reach the top of the wall. Meanwhile, holding firm in firing from the windows of the Military College and other positions, the cadets continued to fire at the swarming attackers, who now seemed to be everywhere and too many to count. Desperate defenders, perhaps some cadets, pushed scaling ladders away off the inner wall, causing climbers to tumble to earth.

But by this time, nothing could now stop the surging tide of attackers, who then began to swarm over the parapet on the commanding summit. One defender described how the cheering throng of elated "Yanquis [now] came through the main door [at the gate where the road that ascended from the southern slope and led to] of the top of the plaza [Military College grounds] trampling over everything" in their path.

Indeed, the bluecoats had surged up the road and then through the main gate, located just before the front of the Military College that led to the open plaza (parade ground or terrace) atop on the level plateau of the summit. Larger numbers of howling Americans then poured over the parapets, including those foremost defenses that protected the Military College, with fixed bayonets and victory cheers.

Colonel Juan Cano, who had already perhaps saved the life of his brother Lorenzo by having prudently dispatched him to Santa Anna's headquarters with a message to the generalissimo, met the first Americans in the open parade ground. These attackers had burst through the main gate, after surging up the road on the southern slope and pouring over the parapet. By this time, the once-solid defense had begun to collapse. After the front-line defenders had fallen back before the onslaught, Colonel Cano stood bravely in the open plaza all alone in the open, while displaying open contempt and defiance for the Yankees. Here, he was "very resolute with gun in hand . . . Two of them asked for his sword [but he refused and] He shut their mouths with the gun [and then] They fell upon him and destroyed him."

Other defenders who attempted to stand up to Pillow's first attackers were likewise quickly wiped out in a flurry of jabbing bayonets and swinging musket-butts. Meanwhile, additional soldados fled rearward to escape the ever-increasing numbers of Americans who had poured over the parapet.

In his journal, Sergeant Thomas Barclay described how he and his comrades surged across the smoke-filled summit: "Company E [2nd Pennsylvania] was the first company of the Volunteer Division in the Castle [and] they were the first full company in either of the Divisions in, for altho Pillow's men had driven in the outposts there were but few of the men into the main building [that included the Military College] and they were without company organization."

Major General Bravo ordered his surviving men to retire in the face of so many onrushing Americans, before it was too late. Indeed, too many Americans to possibly stop had swarmed over the parapet with bayonets flashing in the morning sunlight. But the cadets, still defending their beloved Military College as ordered, remained at their posts and their assigned defensive positions. Here, perhaps in part because they never received Bravo's order to retire or decided to ignore it, they continued to blast away at the bluecoat attackers who continued to spill over the parapet and into the wide plaza now filled with Yankee soldiers and chaos.

Puebla-born Vicente Suárez was one cadet who stood firm at his assigned sentry post position, where he was about to lose his life while faithfully performing his duty to the bitter end. Either refusing Bravo's orders to withdraw or not hearing the command in time, or both, in the confusion and chaos of battle, other cadets continued to fight in defense of their military academy, where they had learned their professions and had been taught to obey all orders by their older instructors.

Then, after seeing cadets failing to fall back with the rest of the retiring troops, General José Mariano Monterde (about to be captured) likewise urgently ordered the cadets to pull back before it was too late. But out of a mixture of sheer courage and defiance, the feisty cadets once again either refused or failed to retreat with the escaping throng of non-cadet soldados, who were now abandoning the summit on the double.

Or as mentioned, perhaps some cadets evidently never received the order in the din of battle, or General Monterde's order to retreat was issued too late amid the nightmarish swirl of close quarter combat. For all practical purposes and for a number of reasons, the cadets were only beginning to fight in the tenacious defense of their Military College on this bloody morning.

First Cadet to Die, Cadet Vincent Suárez

Cadet Vicente Suárez had been born in Puebla on April 3, 1833. He was the son of a cavalry officer. The young cadet possessed a promising future at least until the ill-fated morning of September 13. Now a member of the Second Company of Cadets because of his diminutive stature, the young man had entered the Military College in November 1845 (the month before Texas was annexed by the United States in an illegitimate act because of the acceptance of the bogus Texas claim that the Rio Grande River was the southern border, which Mexico had long emphasized would result in war) when only age twelve.

With open warfare inevitable and only a matter of time, Suárez had then gained entry to the Military College because he most of all desired "to be useful" to his nation during her hour of greatest need. Likewise, Cadet Vincent Suárez was now proving that he was very useful in Chapultepec's spirited defense, after the Americans swarmed over the parapet.

Almost certainly, he was the first cadet to be killed, because of his determination to hold firm at his advanced position at the Castle's entrance: now an isolated position after so many other defenders had retired on the double. Nevertheless, Suárez refused to either run or fall back, while most other garrison members had retired on General

Monterde's orders. Despite being one of the youngest and smallest cadets in stature, he remained defiantly at his assigned sentry post, which was almost certainly located near the front gate, where the road entered the parade ground just before the Military College's main entrance that faced south.

Suárez was most likely stationed near the academy's front door, before the wide parade ground on the terrace atop the summit. Young Cadet Suárez, although slight, thin, and of a "delicate constitution," bravely stood his ground as the charging Americans drew ever-closer. Shouting and firing on the run with fixed bayonets flashing in the sunlight of Chapultepec, General Scott's men seemed now invincible, because of superior numbers and aggressiveness.

Perhaps precisely because of his small size, the cadet compensated for his diminutiveness with a fierce fighting spirit that was displayed in full. According to what he had been long taught at his school, he dutifully and gamely stood his ground, while the Americans closed-in on the small cadet who refused to run like seemingly everyone else. In fact, he even gave the proper command when confronted by the first group of unauthorized interlopers in blue uniforms. Continuing to perform his duties to the last, he ordered the first United States soldiers to halt and advance no closer to the Military College.

When these first attackers naturally ignored his sharply-spoken order to halt, Suárez leveled his shortened musket. He then carefully aimed his musket and shot down the foremost American. But of course, it was now only a matter of time before he was overwhelmed by a number of large-sized grown men, but not before the teenager had bayoneted at least one Yankee in the stomach to inflict what was almost certainly a mortal wound.

Here, at his advanced position near the academy's front door, Cadet Suárez was fatally cut down at his assigned sentry post, where he had made his last stand against the odds. In the end by falling to rise no more exactly where he had been posted and obeying orders to the last as he had long been instructed at his beloved school, this small boyish cadet had remained faithful to what he had been taught. Most importantly, he had remained true to his sacred trust to his Military College, his fellow cadets, his father (distinguished cavalry officer Miguel Suárez), and Mexico during her darkest hour.

In the end, Cadet Suárez had fought and died with the painful knowledge that his own home town of Puebla, founded in 1531 and located in the beautiful Valley of Puebla (southeast of Mexico City), had been captured in mid-May 1847 by General Scott's Army. Even now the cadet's hometown was an occupied city, where his mother, María de la Luz Ortega lived. But of course, this situation partly explained why this faithful cadet had fought tenaciously to the bitter end.

The Tragic End of Cadet Fernando Montes de Oca

As mentioned, Suárez was almost certainly the first cadet to be killed, because of his guardian position near the Castle's entrance. Based on the scanty available primary evidence, Cadet Fernando Montes de Oca, a proud member of the First Company of Cadets like Cadet Márquez, was most likely the second cadet, age eighteen after his May 29 birthday, when the natural beauty of springtime had seemed more promising for Mexico, who was killed.

As a tragic fate have it, Oca was also one of the newest cadets. On January 29, 1847, he had officially requested entry to the Military College. In his official appeal for entry, he had emphasized his burning desire "to serve in the glorious" defense of his nation against the detested invaders from "the United States of the North."

Like Cadet Suárez, he defiantly remained at his post in the Castle, without giving ground in the face of the Americans' onslaught, despite knowing that his widowed mother, whose captain-husband had died, still depended on him: a spirited defiance against the odds that was destined to cost him his life. Atzcapotzalco possessed ample good reason to mourn the loss of one of its most promising sons, who had possessed a bright future. He failed to survive the attack and never again saw his mother, María Rodríguez, or his father.

In the desperate bid to escape so many attackers before it was too late, discouraged Mexican soldiers, who now knew that the Yankees could not be stopped this morning, tumbled off the summit of "Grasshopper Hill" (the old Aztec name that still might have been used by defenders during this period) like grasshoppers before the advance of a hot fire sweeping through a dry field on a windy, summer day.

While many Mexicans attempted to escape off what had become a hill of death, other groups of brave soldados stood firm in stoic, if not suicidal, defiance, facing the swarming attackers. During a true crisis situation, they, including the cadets, demonstrated a truly splendid level of resistance to buy precious time for their fleeing comrades to save themselves, after the collapse of resistance elsewhere.

In his journal, Lieutenant Daniel Harvey Hill, who had entered the open expanse of the terrace by way of the road that ascended the southern slope, described the slaughter of garrison members on the smoke-covered crest: "The havoc among the Mexicans was now horrible in the extreme. Pent up between two fires [the convergence of Pillow's and Quitman's columns] they had but one way [a narrow passageway, or "pass," called the "Belén"] to escape and all crowded toward it like a flock of sheep. I saw dozens hanging from the walls and creeping through holes made for the passage of water & whilst I this position were shot down without making the least resistance. Our men were shouting give no quarters 'to the treacherous scoundrels' and as far as I could observe none was asked by the Mexicans."

Quite likely and although it cannot be determined with any degree of accuracy, some of those soldados who were "hanging from the walls" might have been cadets, if Lieutenant Hill meant the eastern side of the defensive complex. If so, then this chaotic situation (if it also existed in the later stages of the battle) explained why some dead cadets were found sprawled on the steepest and rockiest slope, the eastern side, after the battle.

But the majority of the surviving cadets were not running like these hard-hit and panicked soldados of the regular army and National Guard units. Training at the Military College had hardened the cadets and made them even more determined and patriotic than before their entry into a new life of honor and sacred duty. Consequently, despite their youth and in general, these students were not the kind of individuals who would run, even in a crisis situation and regardless of the odds. Therefore, the vast majority gamely stood their ground assigned to them by their commanders, refusing to fall back like so many others of General Monterde's men, who poured rearward like a flood.

The lessons learned by these young men about the supreme importance of duty to God and country, and commitment at the college now rang true in the midst of a raging battle. Indeed, these lessons had forged a determined soldiery, who were fully committed to performing their duty to the very end and die in the dedicated attempt, if necessary, to save their beloved military school.

Unlike so many older soldiers, the cadets refused to abandon their school and the ancient hill of Chapultepec, especially to the hated Protestant gringos, because they possessed a sacred honor of defending this hallowed ground to the last. Lovers of Mexico's rich heritage and sacred traditions that needed to be protected from heretical invaders, they felt disgust at the mere thought of the Yanquis trespassing on and desecrating the academy's grounds. Consequently, these young men had already made up their minds to commit themselves fully to a desperate last stand to defend this special place on the commanding summit that they loved with their hearts in part because it had become their surrogate homes.

Indeed, the cadets were determined to demonstrate their honor and fidelity which was sorely lacking among many of their cynical Machiavellian leaders, especially General Santa Anna, who had promised reinforcements for Chapultepec that never arrived. In this sense, Santa Anna himself had already doomed the Castle's defense and sealed the tragic fates of half a dozen Boy Cadets long before the American cannon had opened fire at dawn.

Perhaps this sad turn of events was appropriate because the self-serving generalissimo had already doomed Mexico to miserable defeat, since he had taken command of the army because of a long list of his mistakes and miscalculations. Therefore, in this context, perhaps some cadets felt fully justified in basically defying their commander's orders, when it had been first recommended by General Monterde at an earlier date for them to depart Chapultepec and return to their homes, because of the heightened danger of remaining on the summit.

Of course, General Monterde had been thinking humanly and long-term in suggesting that all steps necessary needed to be taken to preserve as many cadet lives as possible, because they were precious and represented Mexico's future. Consequently, in the end, the cadet's heartfelt request to remain to defend their school and not return home as recommended by him had been granted by Monterde, when he learned of their determination to stay faithfully with the garrison and share the same dangers.

After all, with Mexico City now facing its greatest threat and with Major General Bravo needing every man to defend Chapultepec, it must have seemed to the young cadets almost like the end of the world as they knew it. Indeed, every fighting man, including mere boys in gray uniforms, was now needed to save the capital city and the republic.

Meanwhile, the close-quarter combat continued to swirl in and around the Castle, where bloody flurries of close combat raged with intensity. Some enterprising Americans dashed along the top of the parapet, shooting and knocking down defenders with point-blank shots and bayonet thrusts. But most attackers made a rush for the Castle, because of its prominence as the principal target. It was now discovered by the American soldiers that this regal-looking place atop the summit was still more of a palace and residence than a well-designed fortified position.

Although Santa Anna had been allowed ample time to make extensive defensive arrangements and preparations to meet the assault, even the defensive positions atop the summit proved inadequate. Consequently, the Castle complex was early reached by additional attackers, who charged into the former residence of the Spanish Viceroy without stopping to catch their breath.

Engineer Beauregard, the young lieutenant from the bayou country of Louisiana, described the moment when he was engaged in "making a rush for the first open door of the citadel [perhaps the Military College], followed by two or three soldiers—my intention being at the time to take down that Mexican flag, which was waving so gracefully and gently upon all that scene of carnage and bloodshed which was going on under its very shadow! As I rushed in, some Mexicans, who were in it, rushed out, but only to fall into the hands of those who were following me."

The Horror of No Quarter Warfare

But like other cadets, young Escutia still refused to run even while larger numbers of Yankees poured over the parapet, spilling into the parade ground in a tide of blue. Any attempt by the cadets to defend the ancient hilltop of Aztec rulers was now folly, and no longer made any sense, except to salvage and preserve a sense of honor, so as to not tarnish the good name of the Military College. And such were the exact reasons which explained why many cadets remained still defiantly in their assigned defensive positions, continuing to fight against the odds.

As noted, the advancing American soldiers were incensed at this time, but not for any behavior or actions taken by Chapultepec garrison members, especially the cadets. During the last battle at El Molino del Rey (King's Mill), one of the war's ugliest chapters had been played out in an especially brutal fashion, just three-quarters west of Chapultepec on September 8. As a cruel fate would have it, this unforgiveable atrocity had effectively set the stage for the development of an even greater tragedy and horror on the morning of September 13.

At that time less than a week ago, Scott's troops had captured their formidable objective that included the Casa Mata, a powder magazine of stone located near the low, white-colored walls of the lengthy molino, Molino del Rey. In fact, this was the bloodiest attack of the war that had left young American boys laying in clumps across a wide stretch of open ground. After the troops of one assault column had charged and captured a Mexican battery, they were then forced back by heavy losses and a blistering fire.

But one of the most infamous incidents of the war (atrocities were committed by both sides in this increasingly-brutal war, especially as it lengthened and hatreds intensified) developed when Mexican troops had advanced to recapture their lost guns, forcing the Americans rearward and back into the open fields. Taking advantage of the newly-presented tactical opportunity, groups of soldados had then entered the field of fallen American soldiers.

They proceeded to bayonet a large number of American wounded in a slaughter. Some dead were also robbed of valuables, including pocket watches, rings, and wallets of the fallen men who were quickly dispatched in grisly fashion. Sickened by the sight of a massacre, Lieutenant Raphael Semmes described how revenge-seeking soldados scoured the open fields like cold-hearted avenging angels, "bayoneting the wounded with a savage delight!" Ironically, it had been almost as if these soldados had learned bloody lessons from a dark past, inheriting some of the worst traits and qualities of the Spanish Conquistadors.

In addition, finely-uniformed lancers had also contributed to the slaughter by lancing helpless wounded soldiers, who were scattered over a wide area. From a safe distance after the last American attack had been repulsed, Scott's men had watched the cruel murders in the open fields in seething anger. Naturally, they had been horrified by what they saw, but were helpless to save their injured friends and comrades who lay helpless on the ground. After witnessing a horror that he never forgot, Captain Roswell S. Ripley, of General Pillow's staff, wrote how "they murdered every wounded man left on the except" a lucky captain and a private, who were accidently passed over during the killing spree.

Therefore, on the morning of September 13, many attackers were now highly-motivated to not only win victory, but also in exacting revenge on any Mexican soldier in uniform, regardless of their age, because of the infamous massacre at Molino de Rey. Unfortunately and as a tragic fate would have it, the Boy Cadets on the hilltop were now fair game and at no fault of their own. Worst of all, they now had no idea that they had been targeted by the attackers for destruction in an ugly brand of no quarter warfare for what other soldados had committed at Molino del Rey.

Fueled by a potent mix of emotion, revenge, and adrenaline, the enraged Americans with fixed bayonets continued to pour over the crest and across the open terrace, surrounded the Castle, including the Military College, while raising the cry of "no quarter." Unfortunately, for the innocent cadets, who had nothing at all to do with the bayoneting of the American wounded at Molino del Rey, were now in the path of the steam-rolling tide of angry norteamericanos, who were bent on revenge. Intensified by the heat of battle, this rising tide of vengeance now swept over the summit with a momentum and fury all its own, guaranteeing that this morning in hell atop "Grasshopper Hill" would become even bloodier than in a traditional battle under typical circumstances.

In a letter, Lieutenant John James Peck described the systematic slaughter of a large number of soldados at Chapultepec, which was one of the forgotten massacres of the Mexican-American War: "Many of them were bayoneted because of their outrageous conduct towards our wounded at Molino del Rey." However, Lieutenant Peck and other Americans were incorrect and as mentioned, because Chapultepec's defenders, especially the young cadets, were not the murderers of the wounded Americans at Molino de Rey.

During the bloody battle on September 8, the cadets had been performing routine duties at the Military College. Nevertheless, even the throats of some wounded men, perhaps cadets, who defended the Military College and Castle, were later cut on September 13 as part of the no-quarter policy. Initially, these brutal killings not only occurred on the open terrace before the Castle and Military College, but also most likely inside these structures. Enraged Americans repaid the score from Molino del Rey with a terrible retribution on this Monday morning.

As a tragic fate would have it, the entirely innocent Boy Cadets suddenly found themselves at the wrong place at the wrong time. Therefore, half a dozen of these young men in natty gray uniforms of gray were destined to pay a frightfully high price at no fault of their own.

Like the equally enraged Texian and United States volunteers who had killed hundreds of Santa Anna's men without mercy at San Jacinto on bloody April 21, 1836, incensed American soldiers on the summit raised a new battle-cry, "Molino del Rey," that matched the San Jacinto cries of "Remember the Alamo," and "Remember Goliad." Unfortunately for them, General Monterde's men, including the young cadets, found themselves in the worst possible situation, because they were facing an enraged soldiery bent on revenge when possibilities of escape were limited.

Other vengeful Americans cursed the Mexicans as "yellow devils," while screaming their personal war cry to fuel the wrath of their comrades: "give no quarter to the treacherous scoundrels." To the Americans, it did not matter if the soldado was a blue-coated regular, or Guardsman, or a young man in a gray service uniform, when hunting down victims in the savage combat that was merciless.

Larger numbers of howling American soldiers, sounding like fearsome Comanche warriors who had long raided across Chihuahua (Cadet Agustín Melgar's hometown that he would never see again) every autumn like the sudden descent of "blue northers," swarmed into the Military College, after charging across the parade ground of the wide terrace fronting the Military College.

All the while, the cadets remained at their assigned defensive posts in the Castle and, symbolically, in the Military College. Here, they continued to rapidly load and fire their muskets, blasting away at targets. A member of the 2nd Pennsylvania Volunteer Regiment from Greensburg, Pennsylvania, Richard Coulter, described a grim reality for Chapultepec's defenders: "some officers were taken prisoners, but few other were taken alive" in the slaughter, especially of enlisted men who were shown no mercy.

Lieutenant Beauregard, who had gained entry into the Castle that had been transformed into an urban-like battleground, described how: "Finding no stairs [in the Castle to go up and gain the lofty perch to capture the large Mexican flag still waving from the last strategic high ground before Mexico City] or opening in that room, I came out of it to go into some other entrance; but as I came out, I saw one of our soldiers, who seemed to be perfectly exasperated, about to run his bayonet through the neck of a young Mexican officer, who stood in front of him without hat or sword! I mechanically struck a heavy blow with my sabre upon the bayonet, which was about to perform its bloody and deadly deed, and had the good luck to parry the thrust so far as only to let it run through his military coat collar and cravat. I [as an officer] then rebuked the [enlisted rank] soldier, placed the officer in charge of a sentinel and ascertained that his name was Mr. Ximenes, a young Lieutenant of the Corps of Engineers."

Meanwhile, the fighting in and around the Castle continued unabated, reaching new levels of intensity. By this time, the most stalwart of Bravo's men had fallen back to secondary defensive positions to resume fighting with renewed desperation. But many garrison members continued to flee to escape the smoke-filled summit now swarming with fast-moving Americans, who were experts at killing soldados. One of the most effective secondary defensive positions from which to continue the fight against the surging American tide was located on the rooftops. Here, sandbag parapets had been created to make defensive stands from excellent elevated perches that provided very good firing positions to shot down Americans in the plaza below.

While many of General Monterde's men were now in full flight to escape the steamrolling onslaught, especially when faced with the cruel reality of a brutal no-quarter policy, a good many soldados, including the cadets who were still gamely defending the Military College, were fighting back tenaciously. In the words of Lieutenant Beauregard: "the work was filled with our town troops, whilst the enemy, who had taken refuge in the citadel, continued to fire at us from the windows of the second story and the roof."

The cadets were among these final defenders, who were gamely fighting back against the odds that only grew larger with each passing minute. For ample good reason, the panic among Mexican survivors spread across the body-strewn summit, when it was determined that no quarter was being demonstrated with an utter ruthlessness by veteran American soldiers.

Captain Roswell S. Ripley, a member of General Pillow's staff, was shocked by what he saw: "Many Mexicans, in their flight, jumped down the steep eastern side of the rock, regardless of the height." The windows of the eastern edge of the easternmost building, overlooking the steep, rocky eastern slope, provided escape routes to quite a few desperate men hoping to avoid American bayonets, if one survived the jump to the ground below.

But this situation atop the embattled summit was not the usual panic of battle when a defensive position was out-flanked or overrun on a field of strife, but a rout born of a vicious no quarter policy: hence, a fully justified panic under the most grim circumstances, because prisoners were not being taken, as was customary in battle. Indeed, it was now obvious to the soldados that they could not surrender to the Americans who were taking few prisoners, and these were mostly officers.

As mentioned after the front-line defenders were swept aside from the parapet and terrace before the southward-facing front of the Military College, the cadets continued to fight back with spirit from good firing positions at the academy's windows and rooftops, both of the Castle and the Military College, and they now had to be pushed out of their defensive positions at the point of the bayonet.

Lieutenant Beauregard described the vicious struggle for possession of the darkened rooms inside the Castle, including the Military College: "we made another charge into some other parts of the building and bursting open the doors of several rooms filled with Mexican soldiers [mostly of the enlisted ranks] on their knees praying for mercy, and placing sentinels to protect them (whilst they little deserved it, after the cruel treatment of our wounded at Molino del Rey) I left them to search again for those stairs I had been looking for. I at last found them and rushed up them faster than I had ever ascended any flight of stairs before—but arrived only in time to see that Mexican tricolored flag being hauled down by Captain [John G. Barnard and] Those Mexican prisoners had been the cause of my disappointment," for not having captured the green-red-white flag that represented everything that the cadets loved.

With a humanitarian officer like Beauregard, a true Gallic gentleman and Creole officer, present, prisoners were taken instead of killed outright by enraged enlisted men, who were out-of-control. While most soldados in the Military College and Castle had either fled or surrendered by this time, the cadets still continued to fight against impossible odds. It is not known but perhaps some cadets struggled on against overpowering might at this time, because they had not realized that so many of their comrades had capitulated, fled for their lives, or were dispatched because of the savage no-quarter policy.

After all, primary points of resistance had collapsed in every sector, and the battle had turned into a panicked rout. Meanwhile, the cadets at the Military College, now surrounded by large numbers of swarming Yankees, continued to fight in outright desperation in their first battle, firing at the attackers who seemed to be everywhere. As mentioned, the vast majority of defenders were either fleeing or surrendering by this time. Even more, many of the garrison's officers had also either fled or surrendered by this time, leaving the men of the lower ranks, including the cadets, on their own: another fact that had led to an early collapse of resistance and caused the rout.

Therefore and perhaps unknown to them in the noise and confusion of a raging battle, the teenage cadets were now largely on their own, because their less determined elders in uniform, especially officers, had fled or submitted. Major General Bravo and the 40 officers were now entirely out of the fight, including the struggle for possession of the Military College, providing no orders or direction to the cadets who were still fighting back with enthusiasm.

Evidently, these officers had first banded together not long after the initial collapse of resistance along the inner wall that guaranteed the summit's defense was doomed. Here, they had sought shelter in a powder magazine to escape the attackers' unofficial no quarter policy that had resulted in the slaughter of a good many Mexican enlisted men of a lower class and darker skin tone. Without a chance or their own officers now available to lead them, the vast majority of soldados continued to flee and escape the enraged norteamericanos, who could not be stopped.

Even at this point, most cadets were still battling in the confines of the Military College, disputing its possession to the bitter end. However, a small number of cadets were evidently now also positioned in the tower on the summit's eastern side from where the large Mexican flag still flew high in the sulfurous air. It is not known if some cadets had been ordered into the tower as a secondary fall-back position to defend it, or if they had fallen back to rally in the tower during the confusion and chaos of battle. Even now and despite the flight of most defenders who were older and more experienced than themselves, the teenage cadets were putting up a spirited and organized resistance from the Military College and evidently some cadets at the Caballero Alto, while groups of soldados, perhaps including some cadets, also fought from the rooftops.

By this time, most members of the hard-hit garrison were running for their lives, after every defensive line of the inner wall and artillery positions had been pierced at multiple points by these North American devils, who seemingly had been unleashed from hell itself. Therefore, large numbers of General Bravo's men and officers were now only focused on attempting to save themselves by escaping so many war-hardened veterans, who utilized their steel bayonets with a lethal skill in dispatching a good many unfortunate soldados.

In their fury and determined intent to reap revenge, some attackers even bayoneted Mexican wounded men, despite their pleas for mercy in Spanish and perhaps broken words of English, lying on the ground, just like those soldados, who had earlier bayoneted American wounded "with a savage delight" at Molino del Rey. Clearly, the men of both sides in this cruel war had descended into outright savagery that was typical of racial and religious conflicts to this day: the ultimate tragedy of this increasingly vicious war between two neighboring republics.

Lieutenant John James Peck described the savage struggle after breaching the inner wall and swarming across the summit. He penned in a letter how: "At the crest of the hill the work was terrific, but the stormers succeeded in scaling the walls in spite of the iron and lead and rocks and clubs . . . General Bravo and forty officers were found [and taken prisoner] in a [powder] magazine" that was underground to provide protection from the swirling combat above them.

Private Richard Coulter, 2nd Pennsylvania, revealed in his journal how General Bravo and this large group of officers were spared because of their high rank unlike the lower-class and darker-colored enlisted men and also the unlucky young cadets, who became victims of the brutal no-quarter policy: "General Bravo and some officers were taken prisoners, but few others were taken alive."

General Bravo, the former dynamic partisan commander who had often outmaneuvered the Spanish Royalists during the bitter War for Independence and the republic's first vice president, no longer led the resistance effort. While he handed over his diamond studded sword in a formal gesture of submission, and these aristocratic Mexican officers, mostly lieutenants and captains, were taken prisoners, the boy cadets and other more determined fighting men, regulars, and a less number of National Guard troops, continued to battle against the odds in part because they were unaware of the surrender in the "fog" of battle.

This mass surrender of so many officers was another factor that explained why resistance had collapsed so quickly, leaving the common soldiers and the cadets to do or die in a lethal situation of no-quarter warfare. Small wonder that the enlisted men fled for their lives, when abandoned by their officers, which seemed to have been the case to a large extent: an unfortunate and deplorable situation for the young men and boys of the enlisted ranks that helped to set the stage for the deaths of a half dozen cadets and another humiliating disaster suffered by the hard-luck Mexican Army.

By this time, the terrace, plaza, and the smoke-covered crest of Chapultepec had been transformed into a gory slaughter pen, especially because of the unofficial "no quarter" policy. Even the Military College was full of dead and wounded men, including some teenage cadets. Surgeon Richard McSherry, a physician of Scotch-Irish descent and a founder of the Baltimore Academy of Medicine in Baltimore, Maryland, was sickened by what he shortly saw, because of the clumps of Mexican dead and wounded: "Their mangled bodies lay heaped in masses [but] some of them indeed were not yet dead, but were gasping in the last agonies, with their dark faces upturned to the sun, writhing and struggling in death, like fish thrown on shore by the angler. Crushed heads, shattered limbs, torn up bodies, with brains, hearts, and lungs exposed, and eyes torn from their sockets, were among the horrible visions" at Chapultepec.

Some of these men were tragic victims of the forgotten massacre at Chapultepec, including almost certainly some unfortunate cadets, who fell to bayonets and bullets while praying for mercy and deliverance. Clearly, Surgeon McSherry would not eventually administer to as many wounded Mexicans, if a conventional battle had been fought without the horror of an unofficial policy of "no quarter."

It is not known how many cadets were killed because of this brutal policy on the bloody morning of September 13.Some of the more humanitarian American soldiers, including devout Christians, were naturally hesitant about inflicting a fatal shot or savage bayonet thrust into the body of a small-sized cadet, especially the youngest ones who looked almost like children. Consequently, the moral consciences of some American soldiers rose to the fore when they saw these boyish cadets, and they questioned the morality of the vicious "no quarter" policy.

Some Americans, therefore, decided not to shoot or bayonet the finely-uniformed cadets in gray, because of their small size (smaller than the generally larger-boned, taller, more robust, and stronger American soldiers who hailed from a healthy climate) and extreme youth that the attackers noticed even amid the drifting smoke and chaos of battle.

Bitter Fighting Continues Atop the Embattled Summit

Because it could not be seen by them, General Scott's men gave little, if any, thought about the last Mexican flag (much smaller than the large national flag waving from the tower) flying from a window on the Castle's east side just east of the tower, except for one lone cadet, Juan Escutia. Among those few men still engaged in the fighting not concerned about their own safety and desiring to flee as quickly as possible, at least one officer, Captain Alvarado, implored the teenager to save himself by fleeing rearward.

However, Cadet Escutia was not about to flee like seemingly everyone else to escape the slaughter on the summit, despite resistance collapsing around him. After all, he could still not accept the unthinkable possibility that a righteous God would forsake the fighting men of a righteous, faith-based people, who had long devoted their lives to Catholicism, and turn away from brave soldados and cadets in their hour of need during their desperate last stand. Like other cadets, he knew that this was the most unjust war that America had ever waged.

But most of all, Escutia was dedicated to the religious-like principle of fighting to the very end, because it was a righteous duty and his burning obsession with saving the last red-green-white flag that still waved in defiance from the embattled summit: an all-consuming personal goal that was now extremely precious to him, because the sacred banner of silk represented all of Mexico and her people, who needed a measure of salvation like few others in this war against a far more powerful enemy.

Like other cadets still battling on the summit, Cadet Escutia felt that he was bound tightly by this elevated sense of honor and his orders to stand firm against the surging tide of blood-seeking attackers, even though hundreds of Mexican soldiers were now fleeing from Chapultepec that was doomed.

Nevertheless, Cadet Escutia was determined to continue to resist the invaders with every ounce and fiber of his strength, regardless of the situation or cost. If Mexico was to suffer still another disastrous defeat and to lose even more of its dignity, pride, and precious fighting men, then at least Cadet Juan Baptist Pascasio Escutia would have done his very best and part to preserve what relatively little honor and dignity that could be salvaged in such a humiliating no-win situation, because for all practical purposes Chapultepec had fallen by this time.

Like other cadets, especially in their first battle, Escutia almost certainly felt the same pangs of fear as other soldados, but he refused to become a captive of his natural fears and did not panic in this emergency situation. He no doubt had already seen the killing of some non-cadet comrades, who had been attempting to surrender to the infuriated Americans, whose bloodlust had reached unprecedented heights at Chapultepec. Escutia mustered the inner strength of his character and moral bearings to overcome his lingering fears on September 13, resisting the temptation to flee like almost everyone else: a courage that had risen to the fore in a true crisis situation, when the life of the young cadet hung in the balance.

Mortal Wounding of Cadet Agustín Melgar

It is not known but perhaps Cadet Escutia had witnessed the deaths of his comrades, including Cadet Agustín Melgar—the likeable young man who possessed an easy smile, and one of the most popular cadets—from faraway Chihuahua. Like Escutia, Melgar had embraced the pressing need to mount a determined defiance against the blue-uniformed interlopers to the very end.

Therefore and perhaps to honor his father's sacred memory, Lieutenant Colonel Esteban Melgar who had died in the service of his country, Melgar also refused (like Cadet Escutia) to forsake the failing resistance effort and run for his life: rather remarkable and courageous individual decisions, especially because no officers were nearby, because all hope for a successful defense had evaporated by this time, and seemingly everyone else was now attempting to escape the smoke-covered crest swarming with Americans as soon as possible.

By this time, the flat summit broiled by the hot September sun had become not only a raging battlefield, but also an ugly death-trap. Never forgetting his roots or family, Cadet Melgar was the son of an army lieutenant colonel whose early death had left him with only his mother, María de la Luz Sevilla, and his beloved siblings, Favor and Merced.

But most importantly, he was also left with an enduring legacy that remained alive and well at Chapultepec. Melgar was not only fighting for his beloved country on this nightmarish morning, but also for his father's good name and his beloved older sister, who had raised him after his parents' deaths. These sacred memories and enduring legacies of the past had to be protected at all costs, because of what they meant to Cadet Melgar, whose child-like innocence had been noted by one and all.

Refusing to desert his assigned defensive position as long as any rounds remained in his leather cartridge-box, Melgar fought with a fury for the land and people who he loved the most. After most defenders had fled to escape the summit, Melgar stubbornly maintained his ground with stoic resolution, waiting whatever harsh fate that was sure to shortly come his way, which was only a matter of time.

While American soldiers swarmed through the Military College and fought their way through the Castle complex and from room-to-room, Melgar eventually made his way to the large central room that served as the school dormitory, perhaps after ascertaining that a no-quarter policy had been declared, including on unlucky men who attempted in vain to surrender. Preparing to once again confront the Yankees, who were fast-approaching, he and some comrades hurriedly created a make-shift barricade from anything that could be quickly salvaged from nearby beds. Anything handy was hurriedly stacked as high as possible by the young men to create a breastwork that provided some meager protection against the onslaught.

While additional Americans poured into the Castle and just before he received his death stroke, Cadet Melgar loaded and fired his shortened musket as fast as possible at the Yankees. He might now have well wondered if he would ever again see the wide river valleys, beautiful prairies sprinkled with yellow and red wild flowers, and the cool pine forests of the rugged Sierra Madre Occidental Mountains, when the first spring rains brought new life to this land. He had once roamed this picturesque region as a romantic-minded youth, who loved nature and all its endless wonders.

But what no doubt gave Melgar his greatest inspiration, especially when the no win situation at Chapultepec grew darker and increasingly grim, were the many vivid memories of his beloved Cathedral of Chihuahua. Distinguished by a highly-decorative Spanish Baroque style, this magnificent Cathedral dominated the Plaza de Armas, which was located more than 1,000 miles away from the Military College, where he was destined to meet his tragic end. Although we do not know, these poignant religious influences and vivid memories might well have been some of the last thoughts of Cadet Melgar, who still defiantly refused to either retreat or surrender: the audacious decision which guaranteed that he was about to die for God and country on a remote hilltop far from home.

Suddenly, Cadet Melgar found himself entirely alone in the large dormitory of the Military College, after most, if not all, other soldados around him had been either killed, captured, or had fled to escape certain annihilation. At this time, there were just too many attackers, who were determined to reap their revenge on Mexicans, regardless of age or status.

About to be overwhelmed in defending the Military College as he had been initially ordered by his superiors, Melgar boldly faced the northern invaders of his beloved school that was so precious to him. Therefore, he fought back as if he himself alone now represented the entire Military College, and was now solely responsible for its welfare. All the while, Melgar kept his composure in the most dangerous of combat situations, displaying firm resolve and courage to the very end. All of a sudden, an American soldier, perhaps an officer or even a German or Irish immigrant, who spoke with a Green Isle brogue, dashed upon Melgar with a fixed bayonet. The young cadet promptly shot the attacker down with a well-placed shot.

But before he could reload what might have been his last cartridge, if any rounds remained in his leather cartridge-box by this time, a half dozen United States soldiers finally overwhelmed

Melgar. Enraged about his spirited defiance that had resulted in the cutting down of at least one of their comrades and perhaps additional men, the pitiless Americans bayoneted Cadet Melgar repeatedly, while he attempted in vain to fend off the jabbing blades of cold steel, almost like an ancient Aztec warrior under the blows of the Toledo steel swords of the Spanish Conquistadors. Melgar was cut down in a room—evidently the main cadet dormitory in the Castle's southeast section—with multiple wounds from a combination of bullets and bayonets. He finally fell to rise no more. Melgar dropped to the ground with his light gray uniform splashed with red.

Still refusing to forsake his beloved Military College, another defiant cadet, one of the youngest students, also met a grisly end like Melgar. Only age sixteen, he refused to entertain any thought of surrendering to the invaders, even when a group of Yankees, charging with leveled fixed bayonets, closed in on the lone cadet, who did not stand a chance. He was cocking his musket for taking still another shot at the attackers, when he was overwhelmed by a group of full-grown men, who were much larger and stronger than himself. Then, the lengthy blades of steel bayonets were repeatedly plunged through Melgar's body to end his life that he had sacrificed for what the faithful cadet had long loved the most: God, family, and country.

Meanwhile, watching the savage contest swirling atop the strategic hill through binoculars from the east, General Santa Anna could hardly believe his eyes at the alarming sight of blue-colored waves pouring over the crest of Chapultepec that he had long been convinced was impregnable. He then saw the United States flag raised from the tower on the summit's eastern side, announcing the winner of this intense fight.

In the end, Santa Anna had never believed that Chapultepec was General Scott's primary target on September 13 and not farther east on the city's south. Here, throughout the morning, he still waited in vain for the great attack that never came. As penned in his journal, Sergeant Thomas Barclay described how a German-born private named Henry Kelsar, of the 2nd Pennsylvania, played a memorable role "in hoisting the first [United States] flag which went up" the flagpole and then waved over the embattled summit of Chapultepec.

Clearly, for much too long, a smug Santa Anna, who had always overestimated his limited tactical and strategic abilities as a general, had continued to believe that the main attack was coming from the south. But, of course now when it was too late, he finally realized the full extent of his tactical error that had doomed Chapultepec, the Military College, and the cadets to an unkind fate. When Santa Anna realized that Chapultepec was the primary target on the morning of September 13, it was far too late for him to send reinforcements to assist the doomed defenders, including the cadets, who were on their own: the recipe that guaranteed that the garrison was destined to suffer a humiliating defeat.

The Sad End of Francisco Márquez

Unlucky cadets, now literally fighting against a tragic fate, caught by the swirl of the swiftly-moving Americans, who were now basically hunters seeking prey in the Castle, which had become the scene of urban combat, including inside of the Military College, were quickly dispatched with close-range shots or bayonets, while a few fortunate cadets were taken prisoner.

But nothing could save Cadet Francisco Márquez, who was a member of the First Company of Cadets. Although only age thirteen and appearing even younger with his boyish face that was moon-shaped and extremely innocent-looking, he was another defender who defiantly remained at his post and refused to run. He still maintained his position, while even the most seasoned fighting men withdrew without order or directives.

Cadet Márquez, the step son of a respected cavalry captain, met his grisly end in the eastern section of the summit, when overwhelmed by seemingly too many attackers to count. He was the youngest cadet, born on October 8, 1834, who was destined to die in this bloody battle less than a month before reaching his thirteenth birthday.

Márquez was one of the newest cadets, but Cadet Juan Escutia was actually the most recent cadet because he had been admitted to the school on September 8, 1847. Márquez had gained entry into the Military College on January 14, 1847, when this savage war had been still far-away from Mexico City. Márquez was later found riddled with bullets when his body lay on the hill's eastern slope: a located that revealed that the young cadet fought to the bitter end in this sector, where the last flurry of spirited resistance on the summit occurred.

What had started out as such a promising life when pretty Micaela Paniaguaand held her son during a solemn ceremonial baptismal in the quiet reverence in the Parochial Church of the Shrine of Guadalajara on October 18, 1834 ten days after his birth, finally ended in ugly, but heroic, fashion on the body-strewn hilltop.

A meager existing amount of primary evidence exists that some cadets, including Márquez, were trapped in the upper story of the Military College, after the Americans swarmed into the lower floors of the stately academy. Attackers had then poured up the stairs with fixed bayonets to eliminate deadly snipers on the rooftops and remaining pockets of resistance.

Large numbers of shouting and screaming Americans were soon swarming inside the Military College and wiping out the pockets of resistance. A few surviving cadets, consequently, followed Captain Alvarado to the windows of the last large building that overlooked the easternmost side in the hope of escaping the attackers. But as the multiple gunshot wounds to his body later verified when found by soldado prisoners who were used by the victorious Americans to bury the dead, Cadet Márquez was killed in close-range combat rather than falling on the eastern slope. This situation was contrary to the popular view that the young man jumped from the window of the easternmost building.

But, of course, the distinct possibility existed by Márquez was shot and then fell from the edge of the easternmost building to the slope below. If so, then it appears that the youngest cadet of those students killed this morning was perhaps obeying the orders of the captain, who he had followed to the window. Captain Alvarado's fate is not known, but it seems that he might have survived the attack. Since he was a fully-grown man, Captain Alvarado was larger-sized and more mature than the younger cadets. This evidence suggests that he was too big to fit through the window and make a leap to the eastern slope. Therefore, unlike Márquez, the captain evidently was captured when the Americans overran the upper part of the Castle.

If he had witnessed the last moments in the lives of his comrades, like Márquez, Cadet Escutia would have been horror-struck upon seeing the systematic deaths of his friends. He might have even seen the death of handsome Lieutenant de la Barrera, who had fought bravely at the battery (he was assigned to his battery, after having officially exited from the Military College less than a month before) near the front gate. The possibility existed that Escutia might have seen the fall of Cadet Márquez, when he tumbled out the window and down to the rocks on the steep eastern slope.

In having become one of the last defenders in the academy after the vast majority of defenders had already fled, the mortally wounded Melgar was destined to finally breathe his last breath as a prisoner at a makeshift hospital on September 14. Here, he died when only age fifteen.

Young and innocent Melgar never had a chance to wear his dress uniform on the final day of his short life: a neat, finely-tailored blue coat distinguished by a scarlet collar and white trousers to bestow a very stylish appearance that was most distinctive, especially while drilling and marching on the parade ground before the main entrance of the college on the southern terrace. Like the other cadets, Melgar wore the service dress uniform of gray when he had been fatally cut down by the attackers.

After having been felled by the Americans inside the Military College, the red trim, or piping, on the high, gray collar now matched the blood stains on Melgar's uniform. These red stains were especially conspicuous when splattered on his stylish gray pants that he had never imagined would be streaked with splashes of his own blood, when he had been first issued his trousers at a time when the future had seemed so bright.

Meanwhile, during the confusion of battle, Cadet Escutia hurriedly attempted to reload his cut-down "Brown Bess" musket to fire at additional attackers who were now swarming everywhere. Escutia was now entirely on his own. He could not go to Lieutenant de la Barrera, because his battery near the main gate, where the road ascended the southern slope, at the summit's edge before the front of the Military College, had been early overwhelmed. Here, Lieutenant de la Barrera, the devoted son of an equally brave father-general who had made a career of fighting with distinction, had been fatally cut down at the foremost defenses.

The feisty fighting spirit of Lieutenant de la Barrera, who had died while officially serving as a member of a combat engineer battalion, but at heart was still very much a member of the Military College, after having departed from the academy less than a month before with his promotion, had inspired the remaining survivors, especially those men who had seen him fall. All the while, surviving cadets continued to fight against the odds in the hope of saving Mexico City from the clutches of a far more powerful county bent on taking a broad swath of Mexico's lands, just as Texas had been stolen by massive United States intervention in support of the rebellious Anglo-Celts in 1836.

Embracing an invaluable leadership role in a true crisis situation, Escutia assisted younger cadets out of the remaining secure sections of the Military College in the nick of time just before the Americans reached them. By this time, the academy had become a death-trap. In literally saving the lives of less resourceful fellow cadets during the confusion, Escutia acted almost like a father figure. He provided timely assistance to the youngest cadets trapped inside the Military College, until the older cadet from Tepic found a way out that was not barred by United States soldiers. The exact fates of those youngest cadets, who Escutia had helped to escape the Military College, are not known.

Escaping cadets might have been quickly shot down or captured after escaping the school's claustrophobic rooms and then entering into the open plaza, where they suddenly became more vulnerable. If so, Escutia might have been shaken not only by the sight of the tragic fates of the youngest cadets, who he had just helped to slip out of the Military College, but also the equally dismal fates of fellow fighting men, who had been cut down by Yankees, bullets, and bayonets, inside the embattled academy.

After perhaps witnessing the sickening sights of Melgar and Barrera's deaths or other cadets, Escutia almost certainly became increasingly desperate. For ample good reason, Cadet Escutia felt more alone than ever before. Therefore, he might now have silently implored God's mercy and assistance to give him strength in this crisis situation. For a moment, he might have become briefly unnerved by what he saw, understanding the true horrors of war for the first time. The central tragedy of his beloved Military College having become a raging battleground and his friends dying in savage room-to-room combat was played out before his eyes had become something that was surreal, almost like a Greek tragedy from ancient times: the ugly and bloody last chapter of a dying nation.

Young Escutia had never seen anyone killed violently before, and the sight of his comrades having been slain came as a staggering blow that shattered his last remaining illusions. In such a situation when he was alone and the target of American bullets that whizzed around him, Escutia's thoughts very likely turned to God's salvation that awaited him in a better and more serene place that knew no wartime horrors and tragic deaths, especially no quarter warfare.

Of a thoughtful nature and philosophical bent despite his youth, Cadet Escutia perhaps briefly contemplated the war's horrors now on full display before his eyes. He now realized that this war had evolved into something terrible--an organized means of destroying his fellow man as rapidly as possible and in the cruelest way. He might have wondered how young men and boys of the same age could now slaughter each other with such brutality and an unthinking savagery, just because they had been born on opposite sides of the Río Grande River and possessed different religious faiths of the same God.

Perhaps Escutia wondered if so many of these young American and Mexican soldiers were in fact nothing more than manipulated pawns in a larger geopolitical and strategic game about the less admirable qualities of greed, national pride, and ambitious politicians on both sides of the borders? But Cadet Escutia had no time for deep reflection, because so few defenders were still offering resistance by this time and the Yankees seemed to be everywhere.

After most of Major General Bravo's panicked troops had fled to escape down the steep hillsides in a rout and after the last remaining cadets were wiped out (captured, killed, and wounded in that order) by this time, Cadet Escutia knew that he had to act and fast. A seemingly endless number of American troops, powder-grimed and angry-looking with revenge in their eyes, continued to swarm across the summit and ever closer to the lone cadet, who must have felt that

God and Santa Anna had now deserted him in his hour of greatest need.

With bullets peppering the stone walls around him and after assisting the youngest cadets to escape the Military College that was now full of Americans who systematically eliminated the few remaining defenders still fighting back against the surging blue tide, Cadet Escutia's only hope for escape by this time lay directly above him.

The desperate cadet decided to make a dash to a safe place not yet occupied by the Americans. Consequently, Escutia then raced up the stairs of the lengthy building, evidently a barracks, on the Castle's easternmost side. He now wanted to reach a small window where a Mexican flag (much smaller than the one that had flown from the tower) still flew in the smoky haze, while the last flurries of fighting continued to rage, before the attackers gained the roof and captured the precious silk flag of green, white, and red: the intoxicating and inspirational national colors that he loved like his long-suffering nation.

Against the odds, the breathless Escutia won his race to escape the encroaching groups of attackers, and just in time. He was now close to the highest point of Chapultepec after the tall tower, once he gained the highest roof on the eastern side of the Castle complex that overlooked the cliff that dropped straight down. It now must have seemed to the teenage cadet that he stood atop not only Chapultepec, but also the world that had now seemingly gone mad by the inflamed passions of a savage war that now seemed to have nothing to do with Christianity or man's love for his fellow man, as long preached by the self-sacrificing padres in his hometown of Tepic.

No doubt by this time, Cadet Escutia had become disillusioned by the nightmarish qualities of this vicious war that had brought forth so many horrors, after the tragic deaths of a large number of defenders, including cadets who had fought bravely, but in vain.

Were those once-cherished Christian principles of the first Spanish missionaries who had brought their beautiful faith to the virgin lands of New Spain now longer accepted and practiced by men today? Why had baby-faced Cadet Melgar, Lieutenant de la Barrera, and so many other fighting men, who loved Catholicism and their families, been sacrificed on the blood-soaked "Hill of the

Grasshoppers" that had possessed far too few of Mexico's sons to adequately defend? Had they become martyrs as much to an aggressive war by invaders as to the folly of the military and political leaders of Mexico, especially General Santa Anna? Why had not the deep religious beliefs and core moral values of two Christian nations prevailed instead of relying on the insanity of war that had led to the slaughter of a good many young men who were honorable citizens of two republics that had long embraced the faith of egalitarianism and the majestic eagle as their national symbols?

But like other fighting men, the far more pressing question that had to now dominant Cadet Escutia's mind and thoughts was a basic one: where were all of Chapultepec's defenders (regulars and National Guard troops) at this crucial moment? After all, hundreds of men had seemingly disappeared from the strategic summit, where every soldado was needed for a united defense to save the sacred hilltop of the ancient Aztec.

He almost certainly wondered where had all of Mexico's fighting men gone and why? Hundreds of soldados had disappeared from the summit like fleeting ghosts in the night, because they were not seen by him anywhere on the terrace or plaza of Chapultepec. Quite simply, there were not a sufficient number of dead and wounded fighting men for offer a rational explanation for so many soldados to have simply vanished from the summit at the most critical moment.

Indeed, by this time, almost all of the enlisted men who had been assigned to defending the summit had fled "Grasshopper Hill" never to return, deserting their assigned defensive positions and moral responsibilities to their fellow fighters, including the cadets.

Even the leading Mexican officers were now out of the fight. As mentioned, Major General Bravo and around 40 officers had found a safe refuge in an underground magazine to escape not only the slaughter, but also their moral duties and responsibilities to their men. Cadet Escutia had no idea that Bravo and his group of a large number of officers (more than three dozen) had already surrendered to a lieutenant (Charles B. Brower) of the 2nd New York Volunteers.

A humiliated, if not embarrassed, Major General Bravo had handed over his ornate sword to his captors at 9:30 a.m., which was near the time when the large Mexican tri-color was taken down and the United States flag then raised in its place atop the tower. A most disturbing sight to the band of surviving cadets, especially Escutia, which appeared to their shock, the red, white, and blue colors of "Old Glory" now flew from the top of the Caballero Alto for all to see. However, this sickening sight only fueled the fighting spirit and resolve of surviving cadets on this bloody morning.

Indeed, for Major General Bravo and some 40 officers, the war was over, although the resistance effort continued among only a relative handful of surviving defenders, who were still left alive on their lofty perch. In his journal, Sergeant Thomas Barclay wrote about the capture of the highest ranking officer at Chapultepec: "Gen. Bravo, a General of Division and one of the great men of Mexico" was taken prisoner.

Clearly, by this time, almost everyone on "Grasshopper Hill" now understood that Chapultepec was doomed, and that any continued resistance, no matter how gallant and heroic, was in vain. But this undeniable reality was still not accepted by the relatively few and last surviving Boy Cadets, who continued to fight back against the odds with spirit.

Although it could no longer be denied that this day was now lost, Cadet Escutia felt a sense of rejuvenation in viewing the inspiring sight of Mexico's flag still flowing proudly from a window on the castle's eastern side, after the garrison's main flag atop the tower had already been hauled down.

While the final combat continued to roar unabated below him, Escutia was determined to save this remaining small national flag at any cost. He looked lovingly upon the national tricolor flag that represented all that he loved and held dear in his heart. In this crisis situation and like other defenders, Escutia now more clearly understood the true meaning of the bright colors of red, green, and white as never before, because they represented everything that was good and pure to him.

And to Cadet Escutia, the colorful painted design of the magnificent Mexican Golden Eagle, perched majestically atop a large prickly pear as this symbolic national image appeared on the flag's center, was equally awe-inspiring in its sheer beauty. This enduring symbolism now represented a great deal to the young cadet, who had been born in Tepic, state of Nayarit, northwest of Mexico City, around 1830. Because he was now caught in a losing battle, he might have now known that he would never again see his native homeland and the Pacific's beautiful blue waters and crashing waves located just west of Tepic.

To Cadet Escutia when he knew beyond all doubt that Chapultepec was doomed, the last remaining national flag flying on the summit represented something sacred almost like Holy Mass at the beautiful house of worship, the Immaculate Conception Cathedral which had been built around 1750, in his hometown of Tepic.

With all his heart, the young cadet had loved the large flag—now shell-torn and captured—that had flown over the summit in such splendid defiance, as much as his family and Tepic. Escutia was determined that the last remaining silk flag of Mexico, the much smaller one hanging from the window on the east side of the easternmost building atop the summit, would not be despoiled and desecrated by the heretical Yankees, who worshiped the wrong God and religion in his mind.

If the young man knew about the lessons of ancient history, then perhaps he recalled the heroic memory of the diehard Jewish rebels who had defended the rocky hilltop of Masada, which was not unlike the last stand at Chapultepec in some ways. Indeed, against impossible odds, these brave Hebrew fighting men had remained defiant in the face of Rome's military might from 73 to 74 CE at the tragic end of the First Jewish-Roman War.

This courageous Jewish struggle for liberty by a surrounded band of Hebrew warriors and their wives and children might have flashed through his mind, if Cadet Escutia had read some of the ancient classics. It is not known, but Juan might have read a translated copy of Flavius Josephus, *The Jewish War*. If so, the he would have never forgotten the dramatic story about Masada and its doomed Jewish defenders, who had sacrificed themselves for the preservation of their ancient culture and religion.

When they were about to be overwhelmed by the elite fighting men of the Roman Legions after a lengthy siege, the Jewish rebels had decided to deny their enemies the full fruits of their inevitable victory. They, especially fathers with wives and daughters, were determined to never allow loved ones to become the slaves of the hated Romans.

And now surviving cadets, like Escutia, believed that Mexico and her people would be forever enslaved if conquered by the norteamericanos. After all, the Yankees still embraced the horrific institution of slavery to continue to reap great national wealth, unlike the more egalitarian Mexican nation (poor but proud of its distinguished anti-slavery heritage) that had ended slavery in mid-September 1829.

With many of his comrades dead and with additional American soldiers advancing up the stairs to attack the final defensive positions on the roof of the easternmost building, time was running out for Cadet Escutia. It was only a matter of time before a good many United States soldiers reached the top of the easternmost building of the Castle complex. And these veteran soldiers continued to be in no mood to take prisoners, after the American wounded had been killed at Molina de Rey. But, of course, Cadet Escutia knew nothing about this September 8 horror that had now transformed United States soldiers, even regulars, into brutal killers like Cortéz's Conquistadors so long ago.

For ample good reason, therefore, Cadet Escutia finally discovered the best—and only by this time--way out of the easternmost building to escape the triumphant Americans who were swarming seemingly everywhere. He had reached the roof of the decorative stone building that overlooked the steep and rocky eastern slope. Somehow, Escutia had escaped with his life, after having avoided the humiliation of surrender. Even now, perhaps the vivid images of the smiling faces of Melgar and de la Barrera raced through Escutia's mind, flashing before him as if they were still alive, while sprinting to reach the national flag that flew from the window on the building's eastern side.

He might have recalled the extreme acts of kindness of Lieutenant de la Barrea that often went against strict regulations, and the good humor of Cadet Melgar. But both of these highly-respected young men had been cut down in defending their Military College, and they would never see their homes again. Escutia knew that both friends of sterling moral and military qualities would have willingly sacrificed their own lives to save him in a comparable combat situation.

Perhaps as later claimed, Cadet Escutia even thought momentarily about committing suicide rather than suffering the supreme humiliation of submitting to the hated enemy. As he had early learned from reading the well-worn pages of his Holy Bible and from the teachings of his parish priest, he knew that for any human being to commit suicide was seen as a mortal sin in God's eyes.

Instead of willfully ending the promise of his young life, Escutia thought about what kind of personal act would now be necessary amid another humiliating defeat to vindicate the honor of Mexico, Chapultepec, and the fledgling Military College. In this crisis situation, he finally began to understand how some kind of brave deed and a dramatic gesture of defiance might still bestow a measure of honor and respect upon the all-but-defeated republic that had lost still another crushing defeat: the heartbreaking loss of the sacred ground of "Hill of the Grasshoppers."

To the young cadet from Tepic, the personal decision to deliberately go down fighting seemed like a relatively small and easy sacrifice—only one life in a nation of millions of people—to achieve something special that would be far grander and heroic in the larger scheme of things: something audacious and brave that might perhaps inspire an entire nation in its darkest hour. All alone and with the sound of American soldiers racing up the stairs of the easternmost building and getting ever-closer to the last rooftop still in Mexican hands, Cadet Escutia might have now uttered a solemn prayer and inhaled the fresh September air while atop the structure. But providing some comfort in such a no-win situation, he might also have now felt a significant uplifting in spirit for what he was about to do, almost like a dedicated novice priest about to preside over his first Holy Mass at a new church for impoverished people in a remote rural area of Mexico.

Escutia did not know for sure, but perhaps he had been first given life at Tepic by God for exactly this seemingly ill-fated moment when he suddenly found himself alone on a bleak rooftop at the eastern edge of Chapultepec, and his life had been deliberately set on a preordained course just for the final playing out of this dramatic role at Chapultepec. Had not the revered San Sebastian, a martyred Christian saint whose body had been filled with arrows because of the power of his faith in God, survived by a miracle, until finally killed upon the orders of a Roman emperor? Was not Jesus Christ crucified and gave his life to save mankind?

Of course, he did not know but perhaps God's mysterious ways, which Cadet Escutia could never hope to fully comprehend, were somehow personified in what would be the most desperate of individual acts performed by any soldier at Chapultepec, and one that his long-suffering nation would never forget. In this way, perhaps young Escutia might have believed that he would be emulating the heroic self-sacrifice of those revered Catholic saints, who had bravely died for their religious faith that could not be broken.

Nevertheless, the young man's resolution for the undertaking of a dramatic final act of defiance and spiritual redemption (symbolically on behalf of a dying nation and army) became stronger, while he raced across the roof toward the small red-white-green flag that was still hanging from the window overlooking the steep eastern slope. It is not known but perhaps a strange calm (a final stoic acceptance of his ultimate heroic fate., although it was a tragic one) now possessed the teenage cadet to consume him like a comfortable cloak to bestow a sense of peace and well-being, as if God himself had now suddenly touched his shoulder and blessed him in his darkest hour.

In a strange way, he seemed almost to have now moved beyond normal limits of time, place, and space, feeling somehow that God had given him an inner strength and spiritual calm for what he was about to do, because it was a special mission of heroic self-sacrifice that he considered was absolutely necessary on behalf of his nearly-vanquished nation.

Most important for him personally, Cadet Escutia now felt that he was doing the right thing in overall spiritual terms, however frowned upon in the eyes of his family, people, and even God. But on this terrible morning just outside Mexico City, these were desperate circumstances in which past teachings of a more peaceful time and place no longer applied as before. Although Major General Bravo and so many other defenders had already surrendered on the parade ground, the terrace, and in the plaza, Escutia was still not about to give up or surrender.

Again, Chapultepec had all but fallen by this time. The largest Mexican flag flying at Chapultepec had already been lowered from the exquisite tower and handed over to the detested Americans, who raised a great triumph cheer that sent chills down the backs of surviving soldados who were sickened by the sound. This chorus of cheers echoed over the ancient hilltop of the Aztec now strewn with bodies, far more Mexicans, including cadets, than Americans.

In consequence and despite the danger, the young cadet from Tepic was still determined to gain possession of the last national colors still flying at Chapultepec at any cost. Now possessed with the frantic determination that the blood-stained hands of the norteamericano heretics would never touch the last free-flying banner of Mexico that flew from the summit and with a careful reverence for what was most sacred, as taught at the Military College, he finally gained the point where the flag still waved over the eastern slope.

In one swift motion, Escutia then reached down and grabbed the small flagpole. Cadet Escutia then pulled the national flag that hung from a window overlooking the eastern slope to him. The young cadet tripped the sacred banner from its wooden staff. With a sigh of relief and sense of inner calm, he now possessed his nation's colors and the last one not captured on the summit.

It is not known but perhaps at this time Escutia might have recalled the stories of how other soldados, usually officers or members of color guards, had courageously saved the national flags from capture during hand-to-hand combat in the recent battles for possession of Mexico City.

After the flag had been almost lovingly taken down by him in a saving gesture, he then closely embraced its warm folds of silk with a passion that brought instant exhilaration, almost as if the colorful banner was a young, pretty female lover from Tepic. The flag's beauty and bright colors—the eagle and snake design had been hand-painted on the center by skilled artists—also no doubt gave him a warm inner sense of comfort. Like enveloped in a holy shroud, he literally emerged himself into the warmth of its red, white, and green silken folds to make doubly sure that he never lost his grip on this sacred banner, so that it would not slip out of his hands to be captured as a trophy by the detested Americans.

With his friends and fellow cadets having become prisoners or now lying dead in ever-widening pools of blood like Lieutenant de la Barrera and Melgar, who had given their all to save their Military College, the national flag had now become his only friend on the high rooftop, while Cadet Escutia stood alone atop the red-tiled roof on the Castle's eastern side. He almost seemed to now have become part of the fabric of the flag's bright colors, which represented all that was good about Mexico and her people.

With cheering Americans, knowing that they had won still another resounding victory—perhaps the most impressive one of all—that ensured Mexico City's fall, surging up the staircase, there now seemed to be absolutely no hope for Escutia to escape from the isolated rooftop of the easternmost building. All the while, the footsteps, cheers, and shouts of United States soldiers charging up the stairs grew louder and more ominous. No doubt when on his own and facing a truly frightening situation from which there appeared no escape, a degree of fear (which was only natural under the circumstances) now affected Cadet Escutia. However, he kept his head in a desperate and doomed situation, while alone on the rooftop high above the summit, despite somewhat bewildered in the confusion of his first fight by the unpredictable swirl of battle that had a life of his own.

It is not known, but perhaps Escutia now might have believed that his fate had been preordained like that of Chapultepec itself. When growing up in Tepic, he might have dreamed of the glory of battle of famous heroes, including the legendary El Cid in courageously fighting the Islamic Moors to save Spain for Christianity, while other boys had played childish games when they had been consumed childish thoughts.

As the son of a highly-respected military man, he might have read Homer's *Iliad*, which chronicled the most famous stories of ancient western history. The glowing tales of the ancient Greek warriors, especially the greatest of all fighting men, Achilles, might have caused him to dream as a boy about the alleged glory and majesty of war that he now realized were utterly false and a complete lie: dangerous youthful illusions that had been fully exposed in the horror of this morning's vicious combat, including the unofficial American policy of "no quarter" that had transformed the hilltop into a gory killing field. Before meeting the Yankees in combat, Juan perhaps had even imagined that he was a modern-day Achilles, who had won everlasting fame for his battlefield heroics long celebrated in the ancient Greek world that was no more.

But as young Juan had discovered in his first battle to his horror, especially after having seen the grisly deaths (bayoneted and shown no quarter) of fellow cadets, there was simply no romance or glory in the mortal combat that he had witnessed at Chapultepec. As he now fully realized, such long-existing romantic concepts were nothing, but a dangerous illusions and myths that had fooled young men, regardless of race and culture, since time immemorial. As a cruel fate would have it, this was especially the case with the cadets, who had known nothing about the ugly truths the horrors of war until this morning in hell.

Sadly, such naïve delusions that revealed the depth of youthful innocence had already played a part in the deaths of his fellow cadets, who had only recently believed that war was nothing more than a romantic, glorious adventure without bloodshed or grievous losses that had already decimated Chapultepec's garrison.

Indeed, the grotesque, ugly realities of this bloody morning were in fact far more horrible than could have been possibly imagined by the cadets before the final showdown at Chapultepec: young men and boys with arms, heads and legs blown off; steel bayonets plunged into bellies and into faces to knock-out teeth and eye balls, and musket-butts shattering skulls like egg shells, intestines spilling out from saber and bayonet cuts, and grown men screaming for mercy, praying for help, and crying out to see their mothers one last time before they died. Only belatedly, Cadet Juan Escutia realized that there were no Homeric glories or romance in this terrible war, as he had once imagined during his peaceful childhood days at Tepic.

Now fully realized but only belatedly, Escutia was disgusted by the high price that had to be paid for the mistakes of leadership, because he had seen so many young comrades, including fellow cadets, taken from him and this world of sorrow on this nightmarish morning. For such reasons, Cadet Escutia now only wanted a means to gain a measure of redemption and distinguish himself by some final means of preserving the Military College's and Mexico's honor. This was Escutia's last opportunity and he knew it, before the awful destructiveness of this vicious war finally consumed and destroyed him like other many others, including his best friends who were no more.

Then, all of a sudden and just before it was too late, Cadet Escutia dashed along the eastern edge of the red-tiled roof with his flag in his possession to save the precious national banner, because additional Yankees had gained the roof by this time. Then, he wrapped the white-red-green flag more tightly around the upper part of his body to make it more secure around his slim body that was decidedly boyish and youthful, while he fronted the eastern edge of the Lomas de Chapultepec that overlooked the steep, rocky eastern slope.

In saving the national colors from capture, Cadet Escutia emulated the recent heroics of a brave lieutenant, of the Mina National Guard Artillery (whose members had manned the guns of Chapultepec, who saved his unit's colors by wrapping them around his body, before carrying the flag to safety with the victorious Yankees in close pursuit.

In addition, the commander of the decimated San Blas Battalion (three companies that had been annihilated by the attackers on the slopes below Chapultepec's crest), Felipe de Santiago Xicoténcatl, had saved his command's flag by wrapping it around his body and narrowly escaping in the nick of time. But the courageous hero later died from multiple wounds, after his heroics and noble self-sacrifice.

Demonstrating cat-like agility while on the move to evade the increasing numbers of fast-moving Yankees, an increasingly desperate Juan scampered across the thick red tiles of the rooftop, keeping his balance while escaping the encroaching American soldiers, who continued to systematically eliminate any defenders who they discovered. The odds of not only escaping but also surviving were now stacked ever higher against him. However, Juan avoided almost certain death by staying on the move.

However, the grim law of averages was gradually catching up to Cadet Escutia with each passing second. Indeed, it was only a matter of time before the rooftop was completely overwhelmed by additional Yankees, who steadily gained the roof of the easternmost building, which overlooked the eastern slope and the long drop down. All the while, the victory cheers from the Americans echoed louder over the ancient hilltop of the Aztec, signaling a sickening end for Chapultepec's spirited defense and its heroic defenders.

These ill-fated defenders had already been eliminated (killed, wounded, or captured) nearly to the last man. Not one, but two empires of Mexico had been crushed by the relentless advance of foreign invaders of European descent: tragic end which had been played out at or near Mexico City, as a strange destiny would have it.

Meanwhile, the victors of Chapultepec celebrated their sparkling success, which a dismayed Cadet Escutia witnessed high above from atop the red-tiled roof to his ever-lasting disgust. Sergeant Thomas Barclay penned in his journal how some soldiers "were firing upon the enemy retreating across the fields [after they had fled from the summit while]Others [were] watching the chase. Some bread and a barrel of aguardiente [sugar cane rum] attracted the attention of others. The building [Castle] and library [of the Military College] were also ransacked" by American soldiers, who had carried the hilltop by storm.

Clearly, the majestic Golden Mexican Eagle of the ancient Aztec no longer protected this sacred and special place called Chapultepec, and no more glory remained to be salvaged by the defeated defenders, or so it seemed at this time.

Chapter IV

A Final Symbolic and Heroic Act of Defiance

With Mexico's beautiful flag that had been flying from a window still wrapped around his upper body, Cadet Escutia finally reached a point at the extreme edge of the easternmost building of the Castle complex, while looking for a way to escape the ever-encroaching Yankees and save the precious national banner.

To the young man from Tepic, it now must have appeared that he was the last survivor of the Chapultepec garrison except for the large number of prisoners, including Major General Bravo, who were being collected in the plaza below the high rooftop. Despite the fact that Chapultepec had fallen and the vast majority of garrison members had been killed, wounded, or captured by this time, Escutia was still motivated by a fierce pride in country, his Military College, and his role as a cadet that designated him as a future leader.

He hated the Yanqui invaders for systematically destroying his country and the always seemingly unprepared army, which had taken beating in every battle. The mere thought of norteamericanos capturing the last national flag of Chapultepec had made Escutia sick to his stomach, and he had acted accordingly.

As he realized, these hard-fighting men from the north were much like the Spanish Conquistadors, because they were determined to subjugate Mexico City and its people, who he loved with all his heart. In part because he represented the Military College, this determined cadet still desired to do something heroically symbolic to demonstrate the full measure of his devotion to his country not only to the enemy, but also to the nation's corrupt leaders, especially Santa Anna, and the young man's faith-hearted elders, military and civilian. After all, they had doomed Mexico to an early death and their patriotism had quickly faded away because of the army's defeats and failures to stop General Scott's forces.

On the top tier of the eastern edge of the easternmost building and with even more victorious Americans approaching, the breathless Escutia had little time to peer down to survey the long drop all the way down to the steep eastern slope of "Grasshopper Hill." Cadet Escutia was now on the edge of the steepest and most rocky side of the Lomas de Chapultepec. At this point, the sharp drop was straight down to the rocky cliff, which was devoid of trees and underbrush that was unable to grow on the rocky ground, and because of the terrain's steepness.

At this time, the young cadet from Tepic might have thought about the sickening sight of his beloved Military College, now torn and smashed from the bombardment, and the parade ground covered with dead and wounded soldados. The enemy's "Star-Spangled Banner" now waved atop the tower on the compound's east side, situated just west of his rooftop location on Chapultepec's easternmost building, for all to see. All such disgusting sights that revealed evidence of still another gringo victory were intolerable to Escutia, fueling his resolve to never relinquish the small national flag to the Yankees. Escutia was determined that he or this precious banner would never be taken by the invaders, who had already vanquished everything in their path.

Now that he was all alone on the rooftop, perhaps Escutia felt a desire—an inexplicable strong pull—to join his friends and comrades, like Cadets Melgar and Montes de Oca, Suárez, in a soldiers' heaven, a modern Valhalla (the hall for courageous Viking warriors killed in battle), or another such hallowed final resting place for ancient Aztec warriors.

Cadet Escutia would never forget his fellow cadets and their high sacrifice, or why they had died on this bloody morning. By this time, the prestigious military academy and the Cadet Corps, and especially his lost comrades who he had loved like brothers, were now all gone, and nothing more than fond memories of the past, when the world had made more sense to the young man. But Escutia was now determined that the deceased cadets and their battered Military College would never be forgotten.

It was this special place, Chapultepec, and his home that was the Military College, where he truly belonged not only in life, but also in death. Therefore, these two hallowed places, located so far from his native homeland, now represented everything of value to him, and their mutual loss came as crushing blows that had sent him reeling. Consequently, this sacred hilltop of the ancient Aztec was where he now preferred to die more than any other spot on the face of the earth, especially in defending his country to his last breath.

By sacrificing his life here at Chapultepec on this terrible morning when so much was at stake, then Cadet Escutia knew that he would be allowed to once again rejoin his lost comrades by way of a heroic soldier's death, Lieutenant de la Barrera and Cadets Melgar, Suárez, Montes de Oca, and Márquez, who were no more. They had all been fatally cut down by this time. Only Melgar still breathed life, but he had been mortally wounded. Melgar was destined to die on the following day.

For all time in some far-away soldado Valhalla in the sky, then they at least would all be together again as at Chapultepec, where they had fought, died, and belonged together in the end and forever more. Like close family members who loved each other and stayed together even in the most challenging crisis situations, so the cadets would be side-by-side forever and united by ties that could not be broken.

Indeed, the cadets were more than simply brothers in arms, but also best friends and much like loving family members, who had been united by deep, but invisible, bonds that could not have been so strongly forged in civilian life. And like the members of a good family united together by the bonds of blood and love, they had stayed together during the darkest crisis and to the bitter end at Chapultepec.

As if preparing for a routine inspection by de la Barrera last spring, Escutia now might have now straightened out his light gray frock coat one last time to appear as military-like as possible, after having reached the east side of the easternmost building and caught his breath. His service uniform of gray looked pristine and clean compared to the blood-splattered uniform coats of his fallen friends scattered in the plaza and buildings, including the Military College, below the rooftop.

Cadet Escutia stood by himself above the looming steep eastern cliff of Lomis de Chapultepec under the hot Mexican sun, while waves of battle-smoke continued to rise high in the sky, almost as if a strange destiny or God had placed him at this point and at this exact moment for a special symbolic purpose. For the young cadet who now faced too many approaching Americans who were drawing ever-nearer, there was nowhere else for him to now go from the edge of the exposed tiled rooftop, but straight down.

Escutia now faced the steepest and rockiest side on the commanding hill, the eastern slope .Engineer Pierre Gustave Toutant Beauregard, one of General Scott's most promising engineers, described the eastern side as "a very precipitous side of the hill."Less than two miles to the northeast, the sight of Mexico City could be seen in the distance by Escutia: a view that must have emboldened and inspired the young cadet in part because he had fought so hard to save the city and its people. At the forbidding edge of the Castle's eastern side during his final moments on earth and about to meet his ultimate fate, destiny, and Maker, Cadet Escutia now looked almost as if he was about to answer roll call on the parade ground before the Military College like on so many past mornings under the warm Mexican sun.

Not found or mentioned in any military textbook or manual of any nation's army in the world, Escutia embraced his special mission that he had decided upon on his own: to save Chapultepec's last national flag by keeping it out of the enemy's hand for as long as possible, which meant that he had to depart the summit. He loved his family and life itself, but something larger and even more important (an incalculable urge and magnetic-like pull) now beckoned to him, and he could not possibly explain the power of this strange force.

Then, the inevitable finally happened when the first group of American soldiers approached to within close range of Escutia, after they had surged across the rooftop with bayonets flashing in the sun. They immediately opened fire on the lone cadet, who was completely on his own and without assistance by this time. Then, the inevitable finally happened. Cadet Escutia was shot by at least one member of a New York Regiment, Quitman's Division.

But the young man was not killed by the shot, despite hit at close range. Escutia, therefore, was almost certainly seriously wounded, and his chances of survival were now reduced to practically zero, if he remained on the open rooftop. However, Cadet Escutia was not about to give up and surrender to the advancing norteamericanos.

The New York soldiers, volunteers who possessed less training and discipline than regulars, had gained the roof to eliminate the last defenders, until only Escutia remained standing in defiance against impossible odds. As mentioned by this time, the Americans were in a vengeful mood for what had happened on the gory field of Molino del Rey, and this feeling had only increased since storming the summit. At this time and unfortunately for Cadet Escutia, the New York Volunteers were also incensed because their beloved commander, Lieutenant Colonel Charles Baxter, had fallen mortally wounded at the head of his regiment during this morning's assault. Even more, other popular officers of the New York Volunteers had been killed, including Captain Van O'Linda and Lieutenant James W. Cantey, in the attack.

But despite the loss of such fine leaders who had bravely led the way, the Empire State soldiers had stormed the heights and then raised a United States flag on the summit in triumph. And other respected New York officers had been cut down mortally wounded during the assault, like Captain Charles H. Pierson.

Therefore, after bitter hand-to-hand combat that had cost additional lives, the New York Volunteers (more the case in regard to the enlisted men rather than officers) were bent on revenge. The enraged enlisted men, who were from the lower order of society compared to their wealthier officers, called for the taking additional Mexican lives to satisfy their bloodlust, although Chapultepec had already fallen by this time.

Significantly, all available evidence has indicated that these revenge-seekers from New York (volunteers who were far more prone to unleashing "no quarter" warfare than the disciplined regulars) were most responsible for killing the last resisting Boy Cadets, including the mortal wounding of Cadet Escutia.

Indeed, many New Yorkers were now taking no prisoners this morning in hell: the antithesis of the myth that the teenage cadets committed suicide in unison by "stabbing themselves," or allegedly in leaping off the building's eastern edge together and down onto the eastern slope together, as if by prearranged by an alleged suicidal pact.

But both of these improbable scenarios were enduring myths with no validity or substance whatsoever, because the best evidence and documentation have revealed that the six cadets were killed (5) or mortally wounded (1) in combat situations, while defending themselves and their assigned positions to the bitter end.

A Fatal Shot and the End of a Young Cadet and His Dreams

After having been shot by a New York soldier, Cadet Escutia either then fell or deliberately jumped (or a combination of the two) from the highest roof from the eastern edge of Chapultepec Castle. In the end and most important, he had faithfully remained true to his assignment of protecting the Castle and Chapultepec with his life. It is not known if Escutia was asked to surrender, or if he was shot out-of-hand by revenge-seeking Americans, because other Mexican fighting men, including cadets, were captured by the New Yorkers, who swarmed over the rooftop to wipe out the last remaining resistance.

While they took other prisoners from the rooftop, United States soldiers below could hardly believe their eyes at the incredible sight: a young cadet, wearing a neat, gray service uniform, leaping from the rooftop and hurling down like a rock from the easternmost building's edge to shortly meet an inevitable tragic fate upon hitting the jagged ground below, while encased in the flowing, soft folds of red, white, and green silk that flapped around him like a holy shroud from the Cathedral of Saint John the Baptist in Turin, northern Italy. He closely embraced the flapping folds of the flag all the way down in a one-way journey of no return.

In falling through the air at a rapid rate in the descent toward the rocks along the eastern slope, the young cadet perhaps even felt a certain sense of a peace by the heroic symbolism of his last act of defiance on this earth, while wrapped within the comforting cool silk of the flag that he had saved by keeping it out of the Yankees' hands: a final victory to Cadet Escutia, which made him proud. After all, he had achieved the only triumph that was now possible under the most disadvantageous circumstances: a final act of noble and heroic self-sacrifice because he loved his country and people more than life itself.

On this savage morning that was so disastrous for Mexico's fortunes, Escutia had decided on his own free will to embark upon the most desperate of acts that would not be forgotten by the fighting men on both sides. It is not known, but he might have gained some solace in perhaps still feeling an inexplicable sense of comfort in the sacred memory of having long silently knelt in strict observance of Holy Mass in the beautiful Cathedral of Tepic, where he had come to love God and his tender mercies, before the war's insanity had descended to change his life forever.

Almost certainly while falling from the eastern edge of the easternmost building perched atop the summit and like in comparable situations as experienced by others when near death, the entire course of Cadet Juan's brief life of nineteen years might have flashed before him. Consequently, for one last time, he might have thought about his loving parents, dignified Antonio Escutia and his always-smiling mother María Dolores Martínez, who never missed a Holy Mass or uttered a profane word.

Most of all, he fully realized that he would never see his family or his native homeland again.P erhaps if he was fortunate, his family in distant Tepic might hear of his defiant heroics at the end from some lucky survivor of what was the miserable defeat at Chapultepec. Perhaps Juan's family would bring the young man's body back for a proper burial in Tepic instead of being left lying forever in a lonely grave far from home. But for now during his descent through the air toward the rocky eastern slope and as long advised by his parish priest, he totally relied upon the reassuring comfort of "sea pordios," or leave it to God.

Cadet Escutia's fatal fall—in essence a spiritual descent—from the roof on eastern side of the easternmost building was most symbolic for many reasons. His dramatic last gesture of salvaging the last measure of the nation's lost honor and dignity—a notable personal victory in itself—by saving the national flag was even more significant in overall symbolic terms than the lowering of the main Mexican flag, which had been long flying in a silent majesty over the summit from the high tower.

After this main flag had been hauled down by the victors and as mentioned, Cadet Escutia's small national flag now far more profoundly symbolized a spirited last-ditch defiance in the face of the tragic defeat. Indeed, by a symbolic personal sacrifice in the most dramatic possible fashion by the fateful leap into the unknown of a single boyish-looking cadet, he made a profound personal statement and sacrifice that was as meaningful as it was significant.

In addition, Escutia's downward plunge toward the eastern slope was actually in keeping with the final actions of many ancient Roman commanders on past battlefields. They had committed suicide rather than suffer the humiliation of capture by the enemy, who they had considered barbarians, in order to preserve personal honor and dignity. In AD 9, for instance, Publius Quinctilius Varus fell on his sword to commit suicide, when his three legions were surrounded in Germany's Teutoburg Forest and then slaughtered to the last man by large numbers of German tribesmen.

Therefore, in ancient times, suicide was not considered a disgrace to a military man as in modern times, but a necessity under dire circumstances. Even Alexander the Great, when ill with the fever that eventually took his life in Babylon, had attempted to commit suicide by crawling to the Euphrates River to drown himself, before his wife Rhoxana, of a different race and culture, rescued him.

But in fact, Escutia accomplished much more than Varuis in the darkness of the Teutoburg Force. By his final act, Escutia ensured that he and the national colors would not be captured and humiliated, while providing Mexico with a heroic example by a heroic self-sacrifice in his leap of death. Most of all, Escutia and other cadets died in the hope that Mexico would survive and live forever.

Analogies to the Mythical Icarus

In some ways and even more, Escutia's lengthy fall from the highest edge of the easternmost building on the commanding hilltop was almost like the immortal fable of ancient Greek mythology about the ill-fated son of Daedalus, Icarus. Icarus had been warned of the great risks of excessive over-ambition by daring to fly too close to the sun, when the wax of his self-made wings melted and he plunged to earth.

But the fall of Escutia, who was likewise ambitious like Icarus and desired to perform great deeds, was not a myth. Likewise, his drop onto the rocks below was destined to be fatal, proving in part that the ambitious cadet also soared too high. Even more, the original site of Mexico City had been a sacred place of worship to the Aztec Sun God, Huitzilopochtli, who had cleverly taken the shape of an eagle and then flew toward the blazing sun like Icarus.

Indeed, Cadet Escutia's sharp fall onto the rocks strewn across the eastern slope was not unlike the time-honored fable of Icarus, symbolizing the high price of excessive courage. And as noted, the young man from Tepic had long possessed aspirations of reaching greater heights in the military.

Symbolically, Escutia had fallen from the highest point, after the tower known as Caballero Alto, for miles around. But while Mexico City was destined to fall in the days ahead, the legacies of the heroic Boy Cadets, who died in attempting to save the capital city and their people from the invaders, were destined to rise once again like a phoenix emerging out of the ashes of a disastrous defeat that had doomed the capital city.

Fated to die once he leaped from the edge to seal his fate, Escutia had saved not only his nation's flag, but also his nation's sacred honor by his heroic act of noble self-sacrifice: an enduring heroic lesson and core value that had been long taught at the Military College to the young cadets, who had learned their lessons well, because they had demonstrated supreme devotion to their chosen professions and school on bloody September 13.

Clearly, by any measure, cadet Escutia's final sacrifice was most symbolic. No other Chapultepec defender had performed such a symbolic or more dramatic act during the rout of so many panicked soldados, who had left the members of the Cadet Corps at the Military College to fight and die largely on their own. Consequently, in the end, Escutia paid the ultimate price partly because of the rapid collapse of resistance and panic, when his young body crashed on the sharp rocks of the eastern slope. It is not known if the brave cadet was killed instantly upon impact, or lingered in severe pain for an unknown period of time. Most importantly, Cadet Escutia had died for the sins of Mexico's top leaders, especially military, who had failed the fighting men in the ranks.

The Body-Strewn Rocky Eastern Slope of Chapultepec

Very likely, the courageous cadet from Tepic breathed life on the eastern slope for only a short time. Just before he faded away and passed away like so many heroic defenders of Chapultepec, Escutia might have thought about his happy childhood days in Tepic, before the war had suddenly descended upon the ancient land of Montezuma with a vengeance. Like Mexico and its army in the end, Cadet Escutia had also been sacrificed by a cruel fate and circumstances beyond his control.

With bones and a body broken from hitting the rocks on the hill's eastern slope not far from where Cadet Francisco Márquez, who would never see his native Guadalajara again, lay with his body riddled with bullets. Almost certainly, Márquez had been shot by the same soldiers, the incensed New Yorkers, who had shot Cadet Escutia from the same rooftop.

Knowing that death was now swiftly on its way while his body lay battered on the eastern slope, Escutia might have reflected back on what he had loved most in life. Before he breathed his last, Juan Escutia perhaps thought about the beauty of the green hills surrounding Tepic and the fresh waters of the Rio Mololoa, with its shady banks lined with tall cottonwoods, which flowed lazily through Tepic, a Nahuatl word. This ancient river, where an occasional crocodile was seen in its waters, flowed through the town to give ever-lasting life to the farming community and provide fresh fish to the people.

Meanwhile, the scorching heat of this terrible September day at Chapultepec might have briefly faded away from the tortured thoughts of this young cadet lying battered on the rocky slope, especially if he recalled the soothing cool of the swaying tall pines in the windswept mountains of the La Laguna de Santa María and the La Sierra de San Juan, which overlooked the community of Tepic. If still alive after his fall, then perhaps Escutia now imagined or wished that he was now lying in the soft, thick grass of the high country meadows swept by refreshing breezes to ease the scorching midday heat.

If still breathing and fading in and out of consciousness at this time, Cadet Escutia might have felt like his soul and spirit were about to be transported back home to Nayarit's green mountains, groves of stately pines in the cool highlands, and his loving family to be reunited once again in domestic bliss. For one last time, he might now have looked up at the bright and cloudless sky over Chapultepec that was as clear and blue as the Pacific near Tepic.

The young cadet had fallen far in his long, one-way descent to the rugged eastern slope, but the luminous sky over Mexico City now beckoned toward to a better world without the horrors of war. God's paradise now awaited him, because Escutia had always led a righteous and moral life, as he had been taught by his parents and Tepic's priests for as long as he could remember.

The projectile-scarred Chapultepec Castle, which had been transformed into a gory battlefield, might have reminded him of one of the steeples of his beloved Tepic Cathedral. But he knew that the Chapultepec chapter of his life was over forever. While lingering near death on the eastern slope, Escutia might have felt like he was also drifting back to that beautiful church in his native homeland by the hand of God.

Then, after perhaps saying a final prayer, Cadet Escutia knew that the end was fast-approaching and only a matter of time. But he might have possessed just enough physical strength remaining to perhaps tightly clutch a medal of the Virgin Mary, given him by his ever-stoic mother María or another family member, for comfort and solace in his final moments, while his life slowly faded away. The young cadet's loving parents had always sacrificed everything for him and had only wanted only the best for Juan, but destiny itself seemed to have beckoned him for him to play another role at this ancient place called Chapultepec.

A fresh-faced, handsome youth, Juan might have looked skyward one last time, as if beckoning for some kind of a holy deliverance from God, before he died. If so, then the cadet might have asked God for mercy, hoping death would relieve him of his suffering.

High in the cloudless sky, he might have caught sight of a Mexican Golden Eagle gliding high overhead in blue skies with outstretched wings like a guardian angel of the republic. This beautiful Mexican Golden Eagle—just like the one painted on the precious flag of green, white, and red that he still clutched in a loosening grip—might have been the last thing that Cadet Escutia saw on this earth. Far from his family and comrades while feeling the warm silk of the sacred national flag, Escutia finally died. He had given his all to God and country. Escutia was the last cadet of the five who sacrificed their lives on the battlefield this morning, while a sixth cadet, Melgar, was destined to die on September 14.

Here, on the body-strewn eastern slope and on rocks now stained with his blood, Juan's lifeless body still lay protectively over his nation's tri-color flag that represented the beloved homeland for which he had given his life. At least to his way-of-thinking, Cadet Escutia had died without his national flag having ever been desecrated by the norteamericanos: for the young man, a victory in itself and no small accomplishment under the circumstances.

In far-away Tepic, María Dolores Martínez's dark prophetic vision that her son would never return home and that she would never see Juan again was fulfilled on this tragic morning. She would never be the same after the loss of his favorite son. Perhaps the spirit of Our Lady of Guadalupe now shed a tear for Chapultepec's fallen cadets who were no more.

Grim Final Totals of a Futile Resistance in Defending the Sacred Fatherland

Meanwhile, by 9:30 a.m. on this steamy morning just outside Mexico City that was now doomed because of what happened on the bloody morning of September 13, Chapultepec had fallen more swiftly than anyone had expected.

More than 1,800 soldados had been killed, wounded, or captured in a monumental disaster, because once again General Scott's troops once again captured their targeted objective. Incredibly, the attackers only lost 130 men killed, 703 wounded, and 29 missing. Less than 900 American soldiers became casualties in overwhelming the highest and most formidable defensive position before Mexico City.

In his journal, an elated Lieutenant Daniel Harvey Hill, who was cited for valor in the assault while serving as a brave volunteer of the "Forlorn Hope" of Quitman's column, wrote without exaggeration how: "The storming of Chapultepec is looked upon as the most brilliant operation of the whole war. The enemy was in the strongest position he has ever occupied and was twelve thousand strong with ten pieces of cannon."

In a desperate, but ill-fated, attempt to defend the academy and hilltop of the ancient Aztecs, Mexico's Cadet Corps of less than 200 had been decimated. The Cadet Corps suffered a loss of more than one-fourth of its strength. A total of 37 cadets, including Santiago Hernandez, were captured and another 3 cadets fell wounded. However, these totals are incomplete so losses in wounded and captured among the Cadet Corps were actually higher.

Revealing the tragedy and full ugliness of the no quarter policy, the number of cadet dead was higher than the number of wounded youngsters from the Military College. Five cadets and Lieutenant de la Berraca, lay dead or dying in the hot sun.

Symbolically, much of the Military College was now in ruins from the devastating bombardment on two consecutive days, and Mexico herself was now dying, after the fall of the special place called Chapultepec. As a sad fate would have it, twice as many Boy Cadets had been killed than the number of wounded, which was also a testament of the intense combat that had fiercely raged across the summit.

To his utter disbelief and consternation, Santa Anna had suffered still another crushing defeat to an American army that was too well-trained, and too experienced. Even a reliance on high ground defensive positions could not halt the highly-motivated Americans, who were fueled by the spirit of Manifest Destiny. Not even Chapultepec's defenses had been enough to stop the relentless American tide once unleashed by General Scott. From a good distance to the east, Santa Anna saw that the Mexican flag no longer flew from atop the tower of Chapultepec.

One dispirited Mexican officer understood the grim meaning of Chapultepec's fall for the fate of a reeling Mexico that had suffered its most grievous blow in this nightmarish war. No longer able to see the republic's beautiful national colors waving proudly over Chapultepec and knowing that the tragic end had come, after the United States flag had been raised atop the tower, he merely said in disgust to Santa Anna with fatal resignation, "God is a Yankee."

In frustration, an astounded Santa Anna concluded with disbelief: "I believe if we were to plant our batteries in Hell the damned Yankees would take them from us." But it was not a God that had played the leading role in Chapultepec's fall and the decimation (killed, wounded, and captured) of the Boy Cadets, but General Santa Anna's own tactical mistakes and miscalculations. Worst of all, he had failed to reinforce the inadequate garrison as promised, despite a desperate Major General Bravo having repeatedly implored the need for assistance before it was too late, even when the attack was underway and Chapultepec's defenders desperately needed assistance.

Escutia and five other young cadets had sacrificed their lives for God and country. After the last firing of guns had echoed over the smoke-wreathed heights of Chapultepec and while the Stars and Stripes flew from the full height of Caballero Alto in triumph, Lieutenant John James Peck described with pride in a letter how: "Soon the Stars and Stripes were floating over their famed castle, announcing the work was done."

In still another tragedy, the sight of the rising of the "Stars and Stripes" had been the signal for the hanging of 30 crack fighting men of the San Patricio Battalion. From much older countries than the United States and different cultures, these mostly Irish Catholics, who had been captured at Churubusco, had long viewed the crass imperialism of the United States like England's older Protestant-driven and race-based imperialism that had conquered Ireland and then persecuted the Catholic people for generations.

As a tragic fate would have it, these crack fighting men of Mexico now dangled from ropes in a mass hanging to the disgust of Mexicans, including priests, and even other Americans. Like the branding of prisoners with "D" for deserter on their facial cheeks, the mass execution of mostly Catholics by Protestant soldiers shocked those Mexicans who witnessed the brutal execution that stunned the civilized world on both sides of the Atlantic.

A Phoenix Rising

Just beyond the shell-damaged Military College, now containing the dead bodies of a handful of cadets who had fallen in defending their school, the tall stalks of the cornfields, which stretched across the fertile plain below "Grasshopper Hill," waved in the faint breeze rising of the warm evening of September 13 that no one on either side would ever forget.

Perhaps Cadet Escutia had realized just before he died that Mexico was much like these fertile fields of maize that spanned below Chapultepec in all directions like a green carpet: long the primary source of life and prosperity for not only the ancient Aztec, but also the people of Mexico City.

After all, although the broad fields of golden corn might be devastated by the ravages of drought, floods, intense heat, plagues of insects, or plant disease during a single season, the corn would always grow back tall and strong in fresh crops in the following year to always provide its bounty to the people.

Like these omnipresent cornfields of dark green, so the memory of the boy cadets of Chapultepec would likewise not only survive, but also grow in moral strength by the resurrection of "Los Niños Héroes" by the people of Mexico in the future: a classic case of rising out of the ashes of 1847-1848 like a phoenix and evolving into something that was ever-lastingly heroic for all time, despite the humiliating defeat and fall of the legendary "Halls of Montezuma."

While the people of Mexico never forgot what happened at Chapultepec on the fateful morning of September 13, the people of the United States soon forgot about the bloody battle that had raged across the summit, despite that this dramatic victory guaranteed the capture of Mexico City and eventually the war's end.

However, as fate would have it, the enduring memory of the "Halls of Montezuma" and the small battalion of United States Marines who had played a role in storming Chapultepec were enshrined in the official battle-hymn of the United States Marine Corps.

In much the same way, so the cadets' heroics were resurrected from the ashes of the crushing defeat, the capture of Mexico City, and the loss of half of the republic's territory to the invader, whose nation eventually stretched from the Atlantic to the Pacific, thanks to the taking of Mexico's lands.

To a proud nation and liberty-loving people who had long suffered a seemingly endless list of defeats, reversals, and disasters, the enduring legacy of the courage and the sacrifice of the young cadets gained an honored place in the annals of Mexico history. What these young men demonstrated on the morning of September 13 was the remarkable resiliency of a nation and a people, who arose again—not unlike their savior—after so many setbacks that had failed to destroy the heart and soul of Mexico. Out of one of the worst defeats ever suffered the republic's history defeat, the noble sacrifice of the Boy Cadets will never be forgotten, representing the resurrection of Mexico's spirit and a lasting testament to a people's courage in a crisis situation.

Perhaps the most significant lesson that can be glimpsed from the remarkable story of the Boy Cadets is especially important because it is still relevant and valid to this day. Mexico's internal problems that plague the republic today cannot be completely solved without the nation's gifted youth leading the way for Mexico like the brave Military College students, who were among the best and brightest, to provide future leadership, military and civilian.

Like the United States Military Academy at West Point, the Military College at Chapultepec had been established to create a more capable, moral, and competent leadership in the future, which Mexico had sadly lacked, especially in regard to Santa Anna: a fundamental reason that ensured the tragic course of the Mexican-American War.

This timely initiative (the Military College's establishment) was the nation's calculated, but belated, effort to break away from the old corrupt and unethical ways that had long fatally weakened an already internally-divided republic, which had proved incapable of adequately defending itself in 1846-1848. Most importantly, this was a solution that called for the nation to begin anew to resurrect the noble moral legacies of Fathers Hildago and Morelos, who had led the way in the revolutionary effort to create a new republic.

In this sense, the cadets had died for the sins of a corrupt political past and the nation's incompetent, self-serving leaders, especially

Santa Anna. The generalissimo's many strategic and tactical mistakes played a key role in getting the cadets and a good many other defenders killed in vain and in brutal fashion ("no quarter"), because the high ground position could not be adequately defended without reinforcements from Santa Anna. By his own mistakes and in much the same way, he had earlier helped to set the stage for a tragic repeat of the "no quarter" slaughter of more than 650 soldados at San Jacinto, Texas, on April 21, 1836, when Santa Anna lost all of Texas.

As Private Richard Coulter, 2nd Pennsylvania, penned in his journal about the San Jacinto-like repeat on a strategic hilltop within sight of Mexico City, which was one of the jewels of the New World: "After the works were entered but little quarter was shown," including to the cadets, on the bloody morning of September 13.

Surprising Emergence of Reactionary Myths

What should not be forgotten today is that even the darkest lessons of the Mexican nation's tragic past can still play a role in helping to resurrect a brighter future for Mexico and her people in the years ahead. Again and as much as possible, perhaps the best hope for the Republic of Mexico today is simply to avoid the traditional political rule of corrupt, self-serving leaders as much as possible in order to take the nation on a new course in the future.

After all, this lofty goal was a crucial part of the overall national purpose of the Military College and its fiercely-patriotic cadets, who hoped to bring a brighter future for Mexico, by providing a capable moral civilian and military leadership: the antithesis of aristocratic and corrupt strongmen like Santa Anna, who led his nation to ruin by his inept leadership and self-serving ways.

Indeed, Mexico has quite correctly recognized that its youth truly hold the key to a more promising future: like "Los Niños Héroes," who had been disillusioned by the folly of its less than admirable leaders, who had betrayed the republic's vital interests, while these young men had remained true to the nation to the bitter end.

Six Boy Cadets sacrificed their own lives in the heat of battle to preserve the life of Mexico, but their memory and legacy will never die for the Mexican people. Unfortunately, an undue amount of myth and romance has been created about the cadets when so such embellishments are entirely necessary. But perhaps this was only a natural development in a war in which Mexico lost so much of itself, including half of its territory. Most remarkable, even the devastating defeat and humiliation at Chapultepec shined an illuminating golden light on one of the few bright spots of a tragic war: the heroism and sacrifice of the Boy Cadets who had faced impossible odds, but never gave up.

In truth, if there has been any myths created about the young cadets, these have been reactionary and distorted ones that have been largely politically-based. One of these myths was that the cadets allegedly died by committing a group suicide in unison, according to the imaginative writings of some American journalists whose work suddenly appeared in major American newspapers, including the *New York Times*, at the time of President Truman's respectful tribute to the fallen cadets in March 1947.

Ironically, this anti-heroic myth of a group cadet suicide drew partly upon an ancient legacy of Roman military leaders (suicide was considered a heroic gesture of ancient times rather than in 1847) having committed suicide rather than submitting to capture and ultimate humiliation. This reactionary myth emphasized that the Boy Cadets had either stabbed themselves or jumped together off the cliff, when the end was near. However, both of these myths are ridiculous fabrications without factual basis, stemming from self-serving and biased agendas (personal and political) in the twenty-first century. The best existing evidence and most abundant documentation have indicated that the cadet died at different locations and at different times, except in the case of Escutia and Márquez.

Indeed, no solid evidence and documentation, especially from primary sources, has been found to substantiate these most implausible of endings about the cadets' demise in the alleged group suicide. Nor was there any systematic "massacre" of cadets by United States soldiers, which is still another myth, because they had battled to the bitter end and went down fighting. However, some evidence has indicated that at least one cadet was killed because of the unofficial "no quarter" policy of revenge-seeking United States troops, especially the New Yorkers who had lost heavily in the assault, especially in top officers.

Other reactionary interpretations about their deaths were that these half-dozen Boy Cadets had been earlier placed in jail for various infractions and were locked-up and helpless when killed, or that they had been pressured by older soldiers, including officers, to take the fatal plunge together off the easternmost building to the rocky slope in still another version of the alleged mass suicide. One revisionist without the necessary historical facts has even emphasized that the cadets, allegedly in unison, only made their fatal leap onto the eastern slope, because they were either drunk or given drugs to explain their alleged organized suicidal plunge. But again, such was not the case, because their bodies, except for two, were found in different locations.

Some overly class-conscious Marxist historians and writers had even criticized the cadets as representing an aristocratic class and elite members of society: ironically, an early criticism that had been voiced, especially by opposition politicians, across the United States about West Point serving as a haven for the pampered sons of the wealthy upper class. According to the convoluted economic- and politically-based reasoning of these misguided Marxists, this relatively lofty social status of the cadets should disqualify them for the proper recognition and respect that they rightfully deserve for their courage and sacrifice. Other upper class Mexicans have challenged their heroic story because of anti-republican attitudes that have long mocked the nation's military class as allegedly incapable (certainly the case of Santa Anna) of adequately defending Mexico.

Again and most importantly, no primary evidence or documentation has verified any of these anti-heroic and reactionary myths that have attempted to tarnish the distinguished and enduring legacy of "Los Niños Héroes." But the possibility does exist that because of the widespread panic among so many non-cadet defenders, especially after they had ascertained that United States soldiers had unleashed a brutal no-quarter policy, they might well have been left behind on their own in the Military College, which they defended in their rooms or at windows or both, in the general confusion, because the overall collapse of resistance was so swift, after large numbers of American soldiers gained the crest. In the chaos of battle and close-range combat in smoky, darkened rooms, some cadets might have been killed by United States soldiers, who might have never realized their extreme youth until it was too late.

Another myth was that the dramatic showdown at Chapultepec was nothing more than a meaningless "skirmish" of no significance or meaning whatsoever. Again, such was simply not the case as fully revealed in the historical record. In fact, Chapultepec was a most strategic position, and the key to Mexico City. The capture of Chapultepec brought an end of the fighting and set the stage for the final peace treaties.

Quite correctly, the letters, journals, memoirs and diaries of many American soldiers have revealed the battle's supreme importance, because they early emphasized that the struggle for possession of Chapultepec was a key turning point of the war. The fighting men in the ranks correctly viewed the battle of Chapultepec as decisive, because the American victory all but guaranteed Mexico City's fall and the war's end.

But, of course, the greatest myth was that the cadets were nothing more than mere boys who should have still been at home with their mothers instead of engaging in a fierce battle to determine the possession of Mexico City. But this was certainly not the case. They were young soldiers who had been strictly disciplined and vigorously trained for a professional military life and future leadership roles for the overall betterment of the nation and its military establishment.

The cadets were saddled with responsibilities and assignments (defensive positions and guardian roles) that they took most seriously as revealed on the morning of September 13. Their supreme devotion of God, duty and country cost the lives of half a dozen cadets. After all, when directed by the commanding officer—the Military College commandant Major General José Mariano Monterde—they had decided on their own to present a formal appeal that emphasized how they wanted to stay and defend the Military College with the garrison.

In addition, the cadets were the sons of career and professional military officers, and they took their roles most seriously, because they were being groomed for future careers and high-ranking officer positions in the future military establishment. Quite simply, these young men were not children in the traditional sense, but actual soldiers who demonstrated their mettle on the morning of September 13.

Such an all-important life decision to stay and fight to the death, if necessary, was hardly one made by mere children without knowledge of the significant repercussions that it entailed. Many of the cadets had early learned about the stern demands of military life from their fathers who had served as career officers, and they knew what to expect. For all practical purposes, consequently, the cadets were legitimate soldiers and not boys, which they fully and ably demonstrated during the heat of battle.

Even today, in revolutionary and guerrilla struggles around the world, the young, including teenagers, have often proved to be the most determined and diehard fighters in one war after another. In this regard, the cadets of the Military College proved this truism of the value of very young fighting men on September 13.

Another myth, perhaps the most cynical one, was that an overly-glorified depiction of the actions of the Boy Cadets was required by the nation to overcome the shame and humiliation of losing Mexico City and the war: the birth of still another reactionary myth. Indeed, this is not the case, because the existing primary documentation and evidence does fully verify the heroic scenario instead of a less glorious and more fabricated one.

Ironically, despite its history as a nation that is longer than that of Mexico, the United States military establishment does not have a comparable heroic example comparable to "Los Niños Héroes." But the state of Virginia has embraced a comparable heroic legacy of its own. During the American Civil War, the cadets of the Virginia Military Academy (VMI), Lexington, Virginia, played a distinguished role in battle like the Boy Cadets during the previous generation. The young Virginia cadets, who also wore gray uniforms, played their distinguished part in a battle because their presence was needed since the manpower-short South was on the losing end of a lengthy war of attrition. Here, at the battle of New Market, Virginia, in the fertile Shenandoah Valley, the breadbasket of General Lee's Army of Northern Virginia, on May 5, 1864, the Virginia cadets played an impressive combat role.

Interestingly, generations of Americans have never doubted the heroic role and valor of these brave VMI cadets (47), which was nearly the same number of cadets (46) who were killed, wounded, and captured at Chapultepec. Nor were Americans guilty of having created alternative myths of disparage the courage and sacrifice of the VMI cadets, like in the case of some Mexican historians' criticisms of "Los Niños Héroes": a striking contrast that nearly defies rational understanding.

Ten VMI Cadets were killed or mortally wounded at the hard-fought battle of New Market compared to the six cadets of Mexico's Military College. Both the Mexican cadets and the Virginia cadets performed with great courage on behalf of their respective countries, and their heroic examples have served to inspire the youth of the respective republics in successive generations for ample good reason.

Clearly, the heroics of young cadets on the battlefield have crossed cultural lines and various conflicts throughout the course of history. During the Second World War when the German troops of Adolf Hitler's modern war machine pushed toward the fatal rendezvous with destiny on the south Russian steppes at Stalingrad on the Volga River during the summer of 1942, they encountered the exceptionally brave Russian cadets of the Krasnodar Military Academy. Krasnodar was located on the Kuban River northeast of the Black Sea, southern Russia.

In the words of one astounded German soldier, who greatly admired the cadets' heroism: "Red [Russian] Army units have put up a stubborn resistance, but the bravest opponent [were the cadets of] the Krasnodar Officer School [Krasnodar Military Academy].They fought like lions. When we captured about a hundred of them, our divisional commander [a general] lined them up and said the he had seldom seen such brave soldiers."

Clearly, the German soldiers, who were killed by these young Russian cadets, had learned about the harsh reality of facing a formidable opponent, despite their youth and cadet status: just like the American soldiers had learned the same reality when they faced courageous young men of the Cadet Corps at Chapultepec.

Most importantly, the courage and sacrifice of the cadets, "Los Niños Héroes," at Chapultepec were no myth, as General Scott's soldiers fully realized during the intense combat of the hard-fought battle. Again and significantly, this was not unlike the hard lesson learned by Hitler's veteran grenadiers during equally savage combat on the ill-fated road to a rendezvous with a cruel destiny in the ruins of Stalingrad.

Undeniable and Fundamental Truths

Like the heroics of the VMI Cadets at the battle of New Market, so the best existing primary evidence and documentation have continued to demonstrate that all six of the Boy Cadets died fighting primarily in defense of the Military College and Castle, falling at different locations and at different times.

As mentioned, no solid evidence exists that they died together at the same exact place and at the same time in the alleged group suicide. In saving the small red-green-white national flag to keep it out of the victors' hands, Cadet Juan Escutia jumped from a rooftop in a dramatic leap of his death, after having been shot by a New York soldier. No primary or solid evidence has revealed that the Boy Cadets committed suicide as a group on September 13, 1847.

The rather unfortunate recent rise of reactionary and grossly distorted, if not perverse, myths about the Boy Cadets would probably have amused Cadet Agustín Melgar, who fell while battling against impossible odds. He was cut down in a large room— evidently the main dormitory of the Military College—after having just fired a final shot that knocked-down one attacker.

Young Melgar had taken shelter behind mattresses and other bedroom items stacked for meager protection. But there was no shelter from the storm that had swept over Chapultepec with a terrible fury on this morning in hell. Falling with a very bad wound in a main structure guaranteed that Melgar received medical attention from the victors. However, American army surgeons, who were dedicated and treated wounded Mexicans and Americans with equal care, could not save the teenager. He finally died far from home on September 14 from multiple wounds.

What "Los Niños Héroes" also continued was a noble tradition of Mexico's resistance to foreign aggressors that extended back to the invasion by the Spanish Conquistadors. In the frustrated words—that applied to the cadets on September 13—of Hernán Cortéz, who lamented how the Aztec warriors "by no means would they give themselves up, for as long as one of them was left he would fighting." In this regard, a half dozen Boy Cadets remained faithful to their history, culture, and traditions in the end, dying for their beliefs and Military College on the embattled summit that overlooked Mexico City.

Sadly and as fate would have it, the final resting places of the Boy Cadets were known only to God for more than a century. After the battle, the bodies of the six cadets were collected with a large number of Major General Bravo's dead soldados, including the hard-fighting men of the National Guard units, especially the San Blas Battalion, and the regulars of the 10th Infantry Regiment, by Mexican prisoners. Here, the sacred dead of the Republic of Mexico were hastily buried in the deep ditch (the fosse) that surrounded the war-torn Castle.

These saddened prisoners, including perhaps some surviving cadets, who gathered their comrades' lifeless bodies lying along the eastern slope discovered how some fighting men, including cadets like Escutia, had met their grisly ends. Because the six cadets had been killed or died (Melgar died on September 14) in different locations, the cadets were not buried together.

The dead cadets were covered with a thin layer of the dirt of "Grasshopper Hill": a most sacred and symbolic place to die, because of its rich history and symbolism. Besides the six cadets who were killed, several other cadets fell wounded in the attack. As mentioned because of the lack of documentation and accurate records, the losses of the Cadet Corps were actually probably higher. Total losses—killed, wounded, and captured—were more than 25% of the Cadet Corps.

In 1947 and after a diligent search, the remains of the half dozen cadets were found and positively identified. Then, on September 27, 1952, the six cadets, the brave sons of military officers who had faithfully served Mexico with distinction and honor, were re-interred at the Monument of the Heroic Cadets of Chapultepec.

Another Final and Sad Ending

Teenage Cadet Agustín Melgar, born in the northern desert town of Chihuahua, which was captured by the Americans (like Cadet Vicente Suárez's hometown of Puebla which had been captured by General Scott's Army on May 15, 1847, and then occupied at the time of the battle of Chapultepec) on March 2, 1847, had returned to the civilian world, after having been briefly expelled from the Military College for having missed a May 1847 review. Knowing that his fellow cadets and his beloved Military College and Mexico City faced their greatest threat, Melgar had then unexpectedly returned to his prestigious school on September 8, 1847. With considerable pride, he had once again donned his old cadet uniform, almost as if he had never departed the academy perched on the commanding hilltop in splendid fashion.

Following the footsteps of his father whose life was dedicated to serving his country, Lieutenant Colonel Esteban Melgar who died while faithfully serving his country, Cadet Melgar died of his multiple wounds from bullets and bayonets (the attackers' 16- and 18-inch socket bayonet blades) on the following day, September 14, after his leg was amputated. The bone of the young cadet's leg had been shattered by a lead ball fired from a large caliber (.69) flintlock musket. Hard-working American surgeons had well cared for the badly-wounded Melgar, but nothing could save him. Born on August 28, 1829, he died after a great deal of suffering and anguish over not only his tragic fate, but also Chapultepec's capture barely two weeks after his sixteenth birthday. He was the last Boy Cadet to sacrifice his life for his country and school.

Significantly, ample evidence and documentation has fully verified the courageous sacrifice of the Boy Cadets in the heat of battle on the morning of September 13.Therefore, the president of Mexico, Porfirio Diaz, born in Oaxaca, Mexico, made a memorable formal presentation on September 13, 1910 on the battle's anniversary that paid a fitting tribute. He "extolled the heroism of the youthful soldiers who fought valiantly to save the castle from the overwhelming Americans and described them as shining examples for emulation by the youth of the country." Indeed, during a defiant last stand against impossible odds, the six cadets died in a heroic attempt to save Mexico City and their republic from foreign conquest, domination, and rule that would have represented a new dark age for Mexico.

Today, the impressive courage and heroism of the Boy Cadets has become legendary: a powerful inspirational example and enduring symbol to Mexico's defiant resistance and sacrifice during a modern-day Thermopylae. Paradoxically, another enduring chapter of sacrifice and tragedy was also born on September 13, 1847, when Chapultepec's largest flag was lowered by the victors from the top of the tower: the fateful signal for the hanging of 30 soldiers of the crack San Patricio Battalion.

These dual martyrs who had attempted against the odds to save Mexico—the Boy Cadets and San Patricio men who died on the same day, but under entirely different circumstances—were separated by race, culture, and birthplace, but shared the most enlightened republican values, including abolitionism and a hatred of slavery: the most forgotten and overlooked motivations of both distinct groups of Mexico's fighting men. Significantly, they gave their all to the Republic of Mexico and its people, fighting to the end in the most unjust war in American history.

Indeed, what the Boy Cadets and the San Patricio Battalion soldiers shared in common was that they had resisted a more powerful invader if a different religion in an artificially manufactured war in part because it was not only a giant land grab, but also a war to expand slavery. Texas had possessed few slaves during the Spanish period before the arrival of the Anglo-Celtic settlers in the 1820s from the United States. What happened in the loss of Texas was the turning back of the clock on the most progressive and liberal thought of the day: that all men, regardless of color, deserved equality regardless of color.

But when Texas was lost by Santa Anna in April 1836, thanks largely to extensive aid from the United States, the thriving institution of slavery—the foundation of the Anglo-Celtic economy and raced-based society—was saved, becoming a vast empire for slavery. Therefore, the cadets actually fought on September 13 so that President Vincente Guerrero's September 1829 abolition degree would not be negated and repealed in a conquered Mexico, like had been demonstrated earlier in Texas. Indeed, if Mexico was conquered and annexed by the United States, then slavery would once again be reintroduced and reestablished on Mexico soil.

With firm conviction and without hyperbole, General Santa Anna sincerely regretted that if he had only possessed a good many more tough fighting men like the members of the elite San Patricio Battalion, then he could have defeated the invaders. Most significantly, Santa Anna might well have said the same in regard to the cadets of the Military College.

Ironically, in his journal in which he lamented the death of a close friend who was killed (perhaps by the artillery fire from the heights of Chapultepec) during the bloody attack on Molina del Rey, Sergeant Thomas Barclay penned a heartfelt tribute to this lost comrade that might well have applied to the half dozen cadets of Chapultepec, who lost their lives in battling for God and country: "The melancholy consolation of being with him during his last moments was denied us. What were his thoughts, what were his feelings none can tell. But while life remained his thoughts doubtless reverted to the scenes of home, of childhood and in the pangs of death the sorrows of surviving friends caused more generous grief in his generous bosom than all the sufferings which he himself endured. O may he [now] in a brighter and better world again meet with those who loved him so tenderly in this."

In much the same way, the shrill cries of the majestic Golden Eagle of Mexico while circling in the sun-splashed and blue September skies almost seemed to sound a sad lament for the fate of Mexico and so many of her valiant sons, including the virtuous cadets, who were destined to die in vain in this cruel war.

Epilogue

Much more than in the United States today, the past still remains very much alive in the people and soul of Mexico to this day. In truth, the six Boy Cadets died in the heat of combat in a desperate attempt to save everything that they held dear and loved. They fell on the morning of September 13 at the height of the battle, going down as some of the most determined defenders of their Military College, the national flag, and Chapultepec: not unlike the last ancient Spartans, who had bravely defended the strategic pass at Thermopylae in 480 B.C., against the might of the Persian Army to save the people of Greece.

In much the same way and against impossible odds, the cadets had died in defending the strategic avenues leading to Mexico City. Acknowledging heroics where it was due, even an American newspaperman at the time wrote with an appropriate sense of admiration how the cadets died, while "fighting like demons" against the tide of onrushing attackers. These tough fighters, who bravely stood firm in the face of the onslaught, were the famed "Los Niños Héroes," who have become legendary across Mexico.

Most importantly in the end, the celebration of the cadets' supreme sacrifice represented a triumph of Mexican historical consciousness and memory on a national level that helped to compensate for one of the most humiliating defeats of the republic's most tragic war. During a true crisis situation, the young cadets demonstrated considerably more courage and determination than many of their much-touted leaders and a large number of older soldados, including regular troops, who performed below expectations on the battlefield on the bloody morning of September 13.

Most of all, the Boy Cadets fought for the most cherished egalitarian legacies of the American Revolution and the Mexican War of Independence in attempting to keep the foreign invader, including slave-owners who hoped to spread slavery south into Mexico, at bay to preserve what their egalitarian-minded forefathers and heroic revolutionary priests had gained with great sacrifice, after defeating Royalist Spain.

But in the end, all of the hard fighting and the high price paid by Mexico's soldados, including the cadets, who proved to be very good fighting men in a crisis situation of an extremely important battle, could not compensate for the failures at the highest levels of the government and leadership (military and civilian), which failed the soldados, cadets, and people of Mexico.

Today, the Republic of Mexico has continued to face a host of deep internal problems nearly as severe as during the Mexican-American War. Therefore, for Mexico to overcome future challenges to fortify the heart and soul of the republic, the shining example of Cadet Juan Baptist Pascasio Escutia has provided a redeeming moral lesson of the importance of the noble self-sacrifice that was necessary to regain the national honor that had been lost by the army, its overly-confident leaders, and the self-destructive native to the Yankee invaders.

Today, and for ample good reason, the people of Mexico have continued to be inspired by the last words of Cadet Juan Escutia, when he gave his all for his long-suffering country and people, when they faced their greatest threat. In a noble sacrifice of a promising young son of the republic, he literally took flight in the popular Mexican national imagination and consciousness, when he fell toward the eastern slope in a heroic self-sacrifice: symbolically, a dramatic plunge not unlike the swiftly-descending Golden Mexican eagle when diving to snare a water serpent and then devouring the reptile, while sitting atop a tenochtl (the sun plant or prickly pear) near the S-shaped Lake Texcoco, which represented the ultimate fulfillment of a people's destiny, as had been seen in a prophetic Aztec dream long ago.

As mentioned, Cadet Escutia's tragic end was much like the mythological Icarus who had flown too close to the sun and then fell to his death in consequence, because he had aspired higher toward achieving greater things. Most symbolically, the original site of Mexico City had been a sacred place of worship of the Aztec Sun God Huitzilopochitli, and Escutia's heroic sacrifice within sight of the great city was symbolically appropriate. To save his nation's flag from seemingly too many attackers to count, Escutia's long fall from the highest point of the easternmost building's roof and onto the rocky eastern slope was much like the tragic fate of Icarus, because this promising young cadet from Tepic had also aspired to lofty heights that were unattainable by non-cadet soldados.

In defiantly refusing to surrender to the hated Yankees and in despair over what was happening to his beloved country during a systematic conquest by the superior military might of a determined foreign invader and like the other "Los Niños Héroes," who had already died while demonstrating *mucho valor*, Cadet Juan Baptist Pascasio Escutia's dramatic fall to earth left his sacrificed nation with an enduring heroic legacy that the people of Mexico will never forget.

After having been shot on the rooftop and determined to cheat his would be captors and save the national colors at all costs, he leaped from the rooftop edge of the high easternmost building atop the imposing summit of Chapultepec. Escutia dropped like a heavy Aztec stone implement toward the eastern slope, while his upper body was protectively wrapped in the flag's silken folds of green, red, and white, which flapped in the smoky air of a warm September morning during the descent.

As young Cadet Juan Baptist Pascasio Escutia fell toward the eastern slope on this early Monday morning in a living nightmare, he shouted the patriotic words that were the last ever spoken by him in a short life that had been sacrificed much too early. During his lengthy descent of no return, Cadet Escutia shouted "Viva Mexico! Long Live Mexico!"

In the end, the attacking Americans had succeeded in killing, wounding, and capturing 46 cadets on the morning of September 13, 1847. But most importantly, the sacred memory and heroic spirit of the Boy Cadets still lives today in the Mexican republic and the people of this ancient land of the Aztec. To this day, the cadets represent a vibrant sense of Mexican nationalism, patriotism, and most importantly, the undying spirit of the Mexican heart and soul.

Consequently, in this sense and especially in regard to the lofty moral and spiritual realms, the cadets who were killed on that awful September day actually never really died, because their legacy and memory will never die: Vayan Con Dios (They Go With God).

Representing the finest qualities of the heart and soul of Mexico in her darkest hour, these dedicated young men will forever be known as "the Child Heroes," because they have been resurrected by the Mexican nation and people to serve as enduring symbols of courage and sacrifice. In the end, the Boy Cadets nobly fought and died heroically for honor, country, and God.

About the Author

PHILLIP THOMAS TUCKER, Ph.D., has won international acclaim as an original and ground-breaking "new look" historian. One of America's most prolific and accomplished historians in multiple fields of history, Dr. Tucker has authored nearly 40 highly original hand unique books to reveal long-silenced forgotten truths, while correcting and updating the historical record for the twenty-first century.

Dr. Tucker has written nearly a dozen scholarly books solely about the Texas Revolutionary Experience and the African American Experience. The author's expertise in these two dissimilar fields of study has resulted in the writing of two ground-breaking books that have placed the Texas Revolution in a proper and correct historical perspective for the first time, Volume I and Volume II of *America's Forgotten First War for Slavery and Genesis of the Alamo, A New Look at the Texas Revolution 1835-1836.*

Most importantly, these two ground-breaking volumes have given us not only a fresh "new look," but also a new benchmark of literary scholarship on the Texas Revolution and black history. The author has succeeded in fusing these two distinct fields of study, revealing a seldom-explored symbiotic relationship. Significantly, the hidden history and forgotten truths of this extremely important chapter in

American history have been revealed for the first time in these two volumes to update and correct the historical record.

Drawing upon a lifetime of expertise in these two distinct subjects which reveal the events that led to the outbreak of the Mexican-American War, the author has written the most definitive account of the remarkable story of the Boy Cadets of Chapultepec for not only the people of Mexico, but also for the American people.

Bibliography

Alba, Victor, *Mexico*, (New York: American Heritage Publishing Company, Inc., 1973).

Bauer, K. Jack, *The Mexican War, The Mexican War, 1846-1848*, (New York: Macmillan, 1974).

Brack, Gene M., *Mexico Views Manifest Destiny, 1821-1846*, (Albuquerque: University of New Mexico Press, 1975).

Campbell, Duncan B., *Spartan Warrior, 735-331 BC*, (Oxford: Osprey Publishing, 2012).

Campos, Ruben M., *Chapultepec, Its Legend and Its History*, (Mexico: Talleres Graficos De La Nacion, 1922).

Carter, Ruth C., editor, *For Honor Glory and Union, The Mexican and Civil War Letters of Brig. Gen. William Haines Lytle*, (Lexington: University Press of Kentucky, 1999)

Cartledge, Paul, *The Spartans, The World of the Warrior-Heroes of Ancient Greece*, (New York: Vintage Books, 2004).

Casa Museum Juan Escutia, Tepic, Mexico.

Chance, Joseph E., *The Mexican War Journal of Captain Franklin Smith*, (Jackson: University Press of Mississippi, 1991).

Chartrand, Rene, *Santa Anna's Mexican Army 1821-48*, (Oxford: Osprey Publishing Ltd., 2004).

Clary, David A., *Eagles and Empire, The United States, Mexico, and the Struggle for a Continent*, (New York: Bantam Books, 2009).

Cleaves, Freeman, *Meade of Gettysburg*, (Norman: University of Oklahoma Press, 1991).

Coulter, Richard, Journal, Manuscripts Division, William L. Clements Library, University of Michigan, Ann Arbor, Michigan.

Crawford, Mark, *Encyclopedia of the Mexican-American War*, (Santa Barbara, ABC-CLIO, Inc., 1999).

Cutrer, Thomas W., *The Mexican War Diary and Correspondence of George B. McClellan*, (Baton Rouge: Louisiana State University Press, 2009)

Dugard, Martin, *The Training Ground, Grant, Lee, Sherman, and Davis in the Mexican War, 1846-1848*, (New York: Little, Brown and Company, 2008).

Eisenhower, John S., *So Far From God, The U.S. War with Mexico, 1846-1848*, (New York: Random House, 1989).

Fernandez, Justino, *National Museum of History-Chapultepec Castle*, (Mexico City: Instituto Nacional de Antropologiae Historia, 1967).

Fleming, Thomas J., *West Point, The Men and Times of the United States Military Academy*, (New York: William Morrow and Company, 1969).

Grant, Ulysses S., *Personnel Memoirs of U.S. Grant*, (New York: Penguin Classics, 1999).

Greenberg, Amy S., *A Wicked War, Polk, Clay, Lincoln, and the 1846 U.S. Invasion of Mexico*, (New York: Vintage Books, 2012).

Hefter, J., *The Mexican Soldier, 1837-1847*, (Mexico City: Nieto, Brown and Hefter Publishing,1958).

Henry, Robert S., *The Story of the Mexican War*, (Indianapolis: Bobbs-Merrill, 1950).

Herodotus, *The Histories Book 7: Polymnia*, (Radford: Wilder Publications, LLC, 2012).

Hitchcock, Ethan Allen, *Fifty Years in Camp and Field: Diary of Major General Ethan Allen Hitchcock, USA.*, (New York: G. P. Putnam, 1909.

Hogan, Michael, *The Irish Soldiers of Mexico*, (Jalisco: Fondo Editorial Universitario, 1999)

Hughes, Jr., Nathaniel Cheairs, *A Fighter From Way Back, The Mexican War Diary of Lieutenant Daniel Harvey Hill, 4th Artillery U.S.A*, (Kent: Kent State University Press, 2002).

Johnson, Timothy D., *A Gallant Little Army, The Mexico City Campaign*, (Lawrence: University Press of Kansas, 2007).

May, Robert E., *John A. Quitman, Old South Crusader*, (Baton Rouge: Louisiana State University Press, 1985).

McCulloch, David, *Truman*, (New York: Simon and Schuster, 1993.

McNally, Michael, *Teutoburg Forest AD 9*, (Botley: Osprey Publishing, 2011).

Meyer, Jack Allen, *South Carolina in the Mexican War, A History of the Palmetto Regiment of Volunteers 1846-1917*, (Columbia: The South Carolina Department of Archives and History, 1996).

Miller, Robert Ryal, *Shamrock and Sword: The Saint Patrick's Battalion*, (Norman: University of Oklahoma Press, 1989).

Miscellaneous Internet Articles related to the Boy Cadets of Chapultepec.

Miscellaneous Period Newspapers from Mexico.

Nevin, David, *The Mexican War, The Old West*, (Alexandria: Time-Life Books, 1978).

New York Times, New York, New York.

Peskin, Allan, editor, *Volunteers, The Mexican War Journals of Private Richard Coulter and Sergeant Thomas Barclay, Company E, Second Pennsylvania Infantry*, (Kent: The Kent State University Press, 1991).

Pourade, Richard F., editor, *The Sign of the Eagle, A View of Mexico1830 to 1855*, (San Diego: Union-Tribune Publishing Company, 1970).

Ramsey, Albert C., editor, *The Other Side: Or, Notes for the History of the War Between Mexico and the United States, Written in Mexico*, (New York: John Wiley, 1850).

Raat, W. Dirk, editor, *Mexico, from Independence to Revolution, 1810-1910*, (Lincoln: University of Nebraska Press, 1982).

Raat, W. Dirk, *Mexico and the United States, Ambivalent Vistas*, (Athens: University of Georgia Press, 1992).

Riding, Alan, *Distant Neighbors, A Portrait of the Mexicans*, (New York: Vintage Books, 1989).

Scheina, Robert L., *Santa Anna, A Curse upon Mexico*, (Washington, D.C.: Brassey's, Inc.,2002).

Romm, James, *Ghost on the Throne, The Death of Alexander the Great and the War for Crown and Empire*, (New York: Alfred A. Knopf, 2011).

Semmes, Raphael, *The Campaign of General Scott in the Valley of Mexico*, (Cincinnati: More and Anderson Publishers, 1852).

Smith, George Winston and Judah, Charles, *Chronicles of the Gringos, The U.S. Army in the Mexican War ,1846-1848, Accounts of Eyewitnesses and Combatants*, (Albuquerque: University of New Mexico Press, 1968).

Stevens, Peter F., *The Rogue's March: John Riley and the St. Patrick's Battalion, 1846-1848*, (Dulles: Potomac Books, 2007).

Turner, Frederick C., *The Dynamics of Mexican Nationalism*, (Chapel Hill: University of North Carolina Press, 1968)

Washington Post, Washington, D.C.

Weinberg, Albert K., *Manifest Destiny, A Study of Nationalist Expansion in American History*, (Chicago: Quadrangle, 1963)

Wheelan, Joseph, *Invading Mexico, America's Continental Dream and the Mexican War, 1846-1848,* (New York: Carroll and Graf Publications, 2007).

Wilcox, Cadmus M., *History of the Mexican War*, (Washington: Church News, 1892).

Williams, T. Harry, *With Beauregard in Mexico, The Mexican War Reminiscences of P.G. T. Beauregard*, (Baton Rouge: Louisiana State University Press, 1956).

Winders, Richard Bruce, *Mr. Polk's Army, The American Military Experience in the Mexican War*, (College Station: Texas A&M Press, 1997).

CPSIA information can be obtained
at www.ICGtesting.com
Printed in the USA
LVHW080236161219
640628LV00015B/858/P